ATHLETICS IN THE NORDIC COUNTRIES

HISTORY AND DEVELOPMENTS

ATHLETICS IN THE NORDIC COUNTRIES

HISTORY AND DEVELOPMENTS

EDITED BY JÖRG KRIEGER

COMMON GROUND

First published in 2023
as part of the Insert Imprint Name Book Imprint
doi: 10.18848/978-1-957792-52-1/CGP (Full Book)

Common Ground Research Networks
2001 South First St, Suite 201 L
Champaign, IL 61820 USA
Ph: +1-217-328-0405

Library of Congress Cataloging-in-Publication Data

Names: Krieger, Jörg, editor.
Title: Athletics in the Nordic Countries: History and Developments /
    edited by Jörg Krieger.
Description: Champaign, IL: Common Ground Research Networks, 2023 |
    Includes bibliographical references. | Summary: "In the edited
    collection Athletics in the Nordic Countries, scholars from Denmark,
    Finland, Norway, and Sweden explore historical developments and current
    phenomena in the sport of athletics (track and field). The chapters
    provide insight into sport officials, events, and athletes from the
    Nordic countries that have shaped the international athletics scene. The
    authors identify the leading role of sport leaders from Scandinavia in
    the foundation years and highlight how athletics' events held in the
    region were milestones in the transformation of the sport. Athletics'
    international governing body World Athletics was founded in Sweden in
    1912 as the International Amateur Athletic Federation. Seventy years
    later, Finland hosted the first World Athletics Championships in
    Helsinki in 1983. In between those turning points, Nordic officials and
    athletes promoted significant changes in athletics, and their innovative
    approaches continue to shape the development of the sport until today"--
    Provided by publisher.
Identifiers: LCCN 2023009090 (print) | LCCN 2023009091 (ebook) | ISBN
    9781957792507 (hardback) | ISBN 9781957792514 (paperback) | ISBN
    9781957792521 (pdf)
Subjects: LCSH: Sports--Scandinavia--History--20th century. | World
    Athletics (Organization)--History.
Classification: LCC GV625 .A75 2023 (print) | LCC GV625 (ebook) | DDC
    796.0948/0904--dc23/eng/20230306
LC record available at https://lccn.loc.gov/2023009090
LC ebook record available at https://lccn.loc.gov/2023009091

TABLE OF CONTENTS

ACKNOWLEDGEMENTS

This anthology could not have been realized without the support of many people and institutions. Allai Abou-Chaker provided valuable input and support throughout different phases of the project. Student helpers Emilie Møller Ibsen, Mia Christensen, Frederik Kühlwein Pedersen, and Jakob Ravn contributed to the project. Michael Connolly worked on the language of the individual chapters. At Common Ground Research Networks, Patricia Alonso always had an open ear for my updates and ideas. Importantly, the anthology is part of a research project that is funded by a grant received from the Danish "*Kulturministeriets Forskningspulje* 2020." The successful application for the grant initiated the publication process and the support allowed for the organization of a workshop during the 2022 Nordic Sport History Network meeting. I am grateful to the research fund's support. My colleagues of the Research Unit Sport and Body Culture of Aarhus University provided helpful comments and input on various stages of this project. Finally, I would like to acknowledge the role of my family who allowed me the time and focus to finalize the anthology.

AUTHORS' BIOGRAPHIES

John Berg holds a PhD in History and History Didactics. His research has been circling around the heritage making of Swedish sports, yet also Swedish sports history in a wider sense. He is currently working as a senior lecturer in History and History Didactics.

Hans Bolling has a PhD in History and is an independent researcher. His research interest touches on sport and history in the broadest sense. His latest publication, *Kroppens apostlar. Kvinnliga gymnastikdirektörer 1864–2020* [Apostles of the Body], in cooperation with Leif Yttergren, deals with the professional careers and lives of Swedish female gymnastic directors.

Hans Bonde, is a Professor at the Department of Nutrition, Exercise and Sports at the University of Copenhagen, Denmark. He has published several works in English language, amongst them: *Gymnastics and Politics* (2006, Museum Tusculanum Press), *Niels Bukh - A Visual Documentation* (2007, Museum Tusculanum Press), *Football with the Foe* (2008, University of Southern Denmark Press), and *The Politics of the Male Body in Global Sport* (2010, Routledge).

Bieke Gils is an Associate Professor at the University of South-Eastern Norway with competence in the history and sociology of gender and the body. She has a PhD from the University of British Columbia, Canada. Her research to date has focused on female leading figures in a variety of contexts, including the North American entertainment industries around 1900, physical education in Canada in the 1960s-70s, as well as elite coaching in Norway. In her writing and daily life, she is committed to addressing social inequities on the intersections of gender and racial dimensions, to promote inclusion, diversity, and social sustainability.

Matti Goksøyr is a Professor in history at the Norwegian School of Sport Sciences. He obtained his PhD in 1991. He has published several books and articles in Norwegian and English, on the subjects of general sports history, sport, politics and culture; sport and national identity/nationalism, football history, and polar history. His latest book (with Finn Olstad) is entitled *Skjebnekamp. Norsk idrett under okkupasjonen 1940-1945* [Fight for destiny. Norwegian sport during the occupation 1940-1945] (2017, Aschehoug).

Leena Laine is a Historian specialized in the history of sports. She has published and co-published numerous books and articles on the history of Finnish sports organizations and on workers' and women's sports. She has been active in sport historical organizations, such as ISHPES, and in gender and sport networks.

Jouni Lavikainen is a Doctoral Researcher at the University of Helsinki, Finland, and a Special Researcher at the TAHTO Center for Finnish Sports Culture (Sports Museum of Finland). His PhD focuses on the transition from amateurism to professionalism in Finnish elite sport.

Gerd von der Lippe is Professor Emerita at the University of South-Eastern Norway. She created the university's Department of Sports in 1981 and the field of outdoor studies in 1982, and was their first leader. Her PhD was on sport and gender and she worked as a professor in sports sociology with a focus on gender, media and politics. Gerd has written several books and articles on these subjects, among them the two journal articles "Football, Masculinities and Health on the Gaza Strip" (2014, *The International Journal of the History of Sport*) and "We Can! Women`s football in the Occupied West Bank" (2020, European Journal for Sport and Society). In 2022 she interviewed female footballers and coaches in Iran.

Jens Ljunggren is Professor of history, with a focus on sport history, at Stockholm University, Sweden. In addition to sport history, his main research areas have been the history of masculinity and the history of political emotions. Since his defense, he has been active at Stockholm University, Lund University, Uppsala University and as a visiting researcher at Technische Universität Berlin and the German Sport University Cologne.

Anne Tjønndal is Professor of sociology of sport at Nord University, Norway. Currently, she is Head of Department Leadership and Innovation, and Leader of

RESPONSE (Reserarch Group for Sport and Society) at Nord University, Norway. She is also a Visiting Professor at the Norwegian University of Science and Technology (NTNU).

Frida Austmo Wågan is a Doctoral Student and Deputy Leader of RESPONSE (Research Group for Sport and Society) at Nord University, Norway. She is writing her PhD in sociology of sport on the topic of sustainability in sports.

The Nordic Countries' Leading Roles in the History of International Athletics

Jörg Krieger

Athletics has been the core sport of the Olympic Games since their establishment through Pierre de Coubertin in the late nineteenth century. Athletes have competed in the sport at all editions of the Olympic Games, beginning with the 1896 Athens Olympic Games. A symbol of the sport's significance is the men's marathon run, which is traditionally the last event of the Olympic Games. Today, the male and female marathon medalists are the only competitors to receive their medals in the Olympic stadium during the closing ceremony.

However, for the first sixteen years of Olympic history, athletics did not have a governing body to oversee the organization of the sport. Coubertin clung to power over athletics, amidst several attempts to establish an international athletics federation due to his fear that national politics would take over the governing over the sport. It was not until Swedish sport administrator Sigfrid Edström entered the scene and diplomatically convinced Coubertin to agree to the foundation of a governing body for athletics. During a meeting of athletics' administrators, within the framework of the 1912 Stockholm Olympic Games, the International Amateur Athletics Federation (IAAF, later International Association of Athletics' Federations and today World Athletics) was founded on Scandinavian soil. Ever since the IAAF's foundation under Swedish guidance, the Nordic countries have influenced processes of continuity and transformation in international athletics in three main areas: **leadership**, **events**, and **athletes**, like no other region in the world.

With regards to **leadership**, Edström became the organization's first president and remained in this position until 1946. During this time, the IAAF's headquarters remained in Stockholm, Sweden, with several Swedish general secretaries influencing the administration of international athletics prior to the

Second World War. The Swedish leadership often allowed the IAAF to maintain a neutral position in the power games between French and British-American sport administrators. But it was not only the Swedes. Finnish athletics coach and administrator Lauri Pihkala was a founding member of the IAAF, taking on leading roles in various IAAF working groups. During the Cold War period, when the IAAF presidency moved away from Scandinavia to London, Great Britain, several individuals continued to shape decision-making processes within the federation. The Dane Emanuel Rose contributed to the development of the IAAF's legal statutes in the 1960s and 1970s. Swedish medical doctor Arne Ljungqvist occupied a leadership role in the international fight against doping. The leadership of the European Athletics Association (EAA) also profited from Nordic expertise, not least during the presidency of Carl-Olaf Homén, Finland, from 1987 to 1999.

Major cities in the Nordic countries became the sites of important athletics events. Gothenburg, Sweden, played host to the 1926 Women's World Games, at which women competed in twelve athletics disciplines. This was much to the anger of male sport officials who wanted to maintain control over all aspects of the sport. Oslo, Norway, organized the first international athletics event after the Second World War, the 1946 European Athletics Championships. In 1983, the Finnish capital city Helsinki, became the location of the first ever World Athletics Championships. Helsinki hosted the world championships again in 2005, and Gothenburg was host in 1995. All of these events are to be considered milestones of athletics' history, paving the way for significant changes in the sport.

Highly successful athletes have also come from the Nordic countries. Finnish runners dominated the middle- and long-distance races for almost three decades at the start of the twentieth century. The nickname "The Flying Finns" goes back to this period, starting with Hannes Kolehmainen's three gold medals at the 1912 Stockholm Olympic Games, followed by Paavo Nurmi's successes in the 1920s and 1930s. One of the Finns fiercest competitors was the Swede Edvin Wide. In the early 1920s, the Norwegian Charles Hoff set four world records in the pole vault, before ending his athletics career, due to professionalism, in 1926. After the Second World War, athletes from the Nordic region found it much more difficult to achieve international success due to increasing global competition. Only by 1972 did success return in the form of Finnish middle-distance runners around Lasse Viren. In recent years, this dominance has re-emerged in the form of Norwegian success in middle-distance running through the Ingebrigtsen brothers, all European champions in the 1,500 meters, and Swedish pole vaulter Armand Duplantis. Significantly, Danish athletes had considerably less success than their Scandinavian counterparts, but some individuals such as Wilson Kipketer, who migrated to Denmark in the 1990s, and won the 800-meters competition at three successive world athletics championships, are notable exceptions.

Against the background of the Nordic countries' influence on international athletics, this edited collection brings together leading scholars to explore key turning points and processes of continuity in Nordic athletics. Focus lies on historical perspectives to demonstrate how current structures and developments in athletics are shaped by past events and processes. Since the anthology is part of a project to explore the history and current governance of the sport of athletics on the international and regional level, an emphasis is placed on the interaction between these two levels.

The first three chapters deal with early periods of athletics in selected Nordic countries. **Hans Bolling** outlines the role of Swedish sport administrators in the IAAF foundation process, **Hans Bonde** illustrates how Danish athletics became a political tool throughout the German occupation of the country during the Second World War, **Leena Laine** discusses gender, power, and athletics in Finnish athletics until the 1950s, and **Jouni Lavikainen** analyses the rise of commercialism in Finnish athletics, In the second section, authors identify in five chapters milestones of the development of athletics in the Nordic countries between the Second World War and the 1990s. **Matti Erik Goksøyr** and **Jörg Krieger** highlight the significance of the 1946 European Athletics Championships, **Gerd von der Lippe** and **Bieke Gils** put together the history of women and political activism in Norwegian athletics in the 1960s and 1970s, **Jörg Krieger** contextualizes the first World Athletics Championships in Helsinki in 1983, and **John Berg** focuses on media perspectives on Swedish runner Sara Wedlund. The final two chapters deal with athletics more broadly and include current perspectives on the sport. **Jens Ljunggren** presents approaches to youth sport in Sweden between the 1970s and today with a focus on athletics, and **Anne Tjønndal** and **Frida Austmo Wågan** discuss technological innovation in Norwegian athletics, bridging the historical perspectives to present and future scenarios for the sport.

Perspectives from the four Nordic countries of Denmark, Finland, Norway, and Sweden are presented in the book. Unfortunately, it was not possible to secure a contribution on Icelandic athletics. A word on terminology is necessary here since both "Scandinavia" and "Nordic" are mentioned in the texts. All four countries included in this collection fall under the collective noun of "Nordic" and therefore it has been selected for the title of the book. Since the Scandinavian countries of Denmark, Norway, and Sweden, are in some examples analyzed separately from Finland, the term Scandinavia is also used at times.

CHAPTER 1

Sweden and the Foundation of the IAAF. A Harmoniously Developed Body or Citius, Altius, Fortius?

Hans Bolling

Introduction

Athletics have appeared on the program of the Olympic Games from their modern inauguration in Athens in 1896, and remains the most important sport on the Olympic program to this day. Athletics is not only the jewel in the Olympic crown — it is also the most widely disseminated sport with respect to time and place. It is possible to discern a connection between the arenas of the Panhellenic Games of ancient Greece and the stadiums constructed for the modern Olympic Games. At first glance many ingredients in today's athletics seem to have a profound correspondence to the athletics of ancient Greece. It is alleged that the first known Olympic winner was Koroibos, a runner (192.27 meters) from 776 B.C. In the still older *Iliad*, a poetic work attributed to the disputed concept of Homer, competitions in running and throwing (discus as well as javelin) were described dramatically and in some detail. These observations are easy to explain by referring to the natural movement pattern of human beings.[1]

Athletics thus have been practiced in a more or less formalized form for as long as we have evidence of physical activity.[2] In the first half of the nineteenth century, there were organized training and competitions in athletics'

---

[1] Homeros, *Iliaden*, trans. Erland Lagerlöf (Stockholm: Wahlström & Widstrand, 2002), song 23. Donald G. Kyle, *Sport and Spectacle in the Ancient World* (Oxford: Blackwell Publishing, 2007), 105–106.

[2] Åke Svahn, "*Studien über die Anfänge der Körperübungen auf der Grundlage urgeschichtlichen Felsbildmaerials*" (PhD diss., MartinLuther-Universität, Halle-Wittenberg, 1973). Thor Gotaas, *Running: A Global History*, trans. Peter Graves (London: Reaktion Books, 2009).

activities around Europe: Turnen at Hasenheide in Berlin and "Olympic Games" at Ramlösa in Sweden, among others.[3] Modern athletics, however, originated in Great Britain around the middle of the nineteenth century when they were introduced and systematized at schools (especially within the so-called public schools). Gradually special private clubs for athletics were created outside schools.[4]

It has, however, been demonstrated that English sports administrators did not take an active interest in establishing international associations. On the contrary, the English tended to be satisfied with their own national organizations, arguing that they could also be responsible for the leadership that various sports needed in order to function well on an international level. Instead, initiatives for purely international organizations came from other nations, not least from France. It has been pointed out clearly: "While the French lagged behind the British in the invention and diffusion of modern sports, they were unquestionably the leaders when it came to the creation of international sports organizations."[5]

The purpose of this paper is to shed light on the Swedish influence on the process of creating the International Amateur Athletic Federation (IAAF), today called World Athletics. Not only individual contributions and connections will be taken into account, but also what, if any, influence Swedish physical culture had on the formation of the rules of international athletics. The creation of the IAAF is an affair only comprising athletics for men. Before World War I, international athletics was a totally masculine phenomenon. A separate organization for women, Fédération Sportive Féminine Internationale, was founded in 1921. The IAAF, however, did not include female athletics until 1936.[6]

---

[3] Henning Eichberg, "Race-Track and Labyrinth: The Space of Physical Culture in Berlin," *Journal of Sport History* 17, no. 2 (Summer, 1990). Åke Svahn, "Olympiska spelen i Helsingborg 1834 och 1836," *Idrott, historia och samhälle* 1983 (1983), 91–102.

[4] Richard Holt, *Sport and the British: A Modern History* (Oxford: Clarendon, 1989). J.A. Mangan, *Athleticism in the Victorian and Edwardian Public School: The Emergence and Consolidation of an Education Ideology* (London: Falmer, 1986).

[5] Allen Guttmann, "Sports," in *Encyclopedia of European Social History from 1350 to 2000*, volume 5, ed. Peter N. Stearns (Detroit: Scribner, 2001), 175–176.

[6] Jörg Krieger, *Power and Politics in World Athletics: A Critical History* (Routledge: Abingdon, Oxon), 38–43.

Swedish Gymnastics and Athletics

It is fair to say that a hesitant attitude towards English sport in general and athletics in particular existed within Swedish society at the turn of the twentieth
century.[7] Behind this view was a negative perception of specialization within
athletics even if athletes could strive for top results, they should not forget that
the harmonious development of the body was paramount. This view had its
roots in Swedish gymnastics. The unique gymnastics system was designed at
the Royal Central Institute of Gymnastics (RCIG) in Stockholm by Per Henrik
Ling (1776–1839) and systematized by his followers. It was a gymnastic system that was supposed to be based on the needs of the body: harmonious development was the goal, and it was to be achieved through versatile training. Each
part of the body and every organ would get its daily dose of exercise. Symmetry
was one important principle; the right and left half of the body would develop
equally.

During the nineteenth century, the gymnastics promoted from the RCIG was
established as a state-sponsored physical culture that helped improve the physical health of individuals, the general population and the nation. The fact that
gymnastics already claimed "physical activity and health" for itself resulted
in competing, emerging sports put other virtues — such as character building, cohesion, class harmonization and a sense of country — above physical
health-promoting qualities when their place in society was yet to be justified.
In short, state-sanctioned gymnastics was seen as the means of health and re-
habilitation, while sports were designated other functions for both individual
and society.[8]

In 1900, the attitude towards sports from the physical education establishment was thus ambivalent at best, even explicitly hostile at times. It seems that
advocates for the wholesome aspects of physical activity, as well as the medical
community, were caught off guard when competitive sports became established
in Sweden. Through the centuries they had recommended physical exercise as
a method of health promotion, supported by ancient authorities such as Galen.

---

[7] In addition to the criticism noted below, there was a criticism of sport from the political left,
where sport was seen as a means for capitalism to keep the working class down. By extension,
here lies the view of sport as opium for the people.

[8] Hans Bolling, *Sin egen hälsas smed: Idéer, initiativ och organisationer inom svensk motionsidrott
1945–1981* (Stockholm: Acta Universitatis Stockholmiensis, 2005), 44. Henrik Sandblad, *Olympia
och Valhalla: Idéhistoriska aspekter av den moderna idrottsrörelsens framväxt* (Grillby: Lärdoms-
historiska samf., 1985), 355–371.

But when they were taken at their word and physical exercises became a popular movement in the form of sport, they were horrified to see that the ancient rule of moderation was flouted.[9]

One example among many is the medical doctor Henrik Berg, who argued for Swedish gymnastics as an activity which, in addition to strength, provided mastery over the body, noble posture and harmonious physique, while at the same time seeing sport as a mortal danger. Overall, gymnastics was seen as the perfect form of physical exercise, while the competitive aspect of sport inevitably led to excesses that endangered health. It was the root of evil within sport.[10]

Some actors tried to bridge the gap between gymnasts and proponents of sports. Colonel Viktor Balck (1824–1928), even if he is known as the father of Swedish sport, supported the tenets of Swedish gymnastics. He argued that when an all-round physical development through gymnastics had been achieved, one should switch to more suitable and entertaining sports.[11] Balck worked at the RCIG from 1872 to 1910, the last four years as the institute's director. He also initiated or participated in the founding of a number of sports clubs and associations on local, national and international level. He was, among other things, one of the original members of the IOC on which he served until 1920.[12]

Athletics, with its individual and highly specialized expressions, broke in an obvious way against the foundations of Swedish gymnastics with its emphasis on collective participation, symmetrical training and harmonious bodily development. Athletics thus broke the whole into pieces — movements were isolated and, by extension produced runners without muscular upper bodies and throwers with underdeveloped legs. The specialization of the body was seen by

---

[9] PC McIntosh, *Idrotten och samhället*, trans. Lars Ekegren (Stockholm: PAN/Norstedt, 1969), 21–32. According to Hieronymus Mercurialis and his De arte gymnastica, three types of gymnastics had developed in the ancient world: gymnastica medica, that is, exercises whose purpose was to benefit health (the only fully legitimate form of gymnastics); gymnastica bellica, which contained exercises preparatory to war and was therefore partially legitimate; gymnastica vitiosa, physical exercises for their own sake, competition or entertainment. Nancy G. Siraisi, *History, Medicine, and the Traditions of Renaissance learning* (Ann Arbor: University of Michigan Press, 2007), 51.

[10] Benkt Söderberg, *Kroppsövningar i populärmedicinsk litteratur 1900–1960*, unpublished work paper, Idrottshistoriska specialseminariet, Historiska institutionen, Stockholms universitet, 1997.

[11] Oswald Holmberg, *Den svenska gymnastikens utveckling* (Stockholm: Natur och kultur, 1939), 120–124.

[12] Jan Lindroth, *Idrott för kung och fosterland: Den svenska idrottens fader Viktor Balck 1844–1928* (Stockholm: SISU idrottsböcker, 2007).

gymnasts as the greatest exercise sin a person could indulge in and sheer irre-
sponsibility towards one's own body. It was something that, according to one
famous disciple of Ling, only occurred among "crazy Englishmen."[13]

Gymnastics therefore came to have an influence on how athletics was
practiced in Sweden from the outset. A number of the branches of athletics
competed in were made Swedish in accordance with the ideas that Swedish
gymnastics had at its foundation. The way in which good sport was judged
was influenced by gymnastic considerations. For example, an athlete should
not only make it over the bar when jumping, but they should also do it with
perfect form and with the body control and balance of the gymnast. So, it was
not only about making the highest jump or the longest throw, but also about
achieving the feat in an aesthetically pleasing style. In jumping, the jump and
impact should be controlled. If the competitors ended up with the same result,
"the most correctly executed jump, judged according to gymnastic principles, won."[14] In the field events, throws were performed, in true Ling spirit,
with both the left and the right hand, something that was considered the right
and natural way to compete and above all to train. Throwing the discus and
the javelin and putting the shot with the strongest hand only gained Swedish
championship status in 1924.[15]

Style was put on a comparable footing with results, something which was
noted by a sports-obsessed Scotsman on a visit to Gothenburg. He emphasized
to his hosts: "We can run faster, leap longer and jump higher, but we cannot do
it as gracefully as you do."[16]

The gymnastics promoted by the RCIG was seen as a systematic and instrumental form of "scientifically arranged body movements." Moderation was a
key word — better to be average in all branches than invincible champion in
one. A guiding principle in the gymnastics that was promoted from the RCIG
was that there should be a bond between physical exercises and science: gymnastics should be based on the knowledge of the laws of the human organism.
Per Henrik Ling had also been a member of the Swedish Medical Society. The
end goal was the all-round trained body, where no part was neglected and the

---

[13] Lennart K Persson and Thomas Pettersson, *Svensk friidrott 100 år* (Stockholm: Sellin, 1995),
27. The statement has been attributed to Hjalmar Ling, son of Per Henrik and active at the RCIG
from the 1840s to the 1880s.

[14] *Ibid.*, 28.

[15] *Ibid.*, 464–468.

[16] *Ibid.*, 29.

harmonious whole was paramount bodily specialization. Elitism and acrobatics were rejected.[17]

The dominance of gymnastics as the legitimate form of physical exercise has been linked to the primacy of posture as derived from the contemporary medical view of physical exercises. However, this attitude was challenged by developments within the physiological science, sport and the idea of man as an engine. During the first decades of the twentieth century, doctors thus went from a negative, sometimes fearful, attitude towards competitive sports to a more positive one. Today there is an intimate collaboration, even a symbiotic relationship between sports and medical science.[18]

The contradictions that arose from the gymnasts' aberrant attitude to the innovations in body culture brought about by English sport have been described as the most interesting conflict ever experienced within Swedish body culture. The reluctance of the gymnasts was directed towards physically one-sided sports exercises and was kept alive within the gymnastics tradition in Sweden. At first, however, the leaders of the RCIG prematurely viewed emerging sports as a passing fad.[19]

Anarchy in the UK

The athletics competitions at the Olympic Games in London 1908 were marred by bitter and infamous controversies between mainly the British officials and American athletes and their leaders/supporters. In the history of sport, this became known as "the Battle at Shepherd's Bush." The most famous controversies occurred in the tug-of-war, 400 meters and marathon. The fallout stemmed from the Americans feeling wronged by the British officials.[20]

Before the Games in London, representatives of the Swedish Athletics As-

---

[17] Söderberg, *Kroppsövningar i populärmedicinsk litteratur 1900–1960.*

[18] Benkt Söderberg, "A Change in the Medical Model: From Posture to Motor Behavior," in *Sport and Health in History,* ed. Thierry Terret (Sankt Augustin: Academia Verlag, 1999).

[19] Jan Lindroth, *Idrottens väg till folkrörelse: Studier i svensk idrottsrörelse fram till 1915* (Uppsala: Studia historica Upsaliensia, 1974), 261.

[20] Ture Widlund, "Spelen 1896–1908," in *Sverige och OS,* ed. Stig Gustafson and Tomas Glanell (Stockholm: Strömbergs idrottsböcker, 1987), 53. Bill Mallon and Ian Buchanan, *The 1908 Olympic Games: Results for all Competitors in all Events, with Commentary* (Jefferson, NC: McFarland & Company, 2000), 9–12.

sociation (SAA, Svenska Idrottsförbundet) had proposed the creation of an international organization for athletics. The English hosts, however, regarded themselves as readily equipped for carrying through the Olympic event alone, having no time for endeavors outside their main concern.[21] In the end, however, events at the Games clearly demonstrated not only the need for common international rules, but also a generally accepted body for settling disputes. In fact, a lively and easy-going athletic exchange between various countries and continuity within this forum required a set of rules recognized by all competitors. The athletes would also benefit from knowing the rules in advance and thus be able to prepare in the best possible way.

Preludes

The decision of the IOC, in 1909, to select Stockholm/Sweden as the host of the 1912 Olympic Games stimulated the SAA to resume its attempt to create an international athletic federation. The conditions for the creation of such an organization were seen as favorable. In January 1910, the SAA's board thus applied for money to arrange a congress in 1912, where the question could be discussed.[22] The application was directed to the Organizing Committee of the Olympic Games (OCOG). In order not to repeat the failure of the attempt in connection with the 1908 London Games, the applicants underlined that the preparatory work for such a congress must be done well in advance of the forthcoming Stockholm Olympic Games. One argument was that the foreign representatives taking part in such a congress "must be our guests."[23] The most important reason for an international association, however, according to the SAA, was to centre athletics as the jewel in the Olympic crown. The overwhelming consensus prevailed that the repellent example set by British/English and American athletes and representatives in 1908 thus must be avoided.

Despite this, the application was not approved. It was not because the OCOG thought that the idea was flawed. The reason was more related to the intricate bureaucracy that surrounded Swedish sports. Obviously, the application did not

---

[21] Sweden's National Archives, Svenska idrottsförbundet, Board minutes, A2:2, January 16, 1910, § 41.

[22] *Ibid.*

[23] IAAF's archives, General Administration 1913–1914, Letter from the Swedish Athletics Association to the organizing committee of the Olympic Games in Stockholm 1912, January 17, 1910.

fit into the ambitions and obligations of the Olympic organizers. Instead, the Swedish Sports Confederation (SSC, Riksidrottsförbundet), the top organization for all sport clubs and associations in Sweden, was considered the correct authority to deal with such a matter. In an agreement between the different stakeholders in Swedish sport in 1909, the SSC had been assigned the task of leading organized sport at home and abroad.[24]

The SAA thus turned to the SSC with a request for support in December 1910. The request was for a grant in order to arrange a meeting in Sweden, or to cover the costs for three Swedish representatives travelling to London or some other meeting place.[25] And shortly before the annual meeting, the board of the SAA decided to arrange a preparatory congress in the summer of 1911. Provided general consensus could be reached, the intention was to take the next step by discussing specific rules in detail and, thereafter, formally establish an international organization following the Olympic Games in Stockholm.[26]

By April 1911, however, thirteen nations had agreed to the general idea, so it was no longer considered necessary to put resources into a preparatory meeting. The interest was sufficiently high.[27] Undoubtedly, this represented a positive result and it led the SAA to the conclusion that a constituting congress could be held in connection with the Olympic Games in 1912:

> We have also come to the resolution that this first Congress shall restrict its labours to the constituting of the Federation and to any allied questions, and that, later on the course of 1912, a new meeting shall be held for the purpose of settling the amateur question, rules and regulations for competitions.[28]

The SAA thus invited to a congress in Stockholm on July 16, 1912, just after the athletic competitions were completed. According to the invitation, the international organization should be responsible for three main tasks:

---

[24] Lindroth, *Idrottens väg till folkrörelse*, 129.

[25] IAAF's archives, General Administration 1913–1914, Letter from the SAA to the SSC, December 9, 1910.

[26] *Årsbok 1911 för Svenska gymnastik- och idrottsföreningars riksförbund* (Stockholm: Nordiskt Idrottslifs tryckeri, 1912), 77.

[27] Sweden's National Archives, Svenska idrottsförbundet, Board minutes, A2:2, April 22, 1911, § 44.

[28] IAAF's archives, General Administration 1913–1914, Letter from SAA to the national athletic federations, May 11, 1911.

- To establish generally accepted rules for international exchange.
- To register all records (international, national and Olympic) and administer it at a head office.
- To draw up an amateur definition appropriate for international competitions.

Furthermore, it was emphasized that the proposed international organization, already called the International Amateur Athletic Federation (IAAF), would not encroach into the territory of the IOC.[29] The annual report of the SAA contains a scantly concealed boast that the Swedish initiative "had been received with greatest sympathy by all nations" (probably a slight overstatement).[30] The leading force in the effort to create the international association was the president of SAA Leopold Englund (1868–1931). Englund, a wholesaler from Gothenburg, had been one of the founders of SAA in 1895, an organization established in Gothenburg as an alternative to a national federation created by Viktor Balck in Stockholm. Although Stockholm has dominated much of Swedish history, Stockholm and Gothenburg competed to be the sports capital of the nation. In Stockholm, sports were heavily influenced by the RCIG and the military through many deeply committed officers. In Gothenburg, on the other hand, sport was in the hands of civilians who focused their efforts to a much greater extent towards competitive sports. It can also be argued that the Gothenburg approach to sport was international, while Stockholm was more nationalistic in outlook.

Another sports official with roots in Gothenburg's sporting world was Sigfrid Edström (1870–1964). Edström, an engineer by profession, had returned to Sweden and Gothenburg in 1900 after studying and working in Switzerland and the US. He was one of the main actors in creating the SSC in 1903 and the leading person within the organization during its first decade. He has gone down in history as a pragmatic person who had the good sense to surround himself with competent co-workers, both as a leading sport official and as a business leader. One should not overlook that his personal qualities according to Swedish historian Leif Yttergren "made those around him see him as something of a superman, a charismatic leader."[31] Edström came to crown his successful career in sport administration as president of the IOC 1946–1952.

---

[29] IAAF's archives, General Administration 1913–1914, Invitation from SAA, May, 1911.

[30] Sweden's National Archives, Svenska idrottsförbundet, Report of the board, 1911, A2:1.

[31] Leif Yttergren, "Patriarch and a Charismatic Leader? Some Reflections on IOC President J. Sigfrid Edström's Leadership Style Based on Max Weber's Concept of Charisma," in *Pathways: Critiques and Discourse in Olympic Research*. Ninth International Symposium for Olympic Research, ed. Robert K. Barney et al. (London, Ontario: International Centre for Olympic Studies, 2008), 301.

Even if "all nations" had a positive attitude towards the initiative, it did not mean that the initiative was universally supported. The president of the IOC, Pierre de Coubertin (1863–1937), adopted a skeptical position in relation to a new international organization for athletics. In a letter to de Coubertin in February 1911, Englund informed the already-irked leader of the IOC that serious misunderstandings were afoot concerning the new organization for athletics. From the SAA's point of view, no intentions whatsoever existed to accede the IOC and try to take over management of the Olympic Games. Englund emphasized:

> That we have not in any way violated the laws of courtesy, for it has never occurred to us to think that the IOC would bestow any work on these purely technical sporting questions or that the IOC could object to having uniformity introduced in all countries regarding the practical exercise of sport.
>
> You will thus see, that we have not tried to conceal any thing from you, but we were of the opinion that this question did not concern you directly as being outside your immediate sphere of interest. [32]

De Coubertin replied, somewhat less confrontationally, that though they may mean well, that "hell is paved with good intentions."[33] De Coubertin looked for and found arguments by referring to the situation in some other sports. His main argument was that all international federations for specific sports were detrimental to the good of sport as a whole. This was, for example, the case in association football, which had been divided into two fractions, one belonging to the international federation and those outside. The same situation prevailed in swimming according to the Olympic pioneer. Thus, he warned against a similar development in athletics. He was however, careful to emphasize that the opinion was his own and not the official opinion of the IOC.[34]

The strategy from Englund and his allies was to deescalate the tensions and try to calm de Coubertin's fears. They were convinced that an international athletic federation would be created. But it seems de Coubertin was not the only person who worried about the consequences for the Olympic movement

---

[32] IAAF's archives, General Administration 1913–1914, Letter from Leopold Englund to Pierre de Coubertin, February 28, 1911.

[33] IAAF's archives, Members Correspondence 1911–1914, International Correspondence G–Ö, Letter from Pierre de Coubertin to Leopold Englund, March 9, 1911.

[34] IAAF's archives, Members Correspondence 1911–1914, International Correspondence G–Ö, Letters from Pierre de Coubertin to Leopold Englund, February 28 and March 9, 1911.

of the establishment of the federation. Viktor Balck complained to Englund that he had received reactions from colleagues in Austria, England, France and the USA indicating one and the same thing: a new federation threatened to rival the IOC. Balck, effectively the Swedish sports minister for foreign affairs, felt disturbed and lamented that he had to write a lot of letters in order to explain the Swedish initiatives and intentions.[35] On the other side, many international sport administrators agreed on the general need for common rules and methods for their interpretation. In this spirit the American James E. Sullivan (1862–1914) pointed out that:

> it is of greatest importance indeed to have all international competition, Olympic Games, in fact all international games conducted under a positive set of rules. There is no doubt whatever but the point made by you is absolute a sound one.[36]

However, we should keep in mind that Sullivan, with a career in sport publishing and the sporting goods businesses, had both challenged de Coubertin's leadership over the Olympic movement and tried to form an international athletics federation under his leadership before.[37] He was active in competitive sport as one of the founders of the Amateur Athletic Union (AAU), secretary of the US Olympic committee and chief organizer of the 1904 Olympic Games in St. Louis. As a member of the New York City Board of Education he was also strongly committed to strengthening children and young people's opportunities to be physically active.[38] With Irish roots, Sullivan had been one of the more confrontational Americans at London in 1908 and denounced the English officials in the strongest terms upon his return to the USA.[39]

---

[35] AAF's archives, General Administration 1913–1914, Letter from Viktor Balck to Leopold Englund, March 3, 1911.

[36] IAAF's archives, Members Correspondence 1911–1914, International Correspondence G–Ö, Letter from James E. Sullivan to Leopold Englund, March 24, 1911.

[37] Krieger, *Power and Politics in World Athletics,* 16. Kevin B. Wamsley and Guy Schulz, "Rogues and Bedfellows. The IOC and the Incorporation of the FSFI," in *Bridging Three Centuries. Intellectual Crossroads and the Modern Olympic Movement.* Fifth International Symposium for Olympic Research, ed. Kevin B Wamsley et al. (London, Ontario: University of Western Ontario, 2000), 114.

[38] "James E. Sullivan Passes Away," *New York Times,* September 17, 1914, 9. Sullivans made his attitude towards female athletes clear in an interview at Stockholm 1912: "We have not sent women to the competitions, as we in America do not wish to see them doing sport in public. Both sport and they are better off if they practice sport at a distance from public curiosity." Carl G. Laurin, "Post Festum," *Idun,* August 4, 1912, 520.

[39] Mallon and Buchanan, *The 1908 Olympic Games,* 9–12.

At the Olympic Games in Stockholm 1912 the absence of complete, generally accepted set of rules for athletics remained problematic for the committee organizing the athletic events. The official report from the Game states that this fact created "a very great disadvantage" to the hosts. Although the organizers had tried to produce a program which considered all requirements from the various participating nations, it was impossible to satisfy all; a statement that seems quite natural. Thus, the program had been exposed to criticism and insinuations that "Swedish interests had been too much favored."[40] When studying the actual program it cannot be said that the program of the athletic competitions favored Swedish interests to a particularly high degree. But two ingredients can be said to have been influenced by national conditions: the inclusion of both the right and the left hand when throwing the javelin, discus and shotput, and pentathlon and decathlon. On the other hand Sweden did not enter any participants in the 10,000 meters walking race.[41]

Throwing with both hands was so deeply rooted in Sweden that Viktor Balck, at the meeting of the IOC in Budapest in May 1911, threatened to cancel the Stockholm Games if the IOC opposed the inclusion of throwing with both the right and the left hand among the disciplines.[42] The Swedes' fondness for the all-round athlete can help us understand why the Swedish King Gustaf V called the winner of the pentathlon and decathlon Jim Thorpe "the greatest athlete in the world."[43] The words are reputed to have been said at the award ceremony in 1912. The King had been a close ally to Viktor Balck in his efforts to organize Swedish sport for decades.

It is thus reasonable to claim that it was difficult for organizers of international sports competitions to design a program and rules that kept all participants happy, even when they consciously strived towards it. And it is also true that, to a certain extent, there existed a Swedish approach to athletics that did

---

[40] Erik Bergvall, ed., *Olympiska spelen: Officiell redogörelse för Olympiska spelen i Stockholm 1912* (Stockholm: Wahlström & Widstrand, 1913), 391.

[41] Leif Yttergren, Hans Bolling and Ingemar Ekholm, "Counts and Draymen: The Swedish Participants," in *The 1912 Stockholm Olympics: Essays on the Competitions, the People, the City*, ed. Leif Yttergren and Hans Bolling (Jefferson, NC: McFarland & Company, 2012), 102. The lack of walkers may be due to Sigfrid Edström's disdain towards the activity, he compared walking to competing in whispering the loudest.

[42] Sweden's National Archives, Stockholmsolympiaden 1912, Kommittén för allmän idrott, Ö II a:2.

[43] Bill Mallon and Ture Widlund, *The 1912 Olympic Games: Results for all Competitors in all Events, with Commentary* (Jefferson, NC: McFarland & Company, 2009), 22.

not fully correspond to how practitioners and officials elsewhere in the world viewed athletics. The Swedish approach toward athletics was influenced by the aforementioned form of gymnastics created by Per Henrik Ling. Its main point was that the human body should be exercised harmoniously and in an all-round fashion.[44]

Stockholm 1912

On May 16 1912, Sigfrid Edström who also was vice president of the OCOG received a letter from the English Amateur Athletic Association (AAA). It said that the AAA accepted the invitation to take part in the upcoming congress on condition that the agenda presented was followed; the AAA did not intend to support an organization which possibly would be offensive to the IOC or in any way intruded into its territory.[45]

A final invitation to the congress was sent out by the SAA in June. The congress would take place on July 17, three days after the conclusion of the athletic competitions at Stockholm 1912. That the initiative from the Swedish sports officials had support from the Official Sweden is evident from the fact that the meeting was to be held at the Parliament Building, and the Crown Prince Gustaf Adolf acted as the protector of the congress. The agenda remained unchanged. The strategy was prepared by Edström, who had consulted the Crown Prince. Edström and the Crown Prince formed a most influential pairing at the top of the Swedish sports movement at the start of the twentieth century.[46]

The meeting was carried through according to plan. Present were thirty-seven delegates from seventeen nations: Australia, Austria, Belgium, Canada, Chile, Denmark, Egypt, Finland, France, Germany, Great Britain, Greece, Hungary, Norway, Russia, Sweden and the USA. No less than eleven Swedish delegates were present.

The delegates were welcomed by Leopold Englund, who in the interest of Olympic peace emphasized that the interests of the IOC must be respected, wishing:

---

[44] Lindroth, *Idrotten väg till folkrörelse*. Persson and Pettersson, *Svensk friidrott 100 år*, 28–9. Frank Zamowski, *All-Around Men: Heroes of a Forgotten Sport* (Lanham: Scarcrow press, 2005), 31–2.

[45] IAAF's archives, General Administration 1913–1914, Letter from P. L. Fisher to Sigfrid Edström, May 16, 1912.

[46] IAAF's archives, General Administration 1913–1914, Invitation from SAA to take part in the foundation of an international athletics federation, June 1912. Lindroth, *Idrottens väg till folkrörelse*.

that a strong Board may now be formed and that the object of the Board should be, to draw up and agree to rules and regulations for International Athletics, to register all World's, Olympic and National records, and also to draw up an amateur definition for international competitions. Our work should, therefore, be confined to these points, as the organization of the Olympic games is in the hands of the International Olympic Committee. (*Svensk Idrott 1912: Årsbok för Svenska gymnastik- och idrottsföreningars riksförbund* (Stockholm: Nordiskt Idrottslifs tryckeri, 1913), 248–249.)

Sigfrid Edström was elected to chair the congress with Kristian Hellström (1880–1946) as secretary. Hellström, a former middle distance runner who won the bronze medal in 1,500 meters at the Intercalated Games in Athens in 1906, had been handpicked by Edström as general secretary of the OROC in 1910 despite opposition from the committee's chairman, Viktor Balck, who considered him too inexperienced.[47] At last, the time to talk in favor of or against the proposed organization had come. Who were supportive, who were skeptical, who opposed the idea?

The most vocal supporter of the creation of a new organization was Carl Diem (1882–1962) of Germany. Diem was to become a close ally to Edström in the world of sporting bureaucracy for decades to come.[48] The idea, he argued, had met with widespread approval from several nations and all concerned were acquainted with it. If some nations did not want to join at once, they could wait, for example, to the next congress. Support for the proposal was also given from Austria, Chile, Finland, Hungary, Norway and Russia. However, delegates in favor were less forthright with their views than the skeptics and opponents.

The delegate from Greece was concerned with relations with the IOC. He pointed out that de Coubertin was preparing an international Olympic congress in Paris in 1914, where rules, regulations, a standard program, amateur definitions etc. filled the agenda. Here, again, we see how important the Olympic movement, as the older and more prestigious organization, was in the preparations for the IAAF.

The representatives from the English speaking world were more or less negative towards the proposed IAAF from the outset. However, they did sympathize with a new organization as a general idea, appreciating the sentiment behind the Swedish initiative. Some doubt existed as to whether the congress was meant

---

[47] Therese Nordlund Edvinsson, "Organizing the 1912 Games" in *The 1912 Stockholm Olympics: Essays on the Competitions, the People, the City*, ed. Leif Yttergren and Hans Bolling (Jefferson, NC: McFarland & Company, 2012), 65.

[48] Yttergren, "Patriarch and a Charismatic Leader," 301.

to formally establish a new organization, or only to discuss such a step. Several nations were not prepared for the former. They lacked full authorization from their respective home countries. On the other hand, it seems reasonable to wonder why they were not better prepared, since the question had been well-known for a long time. It should be added that decisive opponents — totally rejecting the idea — were not present.

However, the delegates were able to appoint a temporary (ad interim) board with Edström as chairman and Hellström as secretary. Moreover, the congress decided that five more countries should be represented on the new board: France, Germany, Great Britain, Austria and the USA. Austria, however, gave up their place, since the delegate from Hungary expressed his wish to become a member. The following quintet was elected as national representatives: Pierre Roy (France), Carl Diem (Germany), P.L. Fisher (Great Britain), Szilárd Stankovits (Hungary) and James E. Sullivan (USA).[49]

We can see that the Swedish officials succeeded in taking control of the process but the important question of the makeup of the rules of athletics was postponed to future meetings, where the Swedish influence in all probability would be less prominent. To sum up: the need for a special international organization dedicated to athletics was not denied by any country present at the Stockholm congress of 1912. The delegates probably realized that all roads led to the creation of an international federation, in line with sports such as skating, association football, cycling and swimming. But officials from a number of leading sporting nations wanted to proceed cautiously so as not to clash with the IOC and its president.

Berlin 1913

At Stockholm, the delegates decided to meet again the following year in Berlin to form the IAAF. Some problems arose before the sport administrators could meet. A Swedish newspaper illustrated one of them in March 1913 under the headline "Will England cause difficulties?" According to the paper, indications suggested that disagreements were potentially in the offing. The English opinion had shifted, so it was said, to skepticism due to the influence of the president of the IOC, de Coubertin.

The paper added that under no conditions should the congress delegates appointed by the SAA agree to any compromise aimed at diminishing the strength and authority of the new international federation. The SAA was encouraged to

---

[49] *Svensk Idrott 1912*, 249–254.

ignore nations disrupting the foundation process; sooner or later they would come back pleading for acceptance.

It is interesting to notice how this opinion, probably shared by many other papers and sports leaders, railed against two of the traditionally strong forces within international sports: the English and the IOC. Both were expected to withdraw. Regarding England, it was emphasized that this country at that time had lost its leading position — international federations were therefore required to replace English organizations in the leading positions.[50]

When the IAAF was officially formed, in Berlin in August 1913, twenty-seven representatives from sixteen nations took part and a further eleven national associations were recognized at the congress. By broad definition it can thus be argued that all continents had associations recognized by the IAAF.[51]

The results of all proposals, considerations and discussions became the very basis of athletics at the widest possible international level. When the IAAF, thereafter — through the above-mentioned James E. Sullivan and the American Publishing Company — edited protocols and accepted rules, it was said that the Berlin congress undoubtedly formed the most important legislative meeting in the history of athletics.[52]

The Swedish attitude towards the new rules is reflected by the instructions that the Swedish delegates brought with them to Berlin. They can be summarized as follows:

1. The federation ought to be established irrespective of which countries and how many were willing to take part.
2. The federation must not be dependent upon any other sports authority.

---

[50] Jicky, "Den internationella idrottsfederationen," *Svenska Dagbladet,* March 20, 1913, 10.

[51] Federations represented at Berlin 1913: Amateur Athletic Union of Australasia, Österreichischer Leichtathletik-Verband, Ligue Belge d'Athlétisme, Amateur Athletic Union of Canada, Dansk Athletik-Forbund, Union Internationale des Sociétés Sportives d'Egypte, Finlands Gymnastik-och Idrottsförbund, Union des Sociétés Francaises de Sports Athlétiques. Deutsche Sport Behörde für Athletik, Amateur Athletic Association, Magyar Athletikai Szövotsog, Norges Turn- og Idraetsforbund, South African Amateur Athletic and Cycling Association, Svenska Idrottsförbundet, Athletischer Ausschuss der Schweizerischen Football-Association, and Amateur Athletic Union of the United States.

[52] National athletic federation not represented but recognized by the Berlin congress 1913: Sociedad Sportiva Argentina, Federation Sportiva Nacional de Chili, Union des Societies Helleniques d'Athletisme et de Gymnastique. Hongkong Amateur Athletic Association, Federazione Italiana Degli Sports Atletici, Federation des Societes Luxemburgeoises de Sports Athletiques, Club Atletico Internacional, New Zealand Amateur Athletic Association, Russischer Landesverband für Leicht-Athletik, Serbischer Leichtathletischer Verband, and Nerderlandsche Athletiek Unie.

3. Propose that a new congress should be held on the demand of at least three countries.
4. A yearly congress for the time being.
5. If the program of the Olympic Games at Berlin would be discussed, the Swedish delegates were instructed to work for it to be the same as what was used at Stockholm in 1912.[53]

The most obvious conclusion from these instructions seems to be that the Swedish leaders demanded a new international organization for athletics to be established at any cost. They were indeed dedicated to their original vision. From the French side an additional proposal was put forward, namely to include professional athletics in the IAAF sphere of interest. Such an inclusion could prevent newspapers or other private interests from arranging professional championships. According to the French representative, Franz Reichel, the IAAF would have the opportunity to control when, where and how such championships were arranged. Reichel had replaced Pierre Roy as French representative on the interim board for health reasons. All other countries were opposed to this proposal, because they thought that the relations between amateur and professional sports should be decided on a national level. Reichel thus withdrew his proposal.[54]

A special committee was appointed to draw up rules: James E. Sullivan was appointed president of the committee with F. Burger (Germany), S.G. Moss (Great Britain), Szilárd Stankovits (Hungary), J.M. Willig (France) and Leopold Englund as members. The committee was given the task to draft a first set of rules between sessions, then use the year before the next congress to get feedback from all member Federations in order to have a final proposal ready to be accepted at the 1914 Congress.

The foundation decision was supplemented by rules and regulations for international competitions, registration of world records and amateur definitions. Moreover, a standard program for Olympic athletics was accepted: Running: 100, 200, 400, 800, 1,500, 5,000 and 10,000 meters flat and marathon (40,200 meters); 3 000 meters steeplechase, 110 and 400 meters hurdle race; walking: 3,000 and 10,000 meter, running high jump, long jump and hop, step and jump, and pole

---

[53] IAAF, *Minutes and proposed rules adopted by the International Amateur Athletic Federation, held at Berlin Germany, Aug. 20–23, 1913* (New York: American Sports Publishing Company, 1914), 3.

[54] IAAF's archives, General Administration 1913–1914, Letter from SAA to Kristian Hellström, August 6, 1913.

jump; throwing the javelin, discus and weight (56 lbs) with the best hand; putting the shot, with the best hand; throwing the hammer; pentathlon: long jump,
throwing the javelin, 200 meters flat, throwing the discus and 1,500 meters flat;
decathlon: 100 meters flat, running broad jump, putting the weight, running high
jump, 400 meters flat, 110 meters hurdle race, throwing the discus, pole jump,
throwing the javelin and 1,500 meters flat; relay races: 4x100 and 4x400 meters;
team races, 3 000 meters, five to run, three to count; tug-of-war: teams of eight;
and cross country race 10,000 meters, individual and team race.[55]

From a Swedish point of view the Olympic program included one disappointment. As stated previously, the Swedish gymnastic ideology remained prev-
alent to some degree in Swedish sports, prescribing all-round capacity. This
brought about throwing competitions where both hands should be used (one
after the other), with the result of both hands being aggregated. But the opposition against such a procedure (favoring the best hand throw) became too strong
even though the proposal was supported by representatives from Finland and
Denmark.[56]

Both Edström and Hellström were re-elected as chairman and secretary for
a period of four years. The minutes from the congress suggests that Edström's
position as president of the IAAF had been strengthened. We can read that
the delegates "wished to thank the Chairman, of whom everyone felt justly
proud, for the extremely able manner in which he had conducted the proceedings." The record continued that Edström "had proved an ideal Chairman and
had certainly endeared himself to everyone" and "acted with great dignity,
and it was greatly due to his personality that the meeting obtained such good
results."[57] Hellström, however, informed his colleagues that he would likely
have to leave his position as secretary prematurely, since his business engage-
ments almost certainly would force him to leave Sweden. He was replaced as
secretary by Hilding Kjellman in 1914. Kjellman, the president of the Swedish National Association for Student Sports, was an advanced scholar and
later became a professor of Romance philology. He had been co-opted by Edström, who in Berlin had been instructed personally to choose a successor to
Hellström. The members of the temporary board appointed in Stockholm —

[55] IAAF, *Minutes and proposed rules*, 11. "the only way to prevent the growth of professionalism
being to control it, as otherwise any newspaper or private body might arrange professional championships, etc., to any extent, whereas this Federation ought to have power to fix the venues and
times for such championships."

[56] *Ibid.*, 29–30.

[57] *Ibid.*, 17–18. "Olympiskt standardprogram antaget," *Svenska Dagbladet,* August 24, 1913, 7.

with Reichel replacing Roy as France's representative — received renewed confidence until the next congress.

The congress also decided that the IAAF, with Sullivan as mediator, should ask a manufacturer of sports tools, A.G. Spalding & Bros, to produce standard tools for athletics to be demonstrated at the 1914 congress for approval. Every member country would receive one set of all tools produced, with the right to reproduce them under appropriate control.[58]

Lyon 1914

At the IAAF congress of 1914 held in Lyon — not Paris as had been initially decided the year before — standard tools were presented and approved of in accordance with the decision made in Berlin. Only one exception to general approval occurred. The javelin of A.G. Spalding & Bros was ruled out in favor of a Finnish prototype. The regulation of athletic tools became the object of still more regulations. For instance, tools without a mark indicating approval by the authorized association could not be used as far as records were concerned. Furthermore, the detailed rules prescribed what material (metals, for example) had to be used for the tools in throwing the hammer etc. Rules for competitions and amateurism were valid from January 1, 1915. A register covering world records was also legitimated. To demonstrate appreciation of the pioneer manufacturer from the USA, the IAAF resolved:

> that in view of the work they have done in producing the standard implements and the consequent expense entailed, Messrs. A.G. Spalding & Bros will be given the opportunity of tendering bids for supplies of implements required by members of the Federation and for which purpose an official stamp shall be supplied to them for each country in which they have establishments. (IAAF's archives, Administration 1913–1914, Resolutions adopted at the Congress of the International Amateur Athletic Federation at Lyons on June 9 & 10, 1914.)

The IAAF was eager to establish a complete, standard program for the Olympic athletic competitions before the IOC congress, which was to open in Paris three days after the ending of the Lyon meeting. The aim of the IOC congress primarily focused on the program question. Among specific items to be discussed and resolved we can distinguish the following: Which sports would be compulsory at Olympic Games? Women's participation? An age limit for participation?

---

[58] IAAF, *Minutes and proposed rules*, 18–19.

Permission for representing more than one country? The amateur rules? In order to consolidate its position the IAAF wrote to de Coubertin during the IOC congress:

> On behalf of the IAAF, which is composed of the active controlling body of each country, we beg to ask you that the IOC will approve of the unanimous decision of the Federation at Berlin, August 1913, confirmed at the meeting at Lyon, 1914, by which the IAAF recommends that at future Olympic Games each competing country shall be entitled to enter 12 and start 6 competitors in each event. (IAAF's archives, Administration 1913–1914, Letter from the IAAF to Pierre de Coubertin, June 22, 1914.)

At a board meeting with the IAAF, just after the end of the IOC congress in Paris, Edström informed his colleagues Diem, Reichel, Stankovits and Sullivan that the IOC had accepted the IAAF's rules as the official ones for athletics at the Olympic Games to come. The amateur rules and events within athletics had been accepted. Moreover, the IAAF was entitled to arrange for the jury present at the athletic competitions. As jury for the Olympic Games in Berlin 1916, the IAAF board elected itself.[59] It is thus fair to conclude that most of the goals set by Leopold Englund and the SAA in 1909 were ultimately realized.

Summary

There is no exaggeration in stating that the most important reason for creating an international athletic federation was the need for common rules. The ever-growing network of international competitions clearly demonstrated the amount of problems caused by the absence of a consistent set of rules. Moreover, a supreme authority was needed for consistent, central administration. Common rules also improved the ability of athletes to prepare for competition, as the exact conditions for the competitions were known in advance. In this paper, however, the purpose has been to shed light on the Swedish influence on the process of creating the IAAF. Attention has been drawn to the contributions of individual officials and sport organizations, but also the supposed influence of Swedish physical culture on the formation of the international rules of athletics.

We have seen that the initiative to create the IAAF came from the Swedish Athletics Association. However, in the creation process sports officials from many

---

[59] *Ibid.*, 16–17.

countries participated. If some key personal contribution should be mentioned, two Swedes and an American stand out as most essential. Their contributions followed one after the other in a logical way. Leopold Englund, the president of the SAA, played the role of initiator, hosting the congress at Stockholm just after the athletic events at the Olympic Games at Stockholm had ended. The strong guiding hand and political skills of Sigfrid Edström made sure that the initiative was successfully carried through, facilitating the subsequent congresses and the continued work within the federation. He continued as president of the IAAF until 1946. With the creation of the IAAF we can also see a generational shift within Swedish sport administration on an international level. An older generation symbolized by Viktor Balck gave way to new, younger one with Edström at the helm. The members of the new generation were not as influenced by the Swedish gymnastic tradition and had a more pragmatic view of sport in general.

The foremost sport administrator from the USA, James E. Sullivan, had the delicate task of being responsible for giving the finishing touches to the detailed rules, a work which completed the creation process. So even though Swedes were behind the formation of the Federation and Swedes managed to take organizational control over the IAAF, the most important post when it came to shaping how athletics should be practiced ended up in American hands. That is: under the influence of a person who was far closer to what the followers of Ling called crazy Englishmen than to healthy Swedish gymnastics.

Only one serious and persistent opposition to the international federation can be found, represented by one single person: Pierre de Coubertin. De Coubertin is given most of the credit for establishing and sustaining the Olympic Games during the early years and part of his success was due to his rejection of rival governing bodies.[60] He feared that a new organization would contribute to a fissure within the organized world of sport. His concern was exclusively linked to the IOC and the most significant competition, the Olympic Games. The fathers of the IAAF, therefore, continuously emphasized that the new organization did not intend to compete with the IOC and managed to appease de Coubertin in time. The events surrounding the creation of the IAAF also confirms that the English did not play a prominent role when international sport federations were formed.

When the decision to form the federation had been taken the IAAF rapidly achieved fundamental results. However the procedures connected with the creation process are interpreted, it must be concluded that the original three goals put forward by the Swedish officials became fulfilled:

---

[60] IAAF's archives, Administration 1913–1914, Board meeting of the IAAF, June 24, 1914.

1.   The creation of a new organization and agreement on common rules.
2.   Registration of records.
3.   A definition of the concept of amateurism.

Moreover, a standard program for future Olympic athletics (for men) was agreed and accepted by the IOC at the same time as the IOC also accepted the IAAF as the supreme authority concerning athletics. With these facts in mind, the creation of the IAAF must be considered an obvious success.

In one respect the Swedish leaders did not succeed: to make the other countries accept the principle of Swedish gymnastics — the harmonious physical development as the predominant goal. Instead, the IAAF promoted an extremely specialized sport (with two exceptions: pentathlon and decathlon) involving stronger athletes going faster and higher. This direction is in line with the seven criteria that Allen Guttmann has presented as typical for the sportification process during modern time: secularization, equality, specialization, rationalization, bureaucratization, quantification and records.[61] In other words, the creation of the IAAF was perfectly compatible with the general development of modern sports.

This gives rise to a further question; which set of rules was the blueprint for the design of the universal rules? In Sweden they were presented as relying on rules created for the Olympic Games of 1912, the Stockholm rules. But the absence of field events using the right and the left hand makes the claim somewhat dubious. The claim from the USA that it was the rules used in American athletics that formed the basis for the new rules for international athletics is thus not without merit.[62] In the autumn of 1914 the activities within the IAAF came to a standstill, a pause which is not solely explained by the outbreak of war. James E. Sullivan passed away in September 1914 — perhaps the most energetic force in the drafting of the federation's rules, statutes and regulations.[63]

---

[61] Wamsley and Schulz, "Rogues and Bedfellows," 116.

[62] Allen Guttmann, *From Ritual to Record: The Nature of Modern Sport* (New York: Colombia University Press, 1978), 16.

[63] "Sullivan Burial Today," *New York Times*, September 19, 1914, 9.

CHAPTER 2

The Politicization of Danish Athletics during German Occupation in the Second World War

Hans Bonde

Introduction

How closely connected can athletics and politics be? The period up to and during the German occupation of Denmark can throw a surprising light on this very subject, because the characteristics of a phenomena are often shown best when it is under pressure. We can gain an insight into sport's potentially explosive force in situations of conflict when the key question is whether sport should contribute to the improvement of democratic citizenship or instead be embedded in a cult of superiority.

Denmark was occupied by Germany on April 9, 1940. The event would prove to have an effect on Danish sport, in general, and athletics in particular. Both professional sport and many of the associations and unions from the larger Sports Federation of Denmark (DIF), not least The Athletics Association, lived and breathed for international sporting relations, which drew in the crowds and provided their economies with important financial injections. The income from home games, especially, yielded well in the associations' cash boxes. As far as athletics was concerned, anticipation of records set by Danish athletes – achieved through fierce competition with foreign athletes – drew large numbers of paying spectators to events.

The collaboration by Danish sporting organizations with the occupying powers became widespread. In the relatively short period from the first games on August 22, 1940 until the last match against a German team – an international handball match on November 22, 1942 – a wealth of international matches, inter-city matches, tournaments, games and series were held, where especially the boxing and wrestling associations together with The Athletics Association were active as organizers.

Banners of the Nazi swastika flew side by side with the Danish flag, *Dannebrog*, while German competitors gave the 'heil' salute and German spectators gave the 'heil' in return. Crowds sang Danish anthems such as *Kong Christian Stod ved Højen Mast*, followed in German by *Deutschland, Deutschland* über *Alles* and the Nazi *Horst Wessel* anthem. Collaboration in sports provided the most comprehensive Danish example of cultural collaboration with the occupying powers. The first years of the occupation became a 'golden age' of Danish-German collaborative sports that was far more intense than any period before or since.

Sporting relations with Germany involved the entire Danish elite-sports world, both amateur and professional. On a personal level, all the top leadership of DIF and decision makers among the associations entered into these collaborative relations, although only a few – such as the leaders of The Athletics Association – became influenced or indeed infatuated by the Nazi ideology of the occupying power. On an organizational level, too, collaboration took hold. Danish trainers, coaches and heads of sport led Danish teams on trips to Germany; Danish sports physicians contributed at Danish-German competitions; Danish referees and judges adjudicated at matches held internally within Germany and at German matches against other countries; and German judges and trainers were regularly active in Denmark.

A typical storyline was of the German soldier called home from the front, pulling on his sportswear, and lining up to compete. The German authorities made sure that elite sport was one of the few civil activities that continued to receive significant resources and the opportunity to function almost at prewar levels – a projected sign of German mastery of the war situation. Danish sportspeople, therefore, competed against soldiers in sportswear, a fact never concealed by the Danish press.[1]

The main questions for analysis in this article are: What was the distinct role of athletics in this process of politicization of Danish sport? Was Danish athletics a moderating or inciting factor in this process? What was the political profile of Danish athletics' leadership? Did Danish athletics differ politically from other Danish sports during the occupation? During the occupation, did changes in

---

[1] The previous overarching introduction to the Danish-German cooperation during the occupation is inspired from Hans Bonde, *Fodbold med Fjenden* (Odense: University of Southern Denmark Press, 2006): 419–438.

the political profile of Danish athletics take place in line with the development of the German war fortune?

As regards leading research into Danish sports during the occupation, my book *Fodbold med fjenden* ('Football with the Enemy') initiated interest from 2006.[2] In 2016 Christian Tolstrup Jensen published an article on the Danish-German sports-collaboration seen from the German perspective.[3] Regarding the development of Norwegian sports under German occupation, which is touched upon in this article, Matti Goksøyr and Finn Olstad have recently carried out extensive work and drawn fruitful comparisons with the development of Danish sports.[4] The development of German sports policies in the occupied countries has been investigated in Hans Joachim Teichler's classic *Internationale Sportpolitik im Dritten Reich* from 1991.[5] The Nazification of Austrian sport after the '*Anschluss*' to Germany in 1938 has also been the object of investigation in several contributions.[6]

This article is based on a differentiation between an 'attentistic' position, whereby the goal was to gain time in respect of German demands through an attitude of reticence, and an 'activistic' position. This meant an active collaborative policy towards the Third Reich that aimed to establish goodwill with the occupying power. In short, this carrying out pro-German actions without the occupying power having demanded it. Another central term in the present article is 'politicization' which can be defined as the actions that cause an activity or event to become political in character.

---

[2] Hans Bonde, *Fodbold med Fjenden* (Odense: University of Southern Denmark Press, 2006). See also Hans Bonde, *Football with the Foe*, (Odense: University of Southern Denmark Press, 2008) and Hans Bonde, 'Revolt: Danish Resistance to Sports Collaboration with Nazi Germany', *The International Journal of the History of Sport* 26, no. 10 (2009): 1481–503, doi: 10.1080/09523360903057500.

[3] Christian Tolstrup Jensen, 'Football with Friends?' How the German Sporting Press Covered the German–Danish Sports Collaboration, 1939–1944', *The International Journal of the History of Sport* 33, no 10 (2016); 1079–98, doi: 10.1080/09523367.2016.1257613.

[4] Matti Goksøyr, 'How Can You Play When Your House Is on Fire? The Norwegian Sports Strike during the Second World War', *Scandinavian Journal of History* 43, no. 4 (2018): 433–56, doi: 10.1080/03468755.2018.1464275; Matti Goksøyr and Finn Olstad, *Skjebnekamp. Norsk idrett under okkupasjonen 1940–1945* (Oslo: Aschehoug, 2017).

[5] Hans Joachim Teichler, *Internationale Sportpolitik im Dritten Reich* (Schorndorf: Karl Hoffmann, 1991).

[6] Matthias Marschik, 'Between Manipulation and Resistance. Viennese Football in the Nazi era', *Journal of Contemporary History* 34, no. 2 (1999): 215–29; Michael John, '"Mit deutschem Gruss.' Fussballsport und Nationalsozialismus," in *Fussball unterm Hakenkreuz in der "Ostmark,"* ed. David Forster, Jakob Rosenberg, and Georg Spitaler (Gottingen: Verlag Die Werkstatt, 2014). For a general introduction to football during WW2 see Markwart Herzog & Fabian Brändle (eds), *European Football During the Second World War: Training and Entertainment, Ideology and Propaganda,* (Oxford: Peter Lang, 2018).

In Danish research on the occupation period, a distinction has developed between the terms "cooperation" and "collaboration." Where "cooperation" is a
value-free concept, "collaboration" signals a collaboration with the occupiers
based on a desire for a German victory. However, since the Danish use of the
word "collaboration" breaks with the English tradition of using the word more
value-free, I will not apply the Danish use of the word in this article.

Concerning the source material, this article is mainly based on the archives
of The Sports Confederation of Denmark in The Danish National Archive (*Rigsarkivet*), newspaper articles and articles in sports periodicals.

Prelude: Danish-German Sports Cooperation
Until the German Occupation

After the Nazi seizure of power in Germany in 1933, a deep fascination developed in parts of Danish sports for the Third Reich's prioritization of sport. At
the 1936 Olympic Games in Berlin, Danish sports officialdom in its near entire-
ty – not least athletics mustered – witnessed the series of impressive German
victories and the Germans' amazing ability to create an atmosphere and a sense
of unity at the most grandiose Olympics until that point. For the German organizers, the Olympics were arranged as one enormous occasion for giving the
international community a positive impression of Nazi attempts to create new
cultural forms, based on the cult of the Führer, the exaltation of the body, mass
displays and a dazzling, blinding aesthetic surface. Only among Communists,
cultural radicals, workers' sports movements, in the social-democratic press[7]
and in Jewish sports[8] was there resistance to a racist, military regime being allowed to hold Games in the name of peace and understanding between peoples.

The Olympics of 1936 provided the Nazi regime with a fantastic opportunity to affect an entire generation of young Danish elite sportspeople and their
leaders. There were 135 Danish sports competitors apart from judges, referees,
seconds, heads, and congress representatives.[9] Many of the sports heads and

---

[7] Jørn Hansen, "Hellere en Sild uden Rogn end en Akilles, hvis Hjerne sidder i hans Albuer! De olympiske lege i Berlin 1936 og diskussionen herom i Danmark," *Idrætshistorisk Årbog* (1993): 119–139, DOI: https://doi.org/10.7146/ffi.v9i0.31831

[8] Nina Skyhøj Olsen, *"Den jødiske idræts historie: En analyse af den jødiske idræt i Danmark 1921–1959."* Thesis, Department of Nutrition, Exercise and Sports, (Copenhagen: Copenhagen University, 2011).

[9] According to the sports periodical *Ungdom og Idræt*, no. 34, 21/08, 1936, 56–61 and 80–83.

sportspeople who came to compete against German athletes during the German occupation of Denmark had taken part in the Olympics of 1936. Among the more prominent athletes that participated in the Olympics in 1936, the long-distance runner Harry Siefert could be mentioned as well as the multi-talented phenomenon Svend Aage Thomsen. Thomsen was a master of a number of athletics disciplines, besides apparatus gymnastics and the decathlon, in which he won the Danish championships from 1940 to 1942.

After the Olympics in 1936, the Nazi regime continued to attract Danish sportspeople – such as the internationally renowned Danish swimming star Jenny Kammersgaard.[10] There was, therefore, a tradition of strong acquaintance between Danish and German competitors that continued in the first years of the Second World War. These well-functioning relations towards German sport helped to prepare the ground for Danish sports to maintain sporting cooperation with the Germans even after their occupation of Denmark on April 9, 1940.

German Occupation

At the beginning of the German occupation of Denmark on April 9, 1940, sport turned out to be *the* cultural activity that the German authorities showed greatest commitment to resuming. The German authorities were enthusiastic about re-establishing sporting relations because Denmark was defined as an Aryan-Germanic region, and it would be beneficial to incorporate the country within the greater German zone of influence. Other countries – especially those in Eastern Europe – were never given the same opportunity for large-scale sporting relations, but were instead brutally treated as nations of inferior people. In addition, there was the propaganda effect of providing sports entertainment for the German people, demonstrating German surplus capacity for competitive sports at a time of war.

In the wake of the German invasion of Denmark, Danish sport entered a state of shock and initially all international sporting relations were brought to a halt. Hitler and Goebbels, however, wanted to use open-air concerts, military parades, and sporting events in Denmark to encourage a chain of Danish mental associations to enter into friendly German relations. Therefore, the first German *Reichsbevollmächtigter* (plenipotentiary) Cecil von Renthe-Fink put pressure

---

[10] Hans Bonde, *Fodbold med Fjenden* (Odense: University of Southern Denmark Press, 2006), 60–66.

on the Danish sporting authorities, which was eventually seconded by the Danish foreign ministry after the appointment of a new Danish Minister for Foreign Affairs on July 8, 1940, the activistic Erik Scavenius. Scavenius regarded sport as a suitable instrument for achieving German goodwill, thereby enabling their collaborative policy to run smoothly. The situation gradually produced a shift in the Danish sports leadership's attitude and , as early as May 1940, it accepted local competitions in Danish cities of the province against Germans.This, in addition to German membership to Danish sports associations and clubs – although these events were denied the ceremony of official games.[11]

Already at the end of April 1940, despite the general Danish ban on international matches, the chairman for the Danish Football Association, *Dansk Boldspil Union-Union*, Leo Frederiksen entered a covert agreement with the German football leadership designed to kick-start sporting relations with an international football match against Germany in the autumn of that year.[12] After Germany forced the capitulation of Belgium, Holland, and France through its *Blitzkrieg* of May and June 1940, the leadership of Danish sports adapted itself to getting international sporting relations up and running again. It seemed that Europe was about to experience a generation of German dominance, and for DIF the aim became to survive with as much autonomy as possible in Europe under the New Order.

These opening moves led to an agreement reached with Renthe-Fink on August 5 that sporting relations should be resumed and that a group of international football matches be held involving German and Swedish teams; allowing the Danish public to realize there was no question of a one-sided collaboration with the occupying power. The plan was to open up with a game against Sweden: a neutral and free neighboring country.

The chairman of DIF, General Castenschiold, opened DIF's board meeting on August 5, 1940,[13] stressing that proceedings were confidential, after which he stated that German patience was coming to an end. Almost all board members agreed that in the new political situation they felt obliged to put their feelings to one side and think of the best interests of sport and the country which meant resuming sports exchange with Germany. The barrister and representative of Funen, Ernst Petersen, was the only representative among the DIF leadership to come out against football with the occupying forces. Later on, Ernst Petersen

---

[11] Bonde, Fodbold med Fjenden, 60–66 and 120–122.

[12] Teichler, Internationale Sport Politik im Dritten Reich, 285.

[13] The archives of The Sports Confederation of Denmark (DIF) in The Danish National Archives (Rigsarkivet) – abbreviated DIF/NA – pakke 14 – Bestyrelsesmøde 05/08, 1940.

also found other ways of protesting. In October 1940, he was instrumental in the founding of *Odense Terrænsportsforening*, an orienteering club practicing semi-military exercises, which later became a recruitment source for the resistance movement.[14]

However, The Athletics Association, in particular, gave a positive response. This was not so surprising, since its head from 1940 to 1943, Svend Jensen, was an organized Nazi.[15] He naturally greeted "with pleasure" the opportunity to resume international relations but regretted the late timing: "We only have two international opponents in athletics – Norway and Germany – and we should have competed against them, at away matches, this year. The Norwegians informed us a while ago they were unable to hold an international game this year, and we've heard nothing from Germany."[16] It would soon become apparent that the Germans were more than willing participants.

The First Games with Germany

As mentioned, the DIF leadership wished to avoid official sporting relations with Germany until after an international match against Sweden, arranged for October 20, 1940. Starting the international sports cooperation with a match against Sweden was planned to give Danish-German sports cooperation a more neutral aspect. However, this decision was not whole-heartedly welcomed in every Danish quarter, and in the late summer DIF's intentions were for the first time knocked off course.

Nazi groups within Danish sport caught the scent of a new dawn and could not wait to begin collaboration. The Athletics Association of Copenhagen, with Johannes Bojesen Barsøe at its head, became the first association to organize an event with German competitors. Unfortunately, the archives of the Copenhagen athletics associations are unable to shed light on the situation leading up to these games, as the minutes taken from the relevant board meetings wherein these games were discussed are, hardly coincidently, missing.

A suitable date for the games turned out to be August 22, 1940. Major interest shown by the occupying powers in getting collaborative sports un-

---

[14] Andreas Skov, For Danmark og demokratiet – Landsretssagfører Ernst Petersen og besættelsen, *Odensebogen* (2008): 52–71.

[15] Bovrup-Kartoteket, Kbh., 1946, Storkøbenhavn, p. 64, as well as Rasmussen, 1981, p. 54 together with OM 10/04 1940.

[16] The Nazi newspaper *Fædrelandet* 28/06 1940.

derway can be demonstrated from how rapidly a team of notable German athletes was quickly put together. Throughout the entire early epoch of Nazi-governed sport, there had been close collaboration between German and Danish athletics at national-team level. This helps to explain why, perhaps, collaboration was so quickly achieved after April 9, 1940. Denmark's largest sports newspaper, *Idrætsbladet*, completely bypassed the point that the games contravened the wishes of the DIF leadershipwho hoped that a resumption should begin with a Swedish international match in football. The magazine, in fact, began discussing the games only a week after the DIF ban had been rescinded.

As a way of indicating the unproblematic attitude held towards collaborative sports in the Danish press, it can be seen how the Danish Labor Party newspaper *Socialdemokraten* published an article on the KAF games on August 20, under the headline "First International Games." On August 21, the newspaper included a photo of the German competitors with the caption "three more Germans." By August 22, it announced "Tonight – international athletics – no Swedish competitors but still exciting." On August 23, under the headline "Danes and Germans share the victory," it was described how there were "outstanding people" among the German competitors.

On the day itself, August 22, the games were front page material for the leading Danish sports magazine *Idrætsbladet*, which also included three large photographs of German athletes during training at *Østerbro Stadium*.[17] What was most exciting about the participation of German athletes was the chance that tough competition might drive the Danish athletes to set new Danish records. The headlines enticing people to the games read "German athletics stars should mean Danish records at the stadium."

The Danish newspapers reported that the first international games of the year with participation of German athletes were now a reality.[18] Thirteen competitors from the club *Berliner Luftwaffe Sport Verein*, with a Major called Reuter in charge, were flown in especially – indicating direct cooperation with the German *Wehrmacht/ Luftwaffe?*. Danish sport thus cooperated with a German air force, which a few weeks later was to begin its *Blitzkrieg* against Great Britain.

The German military Commander-in-Chief, General Lüdke – who had visited the internationally renowned gymnastics pedagogue Niels Bukh's gymnastics academy on Southern Funen June 2, 1940 – was also present at the

---

[17] *Idrætsbladet* 22/08 1940.

[18] *Politiken, Socialdemokraten* and *Berlingske Tidende* 23/08 1940.

stadium, together with the plenipotentiary Renthe-Fink. Through their presence, the German military and political chiefs demonstrated the importance placed on collaborative sports. When the national anthem was played Renthe Fink and other German dignitaries among the spectators, together with the German *Luftwaffe* team, made the Hitler salute, while General Lüdke made a military salute.

The high level of the German athletes was an olive branch to Danish athletics and, via its new concept for games, launched to create maximum spectator appeal. This would be achieved by "showing us in those disciplines where we are strongest: in the events where the chances for setting records are most. Therefore, and because eight out of nine competitions are track races, the program will especially appeal to the crowd, who will experience so many moments of excitement over the tense climax to each race. It will all be finished within just over an hour, but it is likely more will happen in that hour than during most drawn-out competitions."[19]

Further along in the coverage, potential Danish record breakers in the various distances were detailed. Of special interest was a Danish middle-distance runner of international caliber, Harry Siefert. The head of the Copenhagen athletics association, Johannes Bojesen Barsøe, who was pro-German, watched the German training and was extremely satisfied "with their speed and fitness." Barsøe stated that "the Danes will now have a chance to show what they are made of. In this company, it has got to mean a few new records."[20]

Although it was not an official national match, a German orchestra played the national anthems of both countries while the spectators, according to the newspaper of the Danish Nazi party *Fædrelandet* "stood with their heads bared, but the real tension arose when the runners lined up for the 100-meters hurdles." This event was "a great win for Ole Dorph Jensen." The first German place was fourth, but he "was of the German team's weakest man."[21]

Generally, the German runners "set the pace." However, it would not have displeased German guests when, as *Fædrelandet* and the sports editor of the radio news put it,[22] the Danish 800-meter runner Hans Spanheimer won "after a highly tactical race in a tight struggle against the German, Grau." Spanheimer

---

[19] *Idrætsbladet,* 22/08, 1940.

[20] *Ibid.*

[21] *Ibid.*

[22] Centralkartoteket, Pkr. Nr. 1., Anholdelsesprotokol løbenr. 10376.

ran the best Scandinavian time that year; at 1:54.6.[23] What *Idrætsbladet* did not know at the time was that Spanheimer was on his way to run for a German club. His race at *Østerbro Stadium* was a wonderful place to show off his talents to German scouts. But the German athletes, too, received glowing reports, not least the two "superb Berlin sprinters, Mellerowicz and Bönecke, were supreme and their times excellent."[24]

In the picture archives of *Politiken*, a photograph of Spanheimer's win has been preserved. On the rear face, the name of Kurt E.W. Volkmann is stamped, who was a German journalist and sports diplomat, along with his address, which indicates that this German propaganda specialist made sure that *Idrætsbladet* got the right, politically opportune pictures of Danish-German cooperation.[25]

Almost as an omen for the long-term future of Danish-German collaborative sports, the games were drowned out in a torrential shower, which washed away any possible record attempts with it. Nevertheless, *Idrætsbladet* regarded the games as a success, emphasizing the first-rate performances and the skill of the German competitors. The magazine estimated the paying crowd to be around 4,000, plus a good many invited guests. *Fædrelandet* characterized the games as "a huge success!" highlighting that 6,000 spectators had turned out in such bad weather. Renthe-Fink proudly reported back to the German foreign ministry that an inflated? total of 8,000 spectators had watched the games and he could impart that the Danish press had responded to the games with enthusiasm.

The multi-talented athlete Svend Aage Thomsen was singled out, praised for his "exceptional abilities" and "outstanding victory in the 100-meter hurdles." Thomsen had attended the internationally renowned Nazi-inspired gymnastics Niels Bukh's school ran by a Dane, Niels Bukh. Thomson had taken part in athletics events at the Berlin Olympics, and could easily challenge the Germans on the athletics field. In 1938, he won both hurdles and pole jumping in international competitions against Norway and Germany.

In the build up to the games in Copenhagen, Thomsen was coerced towards being used for German propaganda Apictorial from the stadium at Aarhus showed him in training with the well-known German high jumper Martens, who had recently taken on Thomsen's main discipline of decathlon with some success. The friendly relations between the two elite sportsmen were taken as an obvious indication that "in the realm of sport, collaboration between Denmark

---

[23] *Idrætsbladet* 26/08 and 19/12 1940.

[24] *Ibid.*

[25] The Danish newspaper Politiken photo-archives *Polfoto*.

and Germany throughout this war has become a valuable link in the friendship between two neighboring peoples."[26]

In addition, there turned out to be good opportunities for Danish elite sportspeople to "try out" for German clubs. The opportunity was taken by the pride of Frederiksberg Athletics Association, Hans Spanheimer. From the beginning of 1941, he was able to compete for Hannover Sportverein, secure in a new job at a graphic arts studio in Germany.[27] Spanheimer set a new Danish record in 800 meters, in 1940, and in 1000 meters, in 1941. Speaking to *Idrætsbladet*, "our fabulous runner" described his first win for his new club and the excellent conditions in German elite athletics, which were often linked to military facilities.[28] By March 1941, Spanheimer had moved to Berlin, where he was to train together with two track stars, Dieter Giesen and Ludwig Kaindl. The most famous Danish sports reporter, Gunnar Hansen from *Idrætsbladet* and the national Danish Broadcast, concluded that if "Spanheimer does not learn to run 1,500 meters in under 4 minutes with such guides, then he will never learn."[29]

Membership of the Berlin club was obviously decisive for Spanheimer, and in June 1941, at "an evening festival of sport," at the Momsen stadium in Berlin, he ran to second place, achieving the first Danish record of the year by running 1,000 meters in 2:28.2, which was the fifth-best international time that year.[30] Before that, Spanheimer won a 3,000-meter cross country race in Brandenburg.[31] *Idrætsbladet* championed him with the words "Hopefully, this victory will bring Spanheimer further onto track so he can bring home even more wins, bringing luster to Danish athletics." In Denmark's most important sports periodical, no sign could be traced of any reservation in coming forward for the occupying powers. Hans Spanheimer's accomplishments in Germany continued to be reported on in *Idrætsbladet*, regardless that Spanheimer was also editorial secretary and sports correspondent for *Fædrelandet*.[32]

On the whole, the games were effectively used by German propaganda. Rent-he-Fink clearly placed great emphasis on this resumption of sporting relations since he sent a film taken of the games to Berlin, showing just how well every-

---

[26] Kopenhagener Soldatenzeitschrift, 8/9, 1940.

[27] *Idrætsbladet*, 19/12, 1940, p. 2, as well as 06/02 10/02 1941.

[28] *Idrætsbladet*, 06/02, 1941.

[29] *Idrætsbladet*, 28/03, 1941, p. 15.

[30] *Idrætsbladet*, 20/06, 1941.

[31] *Idrætsbladet*, 08/04, 1941.

[32] *Idrætsbladet*, 08/04, 1941.

thing had gone.[33] A Danish radio broadcast was included as part of a German program called Deutsch-dänische Sportveranstaltung im Kopenhagener Stadion. True to form, it was Kurt Volkmann who was the radio man on the spot. On German radio, coverage of the games was transmitted as part of German sports radio.[34]

Athletics Championships in Germany

The administrative leadership of Danish athletics did not sit idly by, but continued to exploit the favorable conditions to compete against the best German athletes. An opportunity now appeared to meet German champions on a German track, and athletics again made the front page of *Idrætsbladet* in March 1941.[35] The event took place in the same month that the Germans intensified their *Blitz* against Great Britain by launching fifteen devastating attacks. The sensation was that Hans Spanheimer would not only meet the so-called" elite of the world" at Deutschlandhalle in Berlin but he would also compete against Germany's great athletic star, Rudolf Harbig, who had run off with a "fantastic world record" in 800 meters in summer 1939. Harbig was shown on *Idrætsbladet*'s cover with his swastika-emblazoned jersey and was portrayed in the Danish sports press as a masculine idol. Given how many countries that had suspended collaborative sports due to war and occupation, the expression "elite of the world" was somewhat overstated, but the magazine did not feel the need to reflect onthis claim. Neither did *Idrætsbladet* mention that two English runners, L.F. Roberts and A.G.K. Brown (recently killed in the line of duty), had both achieved positions among the world's five fastest in 400 meters.

Spanheimer and Harbig's opponents were Per Lie, a Norwegian who in fact thereby broke a Norwegian sports boycott against Nazified Norwegian sport, which will be explained in more detail later. Also present was Lennart Nielsson from Sweden, the powerful German runners Giesen and Grau and two of the best Danes – Svend Aage Thomsen and Harry Siefert. Siefert told the sports

---

[33] *Idrætsbladet,* 26/08, 1940. Also Hans Joachim Teichler, "Internationale Sportpolitik im Dritten Reich," (Verlag Karl Hofmann Schorndorf, 1991): 285.

[34] Auswärtiges Amt, The archives of the German Ministry of Foreign Affairs, copies in the Danish National Archives, Rigsarkivet, – package 311 – which is a 77-page dissertation on the function of radio and the German plans for it 25/11 1940. CF also *Kopenhagener Soldatenzeitschrift,* 08/09, 1940.

[35] *Idrætsbladet* 13/03 1941.

reporter Gunnar Hansen that the German organizers placed great importance on Danish participation, arranging for flights both to and from the championships.[36]

Siefert's most renown opponent over 300 meters was Miklos Szabo, from Hungary – part of the Axis alliance – having joined the tripartite pact between Germany, Italy, and Japan in November 1940. Szabo was one of the world's most versatile runners and achieved numerous titles including European Champion over 800 meters. He also notably set the world record for two miles (3,218 meters); and he had run 10,000 meters in under thirty-one minutes. The championships, however, were a big disappointment for Denmark. Both Siefert and Spanheimer took last place in their respective races. Only Svend Aage Thomsen cut a decent figure over the 70-meter hurdles by winning his preliminary heat, to thereafter give the Swedish favorite Håkon Lidman a close-fought contest in the final. Thomsen took second place in front of the German competition. *Idrætsbladet* wrote that "it was the most exciting hurdles race ever to be held in Deutschlandhalle." According to *Fædrelandet*, Thomsen was so thrilled about the preliminaries that he "amazed the 8,000-strong Berlin crowd with a pair of somersaults."[37]

Spanheimer was overtaken by the three German runners as well as the two Scandinavians. The headline in *Idrætsbladet*, though, stated "No-one could follow Harbig in Berlin," with his time of 2:28.4, in which "the German runner touched his personal record, while Spanheimer, Svend Aage Thompsen and Seifert all produced an honorable performance." Harbig's race "clearly shows that all of Germany's adored 'Rudy' is most likely embarking on his best season yet." In Denmark, too, there was a buzz around Rudolf Harbig. The Danish national coach, Svend Lundgren, wrote part of a serial for *Idrætsbladet* on Dr. Woldemar Gerschler's [Harbig's coach] "excellent" and "captivating" book *Harbigs Aufstieg zum Weltrekord*.[38]

However, Harbig was not so untouchable that American athletes, still unaffected by the war, could not threaten his position. During the American championships in the summer of 1941, Grover Klemmer already came close to/ matched? Harbig's record by running 400 meters in 46 seconds flat. Nevertheless, *Idrætsbladet* introduced this piece of news with a picture of the Italian runner Mario Lanzi and a "fabulous" picture of Rudolf Harbig in action,

---

[36] *Idrætsbladet* 03/03 1941, p. 5.

[37] *Idrætsbladet* 17/03 1941. Cf. also *Fædrelandet* 18/03.

[38] *Idrætsbladet* 08/05 1941.

who was now being called world champion despite only being a record holder. Again, Harbig's body was brought into focus. "We see the wonderful stretch he commands, the fantastic hip work that characterizes all of his races."[39]

Other Danish athletes took part in athletics competitions at the very highest elite levels during the spring of 1941, in Germany. In addition to a number of athletes already mentioned, other significant Danish sportspeople featured, such as the country's best race walker Viggo Ingvorsen, from the Danish club Sparta.[40]

By the end of the occupation, Ingvorsen had won the national Danish championships no less than twelve times, setting eight Danish national records; and from the period between October 1940 to March 1941 he was also a member of the Danish Nazi Party. In addition, there were plans that Ingvorsen should be accompanied to Hamburg by his Sparta club colleague Poul Theisen. These plans came to nothing and, according to *Idrætsbladet*, Ingvorsen also had to pull out of the Berlin race fairly quickly, but there was speculation that perhaps he had been used as a 'pace-setter', instead. At any rate, he could be pleased that he had taken part in a field that contributed to Hermann Schmidt from Hamburg setting a new world record of 2 hours, 20 minutes, and 33.6 seconds. The field included "several of Germany and Italy's best race walkers."[41]

The Nazi-influenced leadership of Danish athletics, and their comprehensive collaboration with German sport, did not seem to worry the large brewery-backed Tuborg Foundation. Tuborg donated DKK 10,000 – more than 30.000 British pounds in today's currency – in May 1941. The editorial column of *Idrætsbladet* believed the award indicated "perspectives that go much deeper than the simple job of promoting Danish athletics. What is remarkable about the Tuborg Foundation award, which in effect provides a kind of stamp of approval, is the fact that for the first time Danish sport has been positioned alongside a number of other cultural pursuits, such as art and science, to name but two." Sport was therefore regarded as "having won recognition within circles that have the power and finance to lend a helping hand, which is what matters," as *Idrætsbladet* put it.[42]

Danish athletes were given further opportunities to meet the supreme stars of German athletics on German soil, which could be used by German propaganda

---

[39] *Idrætsbladet* 04/07 1941.

[40] *Fædrelandet* 15/03, 25/04 and 24/06 1941.

[41] *Idrætsbladet* 29/04 1941, p. 11.

[42] *Idrætsbladet* 16/05 1941.

to create images of German-Nordic unity under the swastika. Judging by the coverage in *Idrætsbladet*, the contact also contributed to a fascination with the masculine running phenomenon Rudolf Harbig. On May 27, 1941, The Athletics Association held yet another large competition with German participation, in Copenhagen. Furthermore, the Copenhagen Athletics Association held an unofficial national match against Hungary, at Østerbro stadium, on July 23, 1941. After the occupation, these games did not receive the same negative attention as did other sporting arrangements; supposedly because the opponents were not direct representatives of the occupying power, and perhaps because not everyone was aware that Hungary had joined the Axis powers from November 1940.[43] Organizing a team was not without its problems for the Hungarian authorities, since Hungarian and Romanian forces were taking part in the invasion of the Soviet Union.

Athletics Games in Norway

However, it was not only to the belligerent nations Germany and Hungary that the Danish Athletics Federation sent its young athletes, but also to Norway. To understand the issues involved in participation in sporting tours of Norway, it is important to keep in mind that the Norwegian Government, under Vidkun Quisling, from the end of 1940, attempted to Nazify all sport, though this did not give an organization such as the Danish Athletics Federation reason to pause. From autumn 1940, the Danish association was constantly producing plans for contact with Norway. For example, Johannes Bojesen Barsøe, the chairman of the Copenhagen Athletics Association and secretary of the Danish Athletics Federation, spoke to *Fædrelandet* in October, stating that his association would very much like to get collaboration with the Norwegians underway. However, the 1941 season would soon begin and the Athletics Federation looked to urgently "to "contact them and make further arrangements."[44]

This plan worked, too. On September 28, 1941, the Danish Athletics Federation took part in a Danish-Norwegian games against Norwegian sports collaborators at Oslo's large national athletics stadium, *Bislett*, with its capacity for

---

[43] *Idrætsbladet* 18/07 1941, p. 10. Cf. also 19/08 1941, p. 3, together with 06/01 1942, frontcover. In addition, see *Fædrelandet* 24/07 1941.

[44] *Fædrelandet* 17/10 1940.

25,000 spectators. The meeting against Norway was welcomed by the Danish Federation, at a time when Germany for a while had opted out of collaborative sports due to the German invasion of the Soviet Union on June 22, 1941.

After going underground, Olaf Helset, a civil Norwegian sports leader, dedicated himself whole-heartedly to mobilizing the resistance movement – particularly through the creation of a so-called *Idrettsfront* (Sporting Front), that took the initiative for a boycott amongst Norwegian sportspeople, lasting from November 1940 until the end of the occupation in 1945. The sports boycott became one of the biggest victories for the popular resistance in Norway. An overwhelming majority of sports competitors and sports leaders declined to organize competitions or take part in them. Conversely, a phenomenon called illegal sports emerged, in which competitions took place in secret, where competitors practiced sports covertly in secret locations in the mountains.[45]

The former Norwegian national sport leadership considered the Norwegian federation to be dissolved, and they refused to cooperate with the new leaders. Consequently, the chairman of DIF, General Castenschiold, believed Norwegian sports remained under Nazi control. Therefore, the DIF chairman had refused to take part in a radio broadcast following an invitation by the Norwegian pro-Nazi Reichborn-Kjennerud, on the grounds that he could not possibly reach a decision before a Nordic conference had taken place. DIF's initial negotiating position was that "to cooperate with the present leadership is undesirable." "The old fellows of [Norwegian] sport" considered this to be a hostile act.[46]

The problem with this line of argumentation was that German sport, too, was entirely politicized: a point that the Nazi head of athletics Svend Jensen was not slow to underline. Why could they play against Germany and not the new Norway? General Castenschiold had and now found himself in a conflicted position. Since he would not exercise control centrally, he had also denied himself the possibility of imposing sanctions against the Athletics Association; so instead opted to exercise moral pressure. Each association was free to do as it chose "but it will be interesting to see who maintain their liaisons."[47]

There was no great support for Svend Jensen, however, among the remaining board members. Consequently, a number of association chairmen declared that

---

[45] Matti Goksøyr and Finn Olstad, Skjebnekamp. *Norsk idrett under okkupasjonen 1940–1945* (Oslo: Aschehoug, 2017), 78–110.

[46] DIF – pakke 14 – bestyrelsesmøde d. 3/3 1941.

[47] *Ibid.*

they would cease cooperation with current Norwegian sports.[48] In other words, continuing sporting relations with Norway was entirely optional – but it would not receive the support of DIF. And the responses were not slow in coming. An idea that Danish and Norwegian sports competitors should be able to move more freely between the two countries came from the Danish head of athletics, Svend Jensen. At the spring general meeting of the Copenhagen Athletics Association (KAF), in 1941, he proposed that they "should exchange sports competitors purely on the basis of a clearing account."[49]

DIF's refusal to implement an outright ban on sporting relations with Norway meant that an athletics association team, headed by their chairman Svend Jensen, could set out for Oslo, in September 1941. Jensen was assisted by his vice-chairman, E. Schnicker-Pedersen, a former chief librarian who on January 8, 1941 had become a member of the DNSAP.[50] Instead of a planned international competition, seven to eight Danish sportspeople had been invited to the Oslo games.[51] The Danish team eventually consisted of five members and was not especially strong. On Sunday, September 28, 1941, the games were finally held, which was not well-received by the Norwegian Sporting Front. According to a BBC broadcast to Denmark,[52] just before the start of the games, the Danish competitors were handed a communiqué from the Sporting Front in which they were urged in the strongest terms to boycott the games in the final minutes:

> If you have the will and courage that becomes a fair sportsman and a patriotic Dane, then we leave it securely to you to decide the best way to avoid bringing disgrace upon yourself. You have perhaps come to Oslo through a misunderstanding, but you are not yet at the stadium. Remember that the contests today are not ladies whist. What is done cannot be undone and a day to give account of yourselves will come. Will you stand among those who bear the iron cross or among those who retain a clear conscience and honor towards their country and towards humanity.

The BBC broadcast ended by pointing out that sport was used as a political weapon by "the Nazi enemies of Denmark" and that sportspeople who wanted

---

[48] DIF/NA – pakke 17 – Forretningsudvalgsmøde 12/06 1941 and pakke 52.

[49] *Idrætsbladet* 28/03 1941, p. 13.

[50] Centralkartoteket løbe no. 38912.

[51] *Fædrelandet* 02/08 1941 and 20/09 1941.

[52] Udenrigsministeriets Arkiver, Rigsarkivet, (the archives of The Danish Ministry of Foreign Affairs, The National Archives) – 84C15, 'Udenlandsk radio og ikke offentliggjort nyhedsstof', 18 November 1941.

to help keep the reputation of Danish sport "can do this best by staying away from participation in sporting events of any kind involving Nazis of whatever type," which was also a blow to Danish-German collaborative sports. The Norwegian communiqué was published in the London periodical *Frit Danmark* (Free Denmark), in November 1941.[53]

The political character of the games at *Bislett* Stadium was underlined in that the Danish winner of the 800 meters was Hans Spanheimmer, a co-worker for the Nazi journal *Fædrelandet*, who won the "Cup for the best result" given by Minister of Labor and Sports Axel Heiberg Stang, against competition that included the middle-distance runner Per Lie. The presentation of this cup, then, on a symbolic level, also bound the event to the Nazis' new structuring of Norwegian sport. In an interview given to *Fritt Folk*, Svend Jensen said before the trip home that "Both the Norwegian Sports Federation organization and its resurrection must stand today as a model that every true friend of sport can be proud of. It is nothing less than our own wishes that are realized today in the New Norway." The Norwegian team under boycott was so weak, however, that the games resulted in five Danish victories.[54] The Danish press did not join the jubilation over Danish participation in the games. *Idrætsbladet*, *Politiken* and *Berlingske Tidende* used only a short Ritzau press bureau announcement, but *Socialdemokraten* chose to ignore the event completely, which also may have been because of the poor sporting quality.[55]

Without being directly involved, DIF managed to avoid engaging with Norwegian collaboration sports.[56] And they held onto this strategy with some success. In August 1942, The Athletics Association received a visit from a Norwegian head of sport, whom they had sent on to DIF with the hope of securing permission for Danish sportspeople to travel to Oslo. At a DIF committee meeting, on August 12, 1942, the DIF chairman, now Colonel Herbert Sander, reiterated that "under no condition will DIF send athletes to Oslo. That is the responsibility of each sports association."[57]

However, in January 1943 the German authorities decided to halt all sporting relations between Germany and other nations. And in the same year, on Febru-

---

[53] *Frit Danmark* 13/11 1941, London.

[54] *Fædrelandet* 29/09 and 30/10 1941.

[55] *Idrætsbladet* 30/09 1941, *Politiken* and *Berlingske Tidende* 28/09 1941.

[56] Officielle Efterretninger – Dansk Athletik-Forbund, 1 April 1941, passim.

[57] DIF/NA – pakke 18 – Forretningsudvalgsmøde dated 12/08 1942.

ary 2, Germany participated for the last time in an international match, while national inter-German sporting events continued well into 1944.[58] But at the same time as more and more German athletes were killed or injured, the Third Reich slowly moved towards a state of total mobilization, in which sporting events made less and less sense.

August Revolt and an International Athletics Match

Germany's growing problems on the battlefield led to Danish athletics gaining a new symbolic value in society. Over the summer of 1943, Danes began to talk about the collapse of the Axis alliance, and many believed that the war was entering its final phase. This led to an increase in resistance actions against the occupying forces, and acts of provocation descended into more-or-less organized street fights involving large numbers.[59] Under these conditions, the large gatherings that came about with sports events could prove to be particularly dangerous for German attempts to keep the peace.

At the same time, acts of sabotage began to escalate, much to the growing irritation of the *Wehrmacht*, who placed guards at key sites such as dockyards. One consequence was that a number of workers went on strike over the course of August, and the strikes eventually spread to several cities in the provinces well-orchestrated by the Danish Communist party.

On August 28, Werner Best delivered an ultimatum to Erik Scavenius, who was prime minister from November 9, 1942, to August 29, 1943, in which a list of demands was presented, including the death penalty for sabotage and the declaration of a state of emergency. When the Danish Government refused, the German military Commander-in-Chief, General von Hanneken, unilaterally placed Denmark onto a state-of-emergency footing, on August 29. Von Hanneken announced that the Government was now dissolved and that the German Army had taken over supreme command. From that day on, Denmark came under the administration of a so-called *departmentchefstyre*. This meant government through the heads of the various governmental departments, under the leadership of the Permanent Secretary for the Ministry of Foreign Affairs of Denmark, Nils Svenningsen.[60]

---

[58] Teichler, Internationale Sportpolitik im Dritten Reich, 358.

[59] Cf. entry in *Gads leksikon* on "Dansk besættelsestid," 2002, 11.

[60] Hans Kirchhoff, *Samarbejde og modstand under besættelsen – en politisk historie*, (Odense: Syddansk Universitetsforlag, 2001), 194–206.

The August revolt took place at the same time as an international athlet-ics competition between Sweden and Denmark, held in Stockholm between August 28 and 29. Although Germany had terminated all sporting associa-tion with Denmark, the German leaders in Denmark allowed continued sports contests between Sweden and Denmark. It was intended that the competition should be heard on radio by sports fans in Denmark, broadcast by the ubiq-uitous Gunnar Hansen. The match against Sweden, a strong athletics nation, gave rise to a good deal of Danish national feeling at the stadium. Niels Holst-Sørensen won the 800-meter race, setting a new Danish record, and he was the anchor man during Denmark's sensational win over Sweden at the four by 400-meter relay race, which also brought the team the B.T. gold medal. As Gunnar Hansen put it,

> For the first time in many years, the Swedish got a taste of their own mortality (...) like a bunch of school kids we all gathered round Niels Holst-Sørensen and Gunnar Bergsten after their gigantic performances at 800 meters, and with pride in our hearts and our eyes welling up we followed them when the public demanded a lap of honor around the flag-filled stadium.[61]

On the Saturday of the competition, after covering the 800-meter race, Gun-nar Hansen complained about the break in transmission for the exciting needle match in the 10-kilometer race, where the hardened, experienced Danish runner Harry Siefert tried to challenge the Swedish favorite, who looked as though he might improve on the Danish 10-kilometer record. At that point, no one at the stadium knew about the wider events taking place in Denmark. They were equally unaware that all telephone communications between Sweden and Denmark had been severed in the wake of Prime Minister Scavenius being pre-sented demands for the country to be put under a military state of emergency.

On Sunday morning, Danes in Stockholm could read about developments back home on bill-board news announcements. Radio connections were re-established, but despite this the transmission was taken off air due to the seriousness of the situation.[62] A few journalists turned up at the national team's hotel, where:

> The gravity of the situation affected everyone. Anxieties were everywhere. We agreed, when the international games resumed in the afternoon, that we'd adopt a calm, composed manner. Of course, we could be pleased if we achieved fine results – but conditions being what they were, there was no reason for getting

---

[61] Gunnar Hansen, *Med mennesker og mikrofon*, (København, 1944).

[62] *Ibid.*

over excited, nor for showing off any great jubilation. It was only through sport that we'd stand up tall.[63]

National sentiments were turned up to full volume. as the crowd sang

> *Der er et yndigt land*, the Danish national anthem. Gun Robertsson, the actor, read a poem by Hjalmar Gullberg, *Hälsning til Danmark* [Salute to Denmark]. In the inner circle, both teams stood in line (...) The stadium was as quiet as a church. Never will the Danes who were present that day forget the build up to the final competitions.[64]

It was an ironic twist of fate that the most activistic Danish sporting association – with its Nazi leadership – became (after its leadership change), through no will of its own, the association most closely associated with a national manifestation directed against Germany, because of a coincidence in timing between the August revolt and an international sporting contest.

The athletics games in Stockholm at the end of August 1943 acquired a special air of pathos since Denmark, at the same time, was under direct German administration. The occasion was ripe for a fierce and angst-ridden sense of unification around ideas of Denmark and Nordic identity, which in the post-war years could be interpreted as a coupling between Danish sport and an anti-German, liberational, national position: a coupling later fronted by the athlete Niels Holst-Sørensen, who was also an officer in the Danish military. According to Holst-Sørensen, though, it was not sport but the military that led him into German opposition.[65]

After August 1943 and the introduction of government through departmental offices, international sporting events against Sweden also came to an end.The German authorities would no longer issue visas though with the exception of a single tennis international in Stockholm, at the late date of January 1944.

The young and talented Danish athlete Niels Holst-Sørensen did not have roots in the German-Danish traditions of the 1930s and, unlike many other competitors, he had not taken part in the impressive Nazi Olympics of 1936. He did not compete against Germans, but did, however, compete against Hungary in July 1941. On his homecoming from Stockholm, Holst-Sørensen was arrested by the Gestapo and sent to an internment camp. By the end of October 1943, he was released, after which he went into the courier service and to the Danish

---

[63] *Ibid.*

[64] *Ibid.*

[65] Interview with Holst-Sørensen 19/07 2006.

military in waiting, both of which provided Danish sports with a much-needed resistance appeal after the liberation.

In the closing years of the war Niels Holst-Sørensen set two new world records and took over the status of main sports star from the Danish pro-Nazi swimming icon Ragnhild Hveger, who in March 1943 was hired as swimming instructor in the city of *Kiel* in Northern Germany.[66]

Despite the rekindling of a Nordic sense of unity upon the liberation of Denmark on May 5, it was Sweden who now became the archrival. This helped bring sporting life back to its pre-war peacetime atmosphere. It was only in badminton and in a single field handball match that Denmark beat Sweden. In football, the Swedish national team beat Denmark 2–1 and 4–3, in June and July 1945, and before the year was out Danish humiliation was complete with yet another defeat – this time 4–1 – on September 30. On top of this there were international defeats to Sweden in tennis, athletics, weightlifting, archery, wrestling, boxing and golf.

Conclusion

What was the distinct role of athletics in this process of politicization of Danish sport? Was Danish athletics a moderating or inciting factor in this process? What was the political profile of Danish athletics' leadership? Did Danish athletics differ politically from other Danish sports during the occupation? During the occupation, did changes in the political profile of Danish athletics take place in line with the development of German fortunes in the war?

After the German occupation of Denmark on April 9, 1940, the leadership of the Danish national sports organization, DIF, wished to imbue collaborative sports with a neutral tone, beginning with a football match against Sweden. However, DIF's decentralization of the decision-making process regarding international joint sporting events allowed that tone to be completely taken over by Nazi sports leaders within Danish athletics.

Since the DIF leadership did not wish to take responsibility for what went on at club and member-association level, the planned resumption of collaborative sports was not brought about by an international match against Sweden because Nazi circles within the leadership of Danish athletics were quicker off the mark and organized a large athletics event on August 22, 1940. The abandonment of Danish athletics in these crucial years is partly due to athletics being one of the

---

[66] Bonde, Fodbold med Fjenden, 348-352.

most popular sports of the day, where achieving records was of great importance for the athletics sporting public.

Around 4,000 spectators watched the competitions at *Østerbro* stadium in
Copenhagen against German athletes from the Berlin *Luftwaffe* under the mu-
sical direction of a German military orchestra. The German military commander-in-chief, Lüdke, and Renthe-Fink both took part as a gesture of German interest for collaborative sports, along with much of the top leadership of the
occupying forces in Denmark. The German organizers took the opportunity
to put their fascist slant on the resumption of joint sports with military music,
broadcasts through both Danish and German radio, and film coverage for the
powers in Berlin, so Renthe-Fink could reassure his superiors about how well
collaboration policies were going in Denmark.

The success was repeated at a Danish-German meeting in the *Deutschlandhalle* in Berlin in March 1941, where the German running phenomenon and
masculine cult symbol Rudolf Harbig cast a spell over the Danish athletes who
paled in comparison.

The Danish Athletics Federation also played sports with other German-allied
sports systems: for instance in Hungary in July 1941 and Norway in September
of the same year. That Swedish organizations consistently said no to relations
with Norwegian collaboration sports put the Danish sports leadership into another frame of mind. But subsequent DIF attempts to avoid participating with
Norway were hardly effective, as DIF would not challenge the German authorities by issuing an outright ban on Norwegian games. The Danish athletics association, therefore, capitulated in September 1941, travelled to *Bislett* stadium
in Oslo for a competition.

During the occupation, changes in the political profile of Danish athletics
took place in line with the development of the German war fortune and Danish
resistance. In light of Germany's struggles on the battlefield and the so-called
August unrest in Danish cities, athletics acquired an enhanced symbolic value.
An international athletics tournament in August 1943 in Stockholm took place
in the middle of the Danish August revolt – a period of increased resistance
activities and widespread strikes – which gave the games a special, defiantat-
mosphere at the Stockholm stadium, where Holst-Sørensen achieved his great
triumphs.

Taken together, DIF was collaborative in relation to the Nazi German authorities, but against DIF's will the Danish Athletics Association constantly pulled
Danish sport further in the direction of full collaboration. Of its own accord, the

Athletics Association of Denmark carried out a Nazi-motivated collaboration with German sports as well as the Nazified Norwegian sports federation; far beyond what DIF advocated. In this process, the Danish Athletics Association became by far the most politicized association during the German occupation. Overall, Danish athletics differed politically from other Danish sports during the occupation by being the most activist federation. Together with a Nazi-inspired leadership, athletics became a catalyst in the German politicization of Danish sports.

This article concludes by following the fate of the biggest German athletics name who took part in Danish-German athletics competition during the occupation: Rudolf Harbig. Germany tried single-mindedly to maintain sporting relations with the outside world, but their sporting old guard consisted of around fifty amateur sports men and women, who took care of sports activities during the first year of the war. The German sports authorities constantly had to struggle to save their sportspeople from being sent to the front.[67] In the beginning of the Second World War, Rudolf Harbig was enlisted to a strict tour of duty in occupied Poland. In a letter from October 1939, Harbig expressed his frustrations about being unable to prepare for the not-yet finalized Olympic Games in Helsingfors:

> In Gnesen, here, all we have is our guard duty. You can surely imagine my annoyance ... I would much rather carry out other duties for the Fatherland in the nature of the great task sport has given me. I have to admit, though, that guard duty is more important for the State than a possible winner's place at the Olympics.[68]

In 1944 Rudolf Harbig died at the age of thirty in Ukraine where he was fighting as part of a parachute division. In the end, the Nazi revolution ate its own children.

---

[67] Teichler, Internationale Sportpolitik im Dritten Reich, 278.
[68] *Ibid.*, 279.

CHAPTER 3

"Too Many Spoons for Women." Women's Athletics in Finland until the 1950s

Leena Laine

Introduction

Women's history in athletics was a popular and much discussed theme in the early feminist research of sport. Athletics was an illustrative example of subjugation of women in sports, and women's experiences challenged the legitimation of male sports in many ways. Since then, other sports, such as strength and fitness sports, and nowadays women's football in particular, have received attention in gender research, largely inspired by the new rise of this game. A return to athletics' history creating a more detailed chronology of it in the light of new research on other sports is a challenge. Looking back allows us to see the long-term developments in a wider context and to re-evaluate the gender discourse of history in female sports.

The topic of this chapter is women's activism in athletics during the decades of fight for place and equality in sports from the end of the nineteenth century to the 1950s. The focus is Finland, and partly Sweden, as well as the international developments in female and male athletics in general.

One of the main starting points here is organizational. I will focus on female activist groups in athletics as well as women's role in the earlier forms of physical activities. I intend to explore the claim that women have participated in sports from the very beginning. I also claim that in the early stages of sports, women's participation was more accepted and supported by the public opinion than is seen later.

The historical narrative of this chapter focuses on the turn of the nineteenth century and the 1920s when women established their athletics organizations, and on the women's fight for the rights in athletics and sports after the Second World War. It must be emphasized that the development of women's sport does not form a continuum but consists of breaks, and backlashes. A new generation does not know about the achievements of those who went before. The breaks and generational gaps are often unknown for researchers, and we easily reach misleading conclusions about the historical nature of sport and interpret it from too narrow a historical perspective. Besides, we have unknown crests of activity in women's sports. I will present here three periods of activity from the 1900s to 1950s, and I shall question the narrowly based interpretations of the feminist crests of activity suggested in earlier research in women's movements.

When defining women's activities in the sports movement(s) in general I have taken into account both women's independent, autonomous movements in addition to women's activities in joint organizations led by men. Inevitably, there were women who were satisfied with their role as "silent" members in a sports club but one could never know when they were ready to "vote on their feet," leaving their male associates to found their own clubs.

The issues of gender, power and athletics in history will be discussed here from the following angles: starting with the basic questions on women's right to participate, nationally and internationally; their desire to participate, and the limits therein. Secondly, when joining the existing male-led athletic organizations, it is of importance to observe how women's participation was organized; in which activities women participated; how the resources were shared; and who made the decisions. And finally, women's separate organizations will be examined by studying the reasons leading to the segregation; what kind of organizations were founded; what kind of activities were developed; and how successful these organizations were. Besides organizations, of importance are individual actors and activist groups. A further underlying factor are the historical and political changes in society related to general gender politics and the development of national and international sports movement.

Women interested in sports, especially in athletics, were living – at least in the Nordic countries – in the atmosphere of hegemony of two ideas concerning the female body and its control. Gymnastics was considered "acceptable" and "suitable" for women and the emerging "sports" activities, including athletics, were considered too challenging for women physically and mentally. Originally, *gymnastics* was conceptualized as the "mother form" of modern physical education with its particular emphasis on ideological, educational, cultural and health issues, representing a holistic view of the body. Actually, all of the modern athletics disciplines, such as running, walking, jumping and throwing were developed within the gymnastics culture as "free exercises." In the Nordic countries women's gymnastics clubs included most of these physical activities, and out-doors sport. However, in feminist research in sports history women's gymnastics is often undervalued and regarded as promoting conservative ideas of womanhood while opposing competitive sports. The borderline between emancipation, feminism and adaption seem to be drawn according to the researchers' view on feminism, in relation to competitive sports. This chapter questions this view because it neglects the feminist and emancipatory nature of women's gymnastics and its challenging attitude towards male power. Additionally, they were fighting for women's right to name their own activity and for sporting space for all women. Therefore, I use the concept "feminism" in the same general meaning as the concept "women's movement," without distinguishing between their meanings.[1]

Women in Popular Games and Early Athletics

Women's participation in athletic sports in Finland developed from the beginning of the twentieth century and results were first recorded between 1900 and 1920. Women's athletics, as well as other sports were a success story during this period: at the end of the 1910s, some female athletes were celebrated as "sports queens" due to their excellent achievements.[2] However, in common knowledge these scarcely documented achievements have been hidden from (women's) sports history, remaining uncovered until the 1990s. Two sports history enthusiasts published a book series on popular physical and athletic activities from the latter half of the nineteenth century to the early 1910s in Finland. The series includes nine compilations of press news material of sports events between 1878 and 1912. The first collection includes data on the supposed athletics competitions between 1878 and 1899,[3] while the other eight collections cover the years 1900 and 1912.[4] The main body of this material comprises press reports

[1] Leena Laine, "Women's Movements in Sport: National and International Issues," in *Crossing Borders. Re-mapping Women's Movements at the Turn of the 21st Century*, ed. Hilda Rømer Christensen (Odense: University Press of Southern Denmark, 2004), 119–133.

[2] Leena Laine, "What Happened to the Early Queens of Sport? – Problematizing the Discontinuity and Breaks in Women's Sport," in *Sport und Sozialer Wandel/Sport and Social Changes/ Sport et Changements Sociaux*, ed. Jürgen Buschmann and Gertrud Pfister (St. Augustin: Academia, 2001), 42–53.

[3] Risto Karasmaa, Suomen yleisurheilu, *1878–1899* [Finnish Athletics 1978–1899] (n.p., 1992).

[4] Esa Laitinen, *Suomen yleisurheilu 1900–1904* (Jyväskylä, 1991); *Suomen yleisurheilu 1905–1906*; *Suomen yleisurheilu 1907* (Jyväskylä, 1992); *Suomen yleisurheilu 1908* (Jyväskylä,

(local, national and sports press) on popular competitions, club contests and national events for both men and women. The precision of the data is not the main point here, more essential is the documented information about women's activity. The information recorded includes the date and the nature of the event, the locality, the organizing body and the three top competitors.

One must be critical when using the information provided by the collection. The publication series categorizes the early popular meetings, such as running and throwing, as "athletics" (*yleisurheilu* in Finnish). However, athletics in its modern form was not introduced in Finland until the twentieth century, as Finnish sport historian Erkki Vettenniemi points out.[5] Furthermore, it is not possible to find or name the "first" competitive event in the period. Accordingly, the popular running event on the ice of a lake in central Finland in 1878 – which also featured female runners – has been commonly regarded as the first "athletics event" in the country. Nevertheless, this occasion cannot be regarded as the first women's "athletic" competition. Popular sports, including athletics, had been part of public festivals organized by students, upper class people or popular organizations since the 1860s.[6] Over decades popular competitions were a sort of entertainment emanating from "nature," often in the context of national awakening rather than real "sports" events in the modern sense. "Athletics" (first called *rata- ja kenttäurheilu* in Finnish, i.e., "track and field sport," only becoming known as *yleisurheilu* in the 1940s) was formed around the turn of the century in Finland. In 1886, the words *idrott* (Swedish) and *sport* were already translated as *urheilu* deducted from the words *urho*, *urheus* (brave, bravery with a specific male connotation).[7]

During the latter part of the nineteenth century, only nine popular running races with female participants are mentioned. Women and girls had separate competitions and only occasionally did they compete with men. The running distances varied from 300 cubits to 1000 meters. Many of the popular races were open for women if they dared to participate. Though, in the source material collections

---

1993); *Suomen yleisurheilu 1909* (Jyväskylä, 1993); *Suomen yleisurheilu 1910* (Jyväskylä, 1995); *Suomen yleisurheilu 1911*; *Suomen yleisurheilu 1912* (Jyväskylä, 1996).

[5] In his history of long-distance running in Finland Erkki Vettenniemi criticizes the miss-use of the term athletics (yleisurheilu) in sports history. Erkki Vettenniemi, *Joutavan juoksun jäljillä. Kestävyysjuoksun varhaisvaiheet Suomessa* (Helsinki: SKS, 2006).

[6] Leena Laine, "Sport for the Nation: Class and Gender in the Formation of Finnish Sporting Life," *The International Journal of the History of Sport* 30, no. 14 (September 2013), 1618–36, https://doi.org/10.1080/09523367.2013.828039.

[7] Leena Laine, *Vapaaehtoisten järjestöjen kehitys ruumiinkulttuurin alueella Suomessa v. 1856–1917 I–II*, (Helsinki: Liikuntatieteellinen Seura, 1984), 54–55 and 161–164.

covering the years 1900–1911 we find information on 319 competitive events in which women took part.[8] From the year 1900, just two meetings organized by youth associations and one by a temperance society are mentioned. In 1903, the number reached to twelve, listing events organized by youth associations, temperance societies and two sports clubs; which were for the first time mentioned as organizing bodies. Compared with men's competitions mentioned (forty-five in 1900, forty-six in 1901, and 197 in 1904), the numbers for women are modest.[9] A real increase occurred in the year 1908 showing thirty-five events for women. Events organized by sports clubs amounted to fifteen events of total thirty-five mentioned while the remaining events were organized by popular associations or as part of public festivals. The year 1908 is a turning point in the data because the recorded number of yearly events mentioned increased significantly after then: fifty in 1909; ninety-three in 1910, and eighty-one in 1911. In 1908, the first national competition in athletics for women, which received public attention, was organized by the new Central Sports Federation (1906, from now on: SVUL). Furthermore, after 1907, many newly founded districts of SVUL organized championships for women.

By 1911, one third of the more than three hundred events presented in the source material were organized by sports clubs. One of the sports clubs is identified as being a distinctly female sports club. One third of events were competitive meetings organized by popular associations such as youth associations, workers associations, temperature societies, and fire-brigades. The rest of the events took place as a part of popular music festivals, or were launched by several types of organizations from political parties to public library associations. In this way a wide range of ideological associations supported the emergence of competitive women's sport. At the same time, the novelty of women on the track may have proved a good crowd-puller. On one hand, the number of events and the organizations behind them shows that women's athletics increased alongside men's (even if in a minor way) and, on the other hand, one may interpret women's physical activity being positively accepted as a part of the national mobilization against the pressure of Russia's imperialist policy. Thereby, it can be said that women's right to vote in Finland (1906) augmented the acceptance of young women on the tracks and organizing via sports clubs.

---

[8] Laitinen, *Suomen yleisurheilu 1900–1904*; *Suomen yleisurheilu 1905–1906*; *Suomen yleisurheilu 1907*; *Suomen yleisurheilu 1908*; *Suomen yleisurheilu 1909*; *Suomen yleisurheilu 1910*; *Suomen yleisurheilu* 1911.

[9] Laitinen, *Suomen yleisurheilu* 1900–1904.

In the beginning, women's competitions in athletics were either running or walking, and the distances varied between eighty and 300 meters. The program was extended around 1905, with long jump, high jump and triple jump, shotput, and later javelin. Remarkably enough, the first medals were presented to women. An addition in the program brought schoolgirl competitions in the Finnish School Sports Association (SLU, 1899). Besides running, girls competed in walking, long jump, triple jump and the shot put.[10]

At the time, the rise of athletics was considered the formative period from the male point of view too; it can be said that the fields were open for experiments without strict regulations or control of the modern sports or their organizations. I interpret this as one explanation for women's ability to be part of early sports.

A New Framework: Sports Organizations

In the second half of the nineteenth century, modern sports in Finland became organized on the local level. Clubs were founded by middle- or upper-class Finns: sports such as sailing, ice-skating, swimming, and cycling. In principle, they were all open to women and men. Gymnastics was the sport with strict gender segregation in all Nordic countries.[11] The sports clubs' names (or rules) did not generally articulate the sex of the members. The exception was for women's gymnastics clubs. For instance, "the Association for Women's Gymnastics in Helsinki." Such factors as the social control of women, and the clubs' male homosocial atmosphere, kept women out of the first single-sport clubs that concentrated on emerging competitive sports such as wrestling.

From the 1890s onwards, the sports movement spread among the lower middle- and working-classes and was usually organized in all-round sports societies, the so-called "gymnastics and sports clubs." After the turn of the century, tens of clubs established women's sections, in which women practiced gymnastics as well as some other sports. This form of organization enabled women to join clubs, but their influence was effectively limited to their own section.[12]

Women gymnasts were the first to establish a national organization, the Finnish women's gymnastics federation in 1896. The first, male-led nationwide federation (1900–1906), was intended for only Finnish-speaking men and women

---

[10] Laitinen, *Suomen yleisurheilu 1905–1906*, 12.

[11] Laine, *Sport for the Nation*.

[12] Laine, *Vapaaehtoisten järjestöjen kehitys*, 444–446.

and favored non-competitive sports. A new bilingual union, the Gymnastics and Sports Federation in Finland (hereafter: the Central Federation, i.e., SVUL) was founded in 1906. The founding of SVUL finally opened the doors for modern competitive sports, concentrating on popular sports of importance among men such as athletics, wrestling, and skiing. At the same time, some new single sports federations were founded in swimming (including women) and in football. Due to linguistic tensions and the growing involvement of the working classes in sports, there were several groups competing for a place in the expanding sports movement. This is the context in which women had to find their place. During the immediate years after SVUL's foundation, competitions in sports became more regulated. This was also visible in women's athletics. In 1908, the women's 4x100m relay and 1,500m run was seen for the first time at a national event of the SVUL.[13]

At SVUL's gymnastics and sports festival of 1909, an exceptional women's "team race," a 4x200m run was included: members of each club team ran its 200 meters alone, one after another; the next club's group ran after it, and the winner was the club with shortest time summed up. Obviously, such an event, meant to avoid over-exertion of participants, was planned by women gymnasts who had been asked to manage women's competitions. However, according to the main sports magazine *Suomen Urheilulehti*, "The girls flew at such a pace that it was a wonder to behold."[14] In the 1910s, the support for women's participation in certain sports, clubs and towns was astonishing. Inter-club competitions took place; the clubs' male trainers prepared women for events, the club paid partly the travelling costs and the audiences enjoyed fierce contests in running events between women. Even some unofficial world records were achieved.[15]

Women in Finland took part in sports competitions earlier and more actively than women in other Nordic countries. In addition to athletics, competitions in swimming and skiing were quite commonplace. However, women did not have any representation in the SVUL, nor in district organizations. In 1911, one of the leading sports clubs, *Turun Urheiluliitto*, suggested that women should have representation in the leadership of the federation and that women's events in athletics should be included in the federation's official program. In response,

---

[13] Laitinen, *Suomen yleisurheilu 1908*, 65.

[14] Laine, *What happened to the Early Queens of Sport?*, 47.

[15] Kata Fabrin, "'Eikä se näyttänyt ensinkään rumalta' – 90 vuotta ensimmäisistä naisten yleisurheilun Suomen mestareista," in *Kynäniekkoja, kivinyrkkejä, mäki-matteja. Suomen urheiluhistoriallisen seuran vuosikirja 2003*, ed. Heikki Roiko-Jokela & Esa Sironen (Jyväskylä: Atena Kustannus Oy, 2003), 168–183.

two women's athletics events were added in the federation's championships (100m and 4x100m relay). Concerning women's role in organizational matters, some male sports leaders tactically contrived that men should not be involved in the "women's sphere," which was controlled by the women's gymnastics federation. Some male leaders, however, considered it unnecessary to spend any resources on women when international events were not organized for them.[16] The SVUL, nevertheless, was the first federation in the Nordic countries to feature women's athletics in its program and in its championships. In Sweden, the decision was made in 1927. Since 1911 the Swedish Athletic Association discussed including athletics in the program of the women's sports badge planned by the central sports federation. After four years of pondering the decision was a negative one.[17]

That said, the participation of women in athletics was not straightforward in Finland either. Women were not allowed any place in the SVUL organization, as aforementioned. Also, women's presence in sports venues was not without issue: some men took to disturbing their training sessions on the track with nasty comments. Therefore, women demanded, and sometimes were allowed, their own training times on the sports fields. Lauri Pihkala, the first sports coach in the country, wrote in 1908 that men used to have "indecent" thoughts about women in sport. Since they had not learned to think decently of women, it was of concern to him to allow women in sports competitions. If one wanted to raise woman to the level of man in her intellectual development, the same goal should concern her physical development, too, he wrote.[18] Later, in the 1920s, Pihkala became a furious opponent of women's athletics, using the same words indicating indecency that he himself had earlier criticized. Anyhow, the two first decades of the twentieth century saw the first active period of the rise of women's sports in Finland. Women did compete and the press supported their activities in the main.

Women gymnasts tried to keep their sisters out of other forms of sporting competitions in their own ways. In 1912, when the SVUL had given the green light for women's championships, women gymnasts established a substitute system of a "sports badge," a training program that included exercises in both gymnastics and various sports, with an emphasis on athletics in particular. The idea originated in Sweden. In 1913, clubs – applied from an international mod-

[16] *Ibid.*

[17] Leena Laine, "Jämlik idrott - ett brutet löfte," in Idrottens själ. Nordiska Museets och Skansens årsbok Fataburen 2000, ed. Bo G. Nilsson (Stockholm: Nordiska Museet, 2000), 54–74.

[18] Lauri Pihkala, *Urheilijan opas* (Jyväskylä: Gummerus, 1908), 187.

el – initiated communal playgrounds and other outdoor activities for working class women and children in several towns.[19] Athletics and sports in general might also have been adopted by many working-class women and girls on communal playgrounds.

During the following years, the sports program was rewritten in the sense of "women's play movement." Women purposely introduced the term play, *leikki* (in Swedish *lek*) instead of the term *peli* (game) in order to avoid connotations with competitive sports, and the women were adamant about naming women's activity by themselves. Consequently, the term "play" received a new meaning as a substitute and an alternative to "sport." Here we can see the difference between women involved in sports and those involved in gymnastics: the former adapted the male model of physical culture without questioning it; it was something new and exciting. The latter served the needs of all women, socially and physically and created a female model for sports.[20]

Backlash in the Beginning of the 1920s

The development of women's athletics after the First World War was striking in Finland. Finnish male athletes had succeeded at the 1920 Antwerp Olympic Games, equaling their achievements in Stockholm in 1912. In 1921 and 1922, the SVUL did not organize championships in athletics for women, and the male public opinion expressed strong disapproval of women's athletics and competition. Articles published in the press demanded women return to gymnastics and swimming, the only sports suited for them. In 1923, the SVUL without any discussion removed women's athletics championships from its program while revising the rules for the athletics competitions of the federation.[21] This can be explained by nationalist intentions connected with issues of resources: athletics was the most important and largest representative sports in the country and there was also the need for sporting tracks and other facilities. According to the signals given by the *International Olympic Committee* (IOC) and the *Interna-*

[19] Leena Laine, "Gymnastics, Play and Sport: An Alternative Model of Women's Physical Culture in Finland in 1910s," in *International Perspectives on Sporting Women in Past and Present. A Festschrift for Gertrud Pfister*, ed. Annette Hofmann & Else Trangbaek (Copenhagen: Institute of Exercise and Sport Sciences, University of Copenhagen, 2005), 111–125.

[20] *Ibid.*

[21] Reijo Häyrinen & Leena Laine, *Suomi urheilun suurvaltana* (Helsinki: Liikuntatieteellinen seura, 1989), 186–188.

tional Amateur Athletics Federation (IAAF), it was not possible for women to represent their country in the Olympic Games in the future. The aim was simply to wipe women out of the way while SVUL was intensively preparing for the 1924 Paris Olympic Games.[22]

However, this backlash took place at the same time as when women's football in Sweden was expelled from sports. The press adopted similar terms in its criticism: women's athletics/football were not respectable, competing or playing made women appear ugly, and their morale was as low as "prostitutes."[23] Female athletics or football had no future in comparison with male sports and had to disappear, and women's football really did disappear in reality from the national and international fields for decades in Europe.[24] In Finland, public opinion towards women's athletics turned negative more than ten years after its initial acceptance and success. It was easy to recall how, in the 1918 Civil War, some leftist women had fought on the "Red" (revolutionary left) front; they wore men's clothes, had short cut hair as many female athletes had, and were famed by reputation. Consequently, an entire generation of female athletics was denigrated.[25]

Finnish society went through a process of transformation at the start of the 1920s. Finland had become an independent country in 1917, and the nationalist ideals of the new independent state coincided with a new gender ideology aimed towards strengthening the state, order and defusing any social conflicts. Within the Finnish women's movement, the radical phase was over, and a new reform policy was formulated. In political parties, and the Finnish Parliament, women were concentrating on social policy, and their voluntary organizations assumed the task of supporting women in carrying the "double burden," as housewives and working/professional women. For them sporting life was, at the most, activities that kept them health and fit, or gymnastics. In contrast, competitive sports became "the male thing." A deepening gender segregation was seen as a natural part of the development in the new society. Sporting life had to support it.

This strong gender segregation laid the foundations of international competitions in which national celebrations have exclusively been held for men's

---

[22] *Ibid.*

[23] Martti Jukola, "Naisurheilu oikeille jäljille," *Suomen Urheilulehti*, 1922, 481–482.

[24] Thorbjörn Andersson, "Naisten jalkapalloilun varhaisvaiheista Ruotsissa," [Women in Early Football in Sweden], in *Alussa oli vesi. Suomen urheiluhistoriallisen seuran vuosikirja*, ed. Heikki Roiko-Jokela and Esa Sironen (Jyväskylä: Atena Kustannus Oy, 2006), 63–84.

[25] Leena Laine, *Työväen urheiluliikkeen naiset*, (Helsinki: Otava, 2000), 42.

achievements. The IOC had been founded in 1894, with national and international federations established to control the emerging competitive sports. During and after World War I, the rise of women's competitive sport became a reality in most countries. This happened partly in parallel with the postwar return to male sports. At the same time, the (male) sports system went through a complicated development towards stabilization, a process which in many cases led to attempts to restrict women's agency.

The first decades of emerging modern sport saw a gendered segregation of sports which also included a hierarchical segregation of "men's" and "women's" sports. This division formed the foundation of the program for the Olympic Games. Segregation was based on the suggested biological construction of two different sexes, which were regarded as complementary.[26] The "complementary" women's sports gained acceptance in the frame of Olympic Games. Sports representing masculinity in different cultures remained a sphere for men only. Maintaining the strict boundaries between the two spheres in sports was inevitable, and that is why athletics has been one of the sports with historically the most contradiction involving opposition to women's participation. It was the first sport in which women performed in front of an audience in scant clothing. For men, women with "half-naked" bodies in public, and their sweating while performing, would ruin the "male sporting spirit and the marvelous fights between heroes" and give "wrong" messages of womanhood. Female athletes were either seen as unmoral or presenting a problematic vision of masculinity.[27]

However, the conservative gender hierarchy in the international sports movement was challenged by the workers' sports federations in the interwar years. The Communist *Red Sport International* (RSI) was established in the Soviet Union in 1921, in which women's participation in sports was regarded as a tool for promoting women's social emancipation and a role in military defense.[28]

---

[26] Thomas Laqueur, *Om könens uppkomst. Hur kroppen blev kvinnlig och manlig* (Stockholm: Brutus Östlings Bokförlag Symposion, 1994). Laquer speaks of two genders' system, based on two sexes' biology, which is a more precise way to define a gender system, as a heterosexual order, a basic element for the modern sports culture.

[27] Susan K. Cahn, *Coming on strong. Gender and Sexuality in Twentieth-Century Women's Sport* (USA: Harvard University Press, 1995). E.g., Chapter 1 (New Type of Athletic Girl) and Chapter 7 (Lesbian Identity and Community in Women's Sport. In USA in the twenties the masculinity of female athletes was the fear; in 1930s it was turned to fear of lesbian athletes. See also Helena Tolvhed, "'Damolympiaden' i Göteborg 1926 och det olympiska spelet kring kvinnlig fri-idrott" in *Idrott, historia och samhälle. Svenska idrottshistoriska föreningens årsskrift 2008*, ed. Johan R. Norberg and Leif Yttergren (Stockholm: SVIF, 2008), 93–102.

[28] James Riordan, *Soviet Sport. Background to the Olympics* (Oxford: Basil Blackwell Publisher, 1980) 130–142

Athletics in the Nordic Countries

The *Socialist Worker Sports International* (SWSI) founded a women's committee in 1929, and it realized a program for promoting women's sports. At the international level, women's events, including athletics, were included in the Worker Olympiads and their winter sports competitions from 1925 to 1937. The RSI organized so called *Spartakiads*, incorporating women's athletic events from 1921. Women had competitive contacts with athletes abroad, also in Norway and Finland.[29] The SWSI and RSI worked separately and SWSI without contacts with the so-called bourgeois sports system. By the late 1930s, the activities of international worker sports movements were obstructed by fascism.

The Finnish *Workers' Sports Federation* (TUL, founded in 1919) functioned as a pioneer in women's athletics in the country in 1920s. Some of the activist female members in the new workers' sports federation came from clubs of the women's gymnastics federation, to be part of founding of the TUL and to share their knowledge and feminist ideas there. Again, part of them came from different leftist organizations. They took the lead in the women's work in the federation, and their work resulted in hiring a women's secretary and launching a journal in addition to women's committees at all levels in the federation.[30] Women's major sporting activity was gymnastics, but they had competitive programs for athletics, in ball games, skiing and swimming, too. The first championships in athletics were held in 1919, with events of running, shot put, and long jump in the program. The competitions were debated in the women's journal, but were mainly accepted and approved. Many worker women were used to heavy physical work, so, there was no sense in denying them strengthening themselves with the help of sport, they argued.[31]

In any case, competition and international success were pivotal for male workers. In 1921, in preparation for the first International Worker Olympics in Prague, TUL sent only one female runner. The gymnasts had to stay at home because the male participants required all the resources.[32] The lack of resources for women were often discussed in the federation. For example, when they demanded two series in athletic competitions (girls and women), comments such

---

[29] Franz Nitsch, "Appendix A: The Two International Worker Sport Organisations," in *The Story of Worker Sport*, ed. Arnd Krüger and James Riordan (Champaign IL: Human Kinetics, 1996), 167–171. About women's contacts within international worker sports, see Laine, *Työväen urheiluliikkeen naiset*.

[30] Leena Laine, *Työväen urheiluliikkeen naiset*, 43–45; 53ff.

[31] *Ibid.*, 57ff.

[32] *Ibid.*, 51ff.

as "Too many spoons for women!" were heard.[33] In 1925, four female athletes from TUL participated successfully in the Workers' Olympiad in Frankfurt, but once more women were left out from the Olympiad in Vienna (1931). After the 1925 games, a German worker female athlete, Wilma Dittmar embarked on a competitive tour of Finland. Her example and critical comments on the backward Finnish sporting culture and, among others, the heavy clothing of our athlete women was well received here.[34]

Movement against Exclusion Politics in Athletics in 1920s and 1930s

For women active in competitive sports – international by nature and structure – unlimited participation was essential. Therefore, the struggle for full rights was an organizing foundation for international co-operation among active woman athletes. In order to gain space in the international field of sport, women had two choices, either to co-operate with men in joint organizations or to establish their own. The former alternative presupposed wider acceptance of women and women's performances at the national level. The latter choice was not easy in the regulated and male-controlled sports system in which a precondition for participation was membership in an internationally recognized federation. In the following, I am going to present the implications of the only independent international women's organization in the history of competitive sports: *The International Women's Sports Federation* (FSFI).

The history of FSFI (the *Fédération Sportive Féminine Internationale*, 1921–1936) is unique. The federation, with its large membership and own Women's Olympics (from 1926 Women's World Games) was the only women's group in history to challenge the worldwide male power centers, such as IOC or IAAF. It facilitated contacts between female athletes within an international framework. Women's Olympics activated sportswomen all around the world. It was based on the model of the male organization: Olympics should be organized every fourth year with national representation. In the beginning, only athletics events were included in the program. In imitating male games women wanted to demonstrate their physical capacity. The goal

---

[33] *Ibid.*,79ff.

[34] *Ibid.*, 95–97.

was to be able to enter the male system on equal terms.[35] But, as yet, these equal terms did not exist for women.

The IAAF and its Swedish President, Sigfrid Edström, realized that their authority was threatened by the success of FSFI. Edström was of the opinion that women's athletics federation should be controlled by men and by IAAF, and that it had to be merged into the worldwide body of athletics.[36] Negotiations between the two organizations between 1924 and 1926 resulted first in founding a (temporary) women's commission in the IAAF then the inclusion of several women's athletics events into the Olympics' program as an experiment, in 1928.[37] Edström was able to reach his goal. The FSFI finally gave up after several compromises and in 1936 it disappeared from history.

In the Nordic countries FSFI's work was also an inspiration to female organization activities in Sweden in the 1920s, in Finland and Norway in the 1930s. Athletics was already popular among Swedish women and especially among schoolgirls.[38] Compared with Finland, female athletics in Sweden was not totally neglected even if the inclusion of women athletics in the Olympic program was strongly opposed. In 1923 the Swedish Athletics Federation founded a propaganda committee to evaluate women's athletics, and in 1925 it was proposed that the Athletics Federation would set up a women's committee. The federation, however, preferred founding an independent women's organization – men did not, by any means, want women to interfere in their federation. The Swedish women's sports association (*Svenska Kvinnors Idrottsförbund*, est. 1925) was ready to host the Second Women's World Games of FSFI in Gothenburg in 1926. The Games was a public success, widely covered by the press, but not without critical tones.[39]

The new federation's work seemed successful in the beginning, but it was operating without sufficient financing. Hoping to earn their share of state sup-

---

[35] F. A. M. Webster, *Athletics of To-day for Women. History, Development & Training* (London and New York: Frederik Warne & CO. Ltd, 1930), 32–33; Gertrud Pfister, "Die Frauenweltspiele und die Beteiligung von Frauen in Olympischen Spielen," in Sport(geschichte) in *Museen und Archiven: Berichte und Materialien*, ed. Martina Behrendt and Gerd Steins (Berlin: Sportsmuseum Berlin und Forum für Sportgeschichte - Fördererverein für das Sportsmuseum Berlin, 2000), 157–171; Allen Guttmann, *Women's Sports. A History* (New York: Columbia University Press, 1991), 167–168.

[36] Jörg Krieger, *Power and Politics in World Athletics. A Critical History* (London: Routledge, 2021), 39ff.

[37] Webster, *Athletics of To-Day*, 98–100; Pfister, "Die Frauenweltspiele;" Guttmann, *Women's Sports*, 168; Krieger, *Power and Politics*.

[38] Laine, "Jämlik idrott," 62–64.

[39] Sara Lindström, Den kvinnliga idrotten i Sverige 1924–1928. C-Uppsats i historia 1999, University of Göteborg.www.rf.se, 7–8; Laine, "Jämlik idrott," 67–68.

port (already enjoyed by male federations), the women's federation applied for a membership in the Swedish Central Sports Federation (*Riksidrottsföbundet*, RF), which dealt with state subsidies in sports. At the same time, another women's sports organization, in 1924 founded feminist association for promoting sports among women (*Svenska Kvinnors Centralförbund för Fysisk Kultur,* SK-CFK), handed in its application to the *Riksidrottsföbundet.* Its board consisted of gymnastics leaders, female doctors, and feminist activists.[40]

The RF rejected the applications and instead, started negotiations on merging the women's associations into the athletic federation, and it is here the IAAF President Edström started to play his own game. He obviously wanted a concrete model for subjugating the women's international separatism. Edström suggested founding a women's committee in the athletics federation with a precondition that the women's association should be abolished. This is what happened in 1927. Both women's associations were represented in the male lead women's committee. After quite an intensive start, the committee's activity seemed to lose its significance because of the political and economic conditions set for its work.[41] The number of female members in the athletics federation doubled during the 1930s amounting to 20,000, but the federation's policy was not supportive. For instance, the Swedish Olympic Committee refused to finance female athlete representatives in the Olympic Games in 1928. Despite this, the three female participants won two bronze medals.

In Finland, the hostility around women's athletics activity was prolonged. The addition of women's events to the Olympic program aroused a wider debate in the press and loud opposition among male sports leaders as well as within the general public in Finland (as in Sweden). The inclusion of women came as a shock to SVUL, which had abolished women's championships in athletics just a few years earlier. In addition, the reform deleted three important events for Finland from the Olympic program by giving space for women. This was interpreted as Edström's attempt to weaken Finnish chances of success at the Olympic Games. In protest the SVUL called for an Olympic boycott in spring 1927, which was formally motivated by a need to promote popular sports. Lauri Pihkala, a SVUL representative in the IAAF organs led the debates.[42] Already in 1926, he had begun an intensive polemic against women's participation in Olympic athletics. For him, the women's entry

[40] Helena Tolvhed, "'... tendenser, som vi icke böra gå in för.' Riksidrottsförbundet och frågan om kvinnors friidrott i Sverige 1925–1939," in *Idrott, historia och samhälle, Svenska idrottshistoriska föreningens årsskrift*, ed. Paul Sjöholm and Helena Tolvhed (Stockholm: TMG Sthlm AB, 2013), 40–69.

[41] Helena Tolvhed, "... tendenser som vi icke böra gå in för."

[42] Häyrinen and Laine, *Suomi urheilun suurvaltana*, 186–187, 190–193.

into athletics was "the five last nails in the coffin of Olympic Games."[43] The boycott call had no effect, however, and it had to be canceled in silence.

The absence of Finnish women from the 1932 Olympic Games generated questions in the international sports press. Why did only men from such an important sporting country participate? After the Games, several male initiatives for founding of sports societies or sections in clubs for women took place in Helsinki. Finally, in the autumn of 1932, women themselves founded the Helsinki Women's Sports Society (HNU). Its leaders were female academics and students who had practiced athletics since the end of the 1920s in academic associations. The HNU took on an active role immediately, especially in promoting women's athletics. It was supported by many male sports leaders such as Urho Kekkonen, the chairman of the new Finnish Athletic Federation (SUL). The HNU joined the athletic federation which founded a women's section and held unofficial championships for women in 1935.[44] During the 1930s, numerous international visitors took part in its competitions. Four women athletes from SUL participated in the Olympic Games in 1936 but without success, thus disappointing male leaders who had no idea about the level of competition within international women's athletics. In general, the burst of activity around women's sports lost its momentum, as it had in other countries.[45]

Athletics and Women's Co-Operation in Sports in the 1940s

Women from the Nordic countries widely challenged the power exercised by the leading male sports organizations after World War II. During the war, women had assumed wider responsibilities in working life. At the same time, they found space to exercise through sports more freely. After the war a conflict situation emerged in sports as well, in that society wanted to push women back into their homes. This conflict formed the basis for a new movement for women's social rights in the 1940s. At the international level most disciplines were open for women. Since the Olympic Games 1948, female sports stars, especially in

---

[43] *Ibid.*, 187–188.

[44] Häyrinen and Laine, *Suomi urheilun suurvaltana*; Lempi Hartikka, 15-vuotiskatsaus [Helsingin Naisurheilijat], Unprinted manuscript, and the HNU Newspaper Clips Collection. HNU Archives.TAHTO: Helsinki.

[45] *Ibid.*

athletics, were celebrated, and women's sports aroused positive attention and interest in the international media.

In Finland, women's sports spread in the second half of the 1940s. The isolation of workers' sports had ended during the war and new competitive opportunities increased women's activity in several sports. During the war there was held two federation matches in women's athletics between the Worker Sports Federation (TUL) and the SUL. In 1947, a new special section for women athletics was founded in the TUL. The *Working Women's Sports Journal* was given a new, modern title *Women's Sports Journal*. In 1951, the HNU followed up with a second publication forum, and started to publish a leaflet which disseminated information about women's training and competitions in athletics.[46]

In the SUL the athletics committee for women was not renamed after 1938. First, in 1944, the committee with four women and two men with a male chair was re-established. The active sportswoman and lawyer Lempi Hartikka acted as secretary. The core of the activism focused on the Women's Sports Club (HNU) in Helsinki. The women were optimistic about the future of their participation in the SUL: there were plans for the reorganization of the women's competition system, education, and training. Female sections were needed in clubs and district organizations and the federation hired a secretary for women's athletic sports. Education of women trainers was also necessary. The SUL began to organize district championships in athletics in 1946. The first (unofficial) Finnish Championships in women's athletics were held in 1945 on the initiative of the Worker Sports Federation. The championships were excellent publicity for women's athletics – there was audiences of over 3,000 people.[47]

After the success of unofficial championships SUL finally decided (after a vote in the SUL Council: nineteen to eight) that the official Finnish Championships in women's athletics would be added in the co-operative program between SUL and TUL in 1946. The federation still refused to open championships for women in SUL until 1948. The prevailing restrictive attitude towards women's demands in the federation manifested in many ways. Indeed, the male chairman of the women's committee resigned because of the negative attitude of the federation leaders towards women's sports in general, and particularly the work of the committee for women's sport. For example, the federation decided not to send female participants to the 1946 European Athletics Cham-

---

[46] Leena Laine, *Työväen urheiluliikkeen naiset*, 142–150, 154–155, 163; HNU's "*Naisurheilija*"-leaflet was published 1951–1963.

[47] Lempi Hartikka, 15-vuotiskatsaus; Laine, *Työväen urheiluliikkeen naiset*, 240.

pionships in Oslo, despite the hosts promising to cover the expenses of one female participant. Instead, the TUL sent one female athlete to represent Finland.
In Oslo, female athletes from the Soviet Union were presented to the world for
the first time. Their performances challenged western sports leaders to rethink
the education of their female athletes (see also the chapter by Goksøyr and Jörg
Krieger in this anthology).[48]

Two women were sent to the Olympic Games in London in 1948 from
the athletic federation SUL and one from the TUL. Kaisa Parviainen (SUL)
won the silver medal in javelin. She was the first Finnish woman to win an
Olympic medal in athletics. The newspapers generally commented in a positive manner about the women's events in London. Fanny Blankers Koen,
the star of the London Olympic Games, visited Finland after the games and
took part in competitions in several towns, eagerly followed and reported
by the press.[49]

In 1948, SUL and TUL women received an invitation from Norway to participate in a federation match entitled "Sweden against other Nordic countries."
However, the SUL rejected the invitation. The journal of the central federation,
Urheilija (The Sportsman) regretted the decision and complained about wom-
en's poor contacts abroad. According to the writer, women had better possibilities for success than men at the time. It was written in the journal that it was
high time to understand the significance of women's sport.[50] Now the target was
the Olympic Games in Helsinki in 1952. Consequently, Helsinki Games 1952
had a positive effect on women's possibilities. Before and after the London
Games, the number of women's national competitions in Finland grew, training was intensified and international co-operation in form of Nordic athletics
competitions started. They were held between Finland, Sweden, and Denmark
in 1951–1952. Until 1957 most common were competitions between Finland
and Sweden.[51]

However, women in the central federation SVUL lacked organizational
forums for developing their sports until the year 1948, when activist wom-
en initiated the establishment of a Women's Central Sports Committee in the
SVUL. The model was adopted from Sweden and Norway, countries where

---

[48] Lempi Hartikka, 15-vuotiskatsaus; Laine, *Työväen urheiluliikkeen* naiset, 242–243.

[49] Newspaper Clips Collection, Helsingin Naisurheilijat, TAHTO.

[50] *Ibid.*

[51] Martti Jukola, *Urheilun pikkujättiläinen* (Porvoo: WSOY, 1958).

women's position in sports in the 1940s were similar.[52] All federations with women members were represented in the central committee. Thereby committees were founded in single sports federations and districts. The aim was to develop co-operation between women, to educate them in organizational work as well as to organize the members training and competitive opportunities at mass level sports for women.

In the SVUL, the women's committees organized competitions and mass sporting events for women, arranged seminars and educated female administrators, coaches, referees and fought for publicity in (sports) journals. During the late 1940s and 1950s, women's committees obtained considerable autonomy concerning women's interests in sport. However, they did not have control of resources and top-level competitions. Co-operation between the Nordic countries was also established. On the organization level, the Central Nordic Federations rejected the idea of the the launch of a permanent Nordic committee for women' sports in 1956. It was regarded as unnecessary and expensive.[53]

It was difficult to change the basic power relations in sport: the number of women in leading positions in the federations, as sports officials or as coaches did not grow significantly. In Norway, the organizational advancement of women, starting from the middle of the 1940s, declined quickly in the late 1940s thanks to the "rationalization" of the central organization. In Finland and Sweden, the committees vanished during the 1970s.[54] The athletic sports had mostly been led by women since the 1950s. The popularity and significance of this rejected sport grew especially during the years of the so-called Cold War because there was intensified sporting competition between East and West. When the international significance of women's sports was finally understood by sports leaders in Finland within this context, the big athletics clubs started training young female talents, and soon training of athlete women was transferred from female to male control. An activist generation of women believed that their aims had been achieved, and they had abandoned the special organization they had created.

---

[52] Gerd von der Lippe, "Kvinneutvalg – organisering av kvinnners särintresser i idretten," *Nytt omkvinneforskning 4/89,* 1989, 34–43; Leena Laine, "How to Cross Borders – Woen and Sports Organisations in the Nordic Countries," *The International Journal of the History of Sport* 15, no. 1 (April 1998): 194–205, https://doi.org/10.1080/09523369808714020.

[53] Laine, "How to Cross Borders," 201–203; Leena Laine, *Työväen urheiluliikkeen naiset,* 241; Jukola, *Urheilun pikkujättiläinen.*

[54] Gerd von der Lippe, "Kvinneutvalg;" Laine *ibid.*; Lennart K. Persson and Thomas Pettersson, *Svensk friidrott 100 år* (Stockholm: Sellin & Partner, 1995), 393ff.

During the Nordic "committee period," a new stage to strive for recognition of women in sports came into being. At the time, women and the position of women in society were made visible in the mainstream sports organizations, and the committees created and promoted co-operation among women. The critical point is, that in committees, women worked on the organizations rather than on their own terms. Women joined in, but nothing was really changed in terms of the way things were framed; women were involved in the "ready-made sports form." They were able to work on the grassroot level, but remained barred from the "upper rooms."

Movements and Activity Crests in Women's Athletics

In my study I present and analyze the ways women's activities were organized in athletics from the early start to the 1950s in Finland within an international context. In Finland women entered the competition tracks in the beginning of the twentieth century when sport was not yet organized and rules remained unformulated. Activity was so intensive that we can describe it as the first (and largely unknown) period of rise in support of women's athletics. At the end of this article, I present a similarly understudied phase between the 1940s and 1950s. In between these two key eras of change, the postwar period was also a significant emancipatory period in female athletics. The gender segregation in sports and society ensued in the interwar period and, surprisingly enough, it represented an essential part of "modernity." The development of athletics in 1920s was led and controlled by men, whose leading idea was that women/female bodies did not belong on the athletic fields.

After the exclusion of the sport from the Olympic Games, women's own international organization FSFI was founded in 1921. However, it lost its historic fight against the major male powers in sport: the IAAF and the IOC. The final result was the compulsory merging of female organizations with male organisations, since the end of the 1920s. At the end of the 1930s, the rise of women's athletics was paralyzed by ideological and political pressure. A return to hetero-sexual patronage ended female rebellions and reinstated male power.

The next step in women's progress was activity organized in the form of stable female committees in national federations, after the Second World War, in the Nordic Countries. These committees helped female cooperation between, for instance, Nordic athletes and in order to bring common demands onto the agenda. Male power set the limits and diminished the work of the committees. The significance of the committees was noticed only when they were abolished. Instead, while adapting to a larger social program to improve women's lives, women's gymnastics movements achieved continuity "from mother to daughter." Conversely, movements within competitive sports that concentrated exclusively on women's rights in sports recurred in shorter periods. One explanation for the breaks in activity is the connection between crest periods and the different generations of women. This is why it is important to speak about women's movements in sports: they make women visible.

CHAPTER 4

"We Cannot Afford to be Amateurs."
The Rise and Fall of Amateurism
in Finnish Athletics

Jouni Lavikainen

Introduction

Throughout the twentieth century, careers of elite track athletes were shaped by amateurism, an ideology rooted in Victorian era Britain, later embraced by the International Olympic Committee (IOC) and the International Amateur Athletic Federation (IAAF). The amateur question became especially pervasive in athletics – a major sport in the Olympic movement since the initiation of the modern Olympics in 1896.

In the Nordic countries, national sports organizations accepted amateurism early on, despite its alien roots. In Finland, the popularity of athletics resulted in the emergence of "shamateurism" soon after the national sports federation *Suomen Voimistelu- ja Urheiluliitto* (SVUL) had devised the first national amateur rules in 1907. "Shamateurism" saw amateur rules circumvented by arranging sinecures for elite athletes, and paying athletes under-the-table rewards in meets.[1]

In the interwar period, Finnish athletics gained a reputation of paying "only lip service" to the ideals of amateurism, with long-distance runners Paavo Nurmi and Ville Ritola defined by Llewellyn and Gleaves as athletes "who perhaps best

---

[1] On the amateur rules and the policies with which they were enforced in the early twentieth century Finland, see Jouni Lavikainen, "Amatöörikysymys Suomessa 1907–1932," [The Amateur Question in Finland between 1907–1932], in *Liikunnan areenat – yhteiskuntatieteellisiä kirjoituksia liikunnasta ja urheilusta*, ed. Kalervo Ilmanen and Hanna Vehmas (Jyväskylä: Jyväskylän yliopisto, 2012), 189–208; Leena Laine, "Sala-ammattilaisuus – urheilun uskottavuuden uhka," [Shamateurism – Threat to the Credibility of Sport], in *Suomi urheilun suurvaltana*, ed. Erkki Vasara (Helsinki: Liikuntatieteellinen Seura, 1989), 305–26.

exemplified the 'shamateur' spirit of the postwar years."[2] Despite widespread international demands to mitigate and modernize the amateur rules during the Cold War, the amateur apostles in the IOC were able to cling to amateurism until the 1980s, during which a combination of commercial pressures, the new leadership of the IOC, and athlete activism finally paved the way for the professional era.[3]

This chapter contributes to the academic research by discussing the long era of amateurism in Finnish athletics from the approval of the first amateur rules in 1907 to the deterioration of the amateur sports system in the 1980s. I approach the culture of shamateurism that emerged in the interwar period Finnish athletics by drawing upon recently digitalized contemporary newspapers and magazines that can be accessed with the online collections service of the National Library of Finland. How did the amateur policies of the international sports federations and governing bodies of sport in Finland affect career paths of athletes in Finland? How did Paavo Nurmi, suspended by the IAAF for under-the-table payments in 1932, compare to other victims of amateurism, and how were they discussed in contemporary Finnish media? By putting the underground labor-relations system[4] that developed in Finnish athletics on the limelight, I aim to demonstrate how different generations of elite Finnish athletes responded to and ameliorated the shackles of amateurism imposed on them from the above.

The First Shamateurs

Hardly anything has wounded our sport as much as the problem of modern amateurs, those veiled professional athletes, Pharisees of the twentieth century, who suck rotten wounds into all healthy and dignified sports. As an unsolved mystery it still haunts in all countries threatening as ever.[5]

Although the 1906 article quoted above deals with veiled professionalism in international cycling, it illustrates that Finnish sports authorities contemplated

[2] Matthew P. Llewellyn and John Gleaves, *The Rise and Fall of Olympic Amateurism* (Urbana: University of Illinois Press, 2016), 20, 61.

[3] Llewellyn and Gleaves, *The Rise and Fall of Olympic Amateurism*, 182–190; Joseph M. Turrini, *The End of Amateurism in American Track and Field* (Urbana: University of Illinois Press, 2010), 154–159.

[4] Turrini, *End of Amateurism*, 114.

[5] "Kilpailukausi 1905 ulkomailla. Kestävyyspyöräily," [Competition season 1905 abroad. Long-distance cycling], *Suomen Urheilulehti*, no. 1 (1906), 45.

the "problem of modern amateurs" before sports were fully codified. All major sports in Finland at the time were incorporated under the umbrella of the central organization SVUL, founded officially in 1906. Highlighting the importance of amateurism, the amateur rules that applied to all sports disciplines of SVUL came into effect already in May 1907. As a result, loosely organized professional cultures in skiing and wrestling were stifled.[6]

Rather than the British ideal that sports should be reserved for gentleman amateurs, the motive for these actions has been interpreted by researchers as one of social control. Amateurism was accepted because it enhanced SVUL's power and helped it pursue societal targets that transcended sporting success. The amateur rules were initially drafted with only the IOC's vague amateur definitions for guidance, but were soon updated based on the IAAF's (founded in 1913) more specific amateur code.[7]

The first Finnish athlete to be cast internationally as a shamateur was long-distance runner Hannes Kolehmainen. During Kolehmainen's gold-medal winning runs in the 1912 Olympics in Stockholm and his subsequent running tour in England, rumors circulated in the British press about his amateur violations, such as systematic training under the guidance of his brother Viljam (aka William) – an openly professional runner himself – and government subsidies that financed his career.[8] Finnish newspapers mostly portrayed Kolehmainen as an exemplary amateur athlete and defended him when he was later investigated for amateur breaches by the Amateur Athletic Union's (AAU) amateur committee.[9]

Even though Hannes Kolehmainen's training costs were financed more by his brother than by any sports association, the suspicions about his amateurism were well founded. In the United States, Hannes and Viljam Kolehmainen embarked on running tours together, Hannes participating in amateur events and Viljam in professional ones, with Hannes' rewards paid under-the-table.[10] In terms of training, Hannes's running career in the 1910s and 1920s contained

[6] Jouni Lavikainen, "Amatöörikysymys Suomessa," 191–197.

[7] Jouni Lavikainen, "Amatöörikysymys ja ammattilaisuuden uhka suomalaisessa kilpaurheilussa 1907–1932," [The amateur question and the threat of professionalism in Finnish sports 1907– 1932], (Master's thesis, University of Helsinki, 2011), 30.

[8] Matthew P. Llewellyn, "'The Best Distance Runner the World Has Ever Produced': Hannes Kolehmainen and the Modernisation of British Athletics," *The International Journal of the History of Sport* 29, no. 7 (2012): 1024–1025, https://doi.org/10.1080/09523367.2012.679026.

[9] Ossi Viita, *Hymyilevä Hannes: työläisurheilija Hannes Kolehmaisen sankaruus porvarillisessa Suomessa,* [Smiling Hannes: working class athlete Hannes Kolehmainen's heroism in bourgeois Finland], (Helsinki: Otava, 2003), 183–184.

[10] *Ibid.*, 184.

months-long periods of full-time training during which he considered running
his vocation, but also equally long periods when he did not have much time for
running, working full-time as a mason.[11]

Hannes Kolehmainen did not benefit from state subsidies as much as was
rumored in the 1910s. During the peak of his career from 1912 to 1920, state
support for sports in Finland was still comparably low. The funding of Finland's
Olympic preparations relied on fundraisings and individual donations which
increased significantly between the 1920 and the 1924 Olympics. A budget of
FIM (Finnish marks) 100,000 (EUR 43,597 in 2022)[12] was reserved for the
coaching of track and field athletes for Antwerp in 1920, rising to FIM 350,000
(EUR 122,627 in 2022) for Paris four years later.[13]

This fundraising system set the benchmark for decades to come. As Kalle
Rantala has argued, the lightweight structure of the coaching organization –
who was primarily one man, athletics coach Jaakko Mikkola – meant that most
of the funding was conveyed directly to athletes to enable their full-time training months before the Olympics.[14] Mikkola contacted directors in suitable business firms and arranged athlete sinecures, compensations for lost earnings, and
monthly stipends. Athletes were also provided as much equipment and massage
as required. Mikkola advised athletes to stay quiet about these arrangements,
and only compete in official qualification events before the Olympics.[15]

Some athletes required more support than others due to their professions.
For example, when long-distance runner Sameli Tala, a farmer by trade, applied for FIM 4,000 to cover the wages of a farmhand taking care of his
farmstead during the eight months spent preparing for and participating in the
Olympics, Mikkola replied that the coaching committee could not afford to
in line with amateur rules. Instead, Mikkola suggested that the sum would be
paid to him privately. Tala's Olympic preparation was eventually funded by
a group of local benefactors that were contacted by the president of his club,
Viipurin Urheilijat.[16]

---

[11] *Ibid.*, 181–182, 199–200.

[12] I converted the currency into 2022's euros with the Bank of Finland Museum's online money
value converter. Bank of Finland Museum. https://app.rahamuseo.fi/calculator?lang=ENG. Accessed October 25, 2022.

[13] Viita, *Hymyilevä Hannes*, 278–282.

[14] Kalle Rantala, "Jaakko Mikkola ammattivalmentajana 1924," [Jaakko Mikkola as a professional
coach in 1924], *Kasvatus & Aika* 11, no. 2 (2017), 61.

[15] Lavikainen, "Amatöörikysymys ja ammattilaisuuden uhka," 75–76.

[16] *Ibid.*

Within this context, it is no wonder that Finland – along with Sweden[17] – was one of the most vocal supporters for broken-time payments in the IOC. At the IOC's congress in 1930, Finland went even further than Sweden by suggesting that athletes could be compensated for their losses not only during the Olympics, but also during the training period preceding the Games.[18] This would have only served to legalize the practice that had been common in Finland since the early 1920s.

Finnish sports leaders interpreted amateurism in a more pragmatic fashion than most of their counterparts in the IOC. In 1917, SVUL investigated expenses compensations of fifty-five athletes in the preceding two years, and found out that four of them demanded excessive payments. One individual athlete – the leading Finnish middle-distance runner, Einari Anttila – was found to have systematically requested excessive payments. The investigations began on the initiative of three of SVUL' district organizations, indicating that athletes' demands were considered problematic in various parts of the country. However, no punishments were given to the individual athletes.[19]

A different approach was taken when, in early 1920, the prize trophies and Finnish championships medals of long-distance runner Albin Stenroos were found in a jeweler's shop in Helsinki. On this occasion SVUL decided to strip the runner – who by his own testimony was not planning to compete anymore – of his amateur status. This represented the first such ruling for a track and field athlete in Finland. After being banned from running for a year, Stenroos – who had returned to running – applied for reinstating his amateur status, arguing that financial hardship had prevented him from buying back the prizes that one of his family members had pawned.[20]

Agreeing that difficult conditions after the Finnish Civil War in 1918 should be considered as a mitigating factor, SVUL decided to return Stenroos' amateur status in 1921. According to the rules of the IAAF, national governing bodies of athletics were entitled to do this – but only for domestic competition. Only national federations could enforce the amateur rules by punishing athletes, which effectively afforded full control over the amateur status of their own athletes. As a result, athletes were treated differently for similar breaches of amateurism.[21]

---

[17] Karin Wikberg, "Amatör eller professionist? Studier rörande amatörfrågan i svensk tävlingsidrott 1903–1967," [Amateur or Professional? A Study of the Amateur Question within Swedish Competitive Sport between 1903–1967], (PhD diss., University of Stockholm, 2005), 153.

[18] Lavikainen, "Amatöörikysymys ja ammattilaisuuden uhka," 66.

[19] *Ibid.*, 33–34.

[20] *Ibid.*, 50.

[21] Lavikainen, "Amatöörikysymys Suomessa," 200.

In 1928, controversial Norwegian pole vaulter Charles Hoff was declared professional by his own federation. Two years earlier he had been caught by the AAU for taking under-the-table money in athletics meets while touring the United States and was subsequently deprived the right to compete in the country.[22] Afterwards, Hoff was reported by *Suomen Urheilulehti* – which paid particularly close attention to such cases – to have become a "professional dancer and a pole vault actor" in the United States, openly using his athletic ability for monetary gain, for example by arranging pole vault exhibitions. This was probably one of the reasons why the Norwegian federation did not return his amateur status before the 1928 Olympics in Amsterdam.[23]

When Albin Stenroos committed his "crime" against amateurism, he was clearly anything but a "shamateur" like Hannes Kolehmainen was, and Paavo Nurmi and Charles Hoff would be proven to be later. During the years of the First World War and the Finnish Civil War, he did not compete in many years, and later reminisced that he thought then that his running days were over.[24] Given that he was born in 1889, the explanation is plausible as time marched on. Even still, when the Olympics in Paris approached in 1924, he was an athlete who had only recently regained his amateur status after being banned by his own federation for breaking the amateur rules.

Probably fully aware of Stenroos' difficult past with the amateur rules, the selection committee of SVUL selected him for the Olympics anyway. Their decision was rewarded as Stenroos won gold in the marathon. The ban was successfully kept hidden from the media both before and after Stenroos' marathon victory. This prevented international controversy that would have surely arisen otherwise.

The Anatomy of Interwar Shamateurism

The IOC's decision to uphold prohibition on broken-time payments at the congresses in Prague (1925) and Berlin (1930) propelled international athletics further towards hidden professionalism practices. Sports clubs and meet organizers in both Europe and the United States offered star athletes, often through

---

[22] Lavikainen, "Amatöörikysymys ja ammattilaisuuden uhka," 69–70.

[23] *Ibid.*

[24] "Albin Stenroos – maratonsankari 50 v. 24.2.39," [Albin Stenroos – marathon hero 50 years February 24, 1939], *Olympia: aikakauskirja Urheilun ja Kansankuntoisuuden kehittämiseksi*, February 1, 1939.

middlemen, increasing sums under-the-table.[25] In Finland, the number of athletics meets increased in the 1920s and 1930s,[26] providing athletes with avenues to secretive earnings, even in their own country. After hugely successful Olympics in 1920, 1924, and 1928, Finland boasted a vast cadre of Olympic medalists in athletics, athletes who guaranteed large crowds wherever they competed in Finland. This was recognized by meet organizers both in Finland and abroad.

Rumors about excessive rewards given to Finnish athletes in Finland and in their tours abroad increased during the 1920s. The authorities in SVUL placed the blame of the unwanted phenomenon on sports clubs.[27] In the mid-1920s, there were fairly detailed plans inside SVUL to found a committee to enforce the amateur rules more effectively on a national scale, but the plans floundered at the last stages after officials failed to find a suitable person to lead the committee. According to influential sports leader and journalist Lauri Pihkala, an organ led by "impartial" sports leaders, who understood the importance of amateurism, would have been best suited for the difficult and thankless task.[28]

In the media, shamateurism was approached differently based on the newspapers' political standing. Since the Civil War in 1918, the society in Finland had been divided into two: in sports, the "bourgeois" camp was led by SVUL and workers' sports movement, the Workers' Sports Federation (*Työväen Urheiluliitto*, TUL). In the working-class newspapers, shamateurism was seen as a confirmation of the corrupted nature of bourgeois sports, with each amateur conflict used as a weapon in the political battle against bourgeoisie. TUL accused bourgeois sports clubs of luring the best athletes in workers' sports clubs into their ranks with money, apartments and work places, which was true.[29] But despite claims that amateurism had stayed pure in workers' sports, monetary rewards also circulated into competitions under TUL.[30]

Shamateurism engendered mostly rumors and hearsay, but not much in terms of concrete evidence. Of the Finnish athletes, there is little doubt that

---

[25] Llewellyn and Gleaves, *The Rise and Fall of Olympic Amateurism*, 79.

[26] Jouko Kokkonen, *Suomalainen liikuntakulttuuri – juuret, nykyisyys ja muuttossuunnat*, [Finnish sports culture – roots, present and future directions], (Helsinki: Suomen Urheilumuseosäätiö, 2015), 94.

[27] "Mihin suuntaan urheiluelämäämme on johdettava," [Into what direction should our sport be led], *Suomen Urheilulehti* (March 1926).

[28] Lavikainen, "Amatöörikysymys ja ammattilaisuuden uhka," 59–61.

[29] Antti Syrjäläinen, "Miksi siksi loikkariksi?: huippu-urheilijoiden loikkaukset TUL:sta SVUL:oon 1919–1939," [Why? The defections of the top-athletes from TUL to SVUL in the years 1919–1939], (PhD diss., University of Joensuu, 2008), 134–140.

[30] Kokkonen, *Suomalainen liikuntakulttuuri*, 91.

nine-time Olympic gold-medalist Paavo Nurmi profited more than anyone else in Finnish, and in all likelihood international, athletics. According to Kalle Virtapohja, "the King of Runners" earned about $2 million dollars from his much-publicized running tour in the United States in 1925.[31] Nurmi sought to maximize his market value with the help of manager Hugo Qvist who was fluent in English, unlike Nurmi, and well connected with meet organizers in the United States.

Cooperating with Qvist was perhaps not as lucrative for Nurmi as he had assumed, because according to Virtapohja, Qvist "betrayed" Nurmi to the tune of FIM 800,000 during the tour. Qvist allegedly later returned the money to Nurmi. Soon after his return from the United States, Nurmi bought a car – disguised as a gift from his Finnish sports club, *Turun Urheiluliitto* – and deposited the rest of his American earnings into a bank account.[32]

Faced with the brazen shamateurism of the likes of Nurmi, the IOC and the IAAF responded with vigorous defense of amateurism. Paavo Nurmi's suspension for under-the-table rewards by the IAAF in 1932 was the culmination of this policy. Finnish sports leaders tried to revoke the ban until the last minute during the Olympics in Los Angeles. Evidence against Nurmi was considered as juridically invalid, and banning one athlete among many that were just as guilty was viewed as unfair. The Finns argued that only national federations had the right to ban athletes for amateur breaches – as the IAAF's rules also stated – but it was exactly this right that the IAAF was intent on enforcing. Nurmi's ban was upheld, and his international career was over.[33]

Just two months before Nurmi, French long-distance runner Jules Ladoumèque was banned for breaching the amateur rules by the French Athletics Federation.[34] Also in the ranks of banished amateurs was a Latvian-Polish runner Stanisław Petkiewicz (or Staņislavs Petkēvičs), who was well known in

---

[31] Kalle Virtapohja, *Mies josta tehtiin patsas. Paavo Nurmen ennätykset, maine ja perintö*, [Man from which a statue was made. Records, reputation and legacy of Paavo Nurmi], (Jyväskylä: Docendo, 2017), 80–81.

[32] *Ibid.*

[33] On the evidence with which Nurmi was banned, and Finnish sports leaders' efforts to overturn the ban, see, Heikki Roiko-Jokela, "Taistelu Nurmesta! Urho Kekkosen toiminta amatööriurheilun puolesta," [Fight for Nurmi! Urho Kekkonen's actions for amateur sport], in *Se toinen Paavo Nurmi – ja varjoon jääneet. Suomen Urheiluhistoriallisen seuran vuosikirja 1997*, ed. Anssi Halmesvirta and Heikki Roiko-Jokela (Jyväskylä: Suomen urheiluhistoriallinen seura, 1997), 59–77; Paavo Karikko and Mauno Koski, *Legendary Runner. A biography of Paavo Nurmi*, (Helsinki: The Sports Museum Foundation of Finland, 2006), 117–130.

[34] "Jääkö Ladoumeque pois Los Angelesista?" [Will Ladoumeque stay out of Los Angeles?], *Uudenmaan Sanomat*, February 2, 1932.

Finland as one of the few runners who had once managed to beat Paavo Nurmi. Nurmi remained the biggest star to be banned, however.

Interestingly, the cause of Petkiewicz's ban was not appearance money for his own runs, but pre-payments of Paavo Nurmi's rewards for meets in Paris and Milan. According to the Finnish press, Petkiewicz had pretended to be Nurmi's manager.[35] He was described as an athlete who was "well versed in means of shamateurism, and whose competition trips never came cheap for meet organizers"[36] – thus much like Nurmi.

In reality, Petkiewicz had not just pretended to be Nurmi's manager. Later research has shown that Nurmi had cooperated with both him and the treasurer of the Polish Athletics Federation, Felix Weinthal, when arranging his tour in Italy during autumn 1931.[37] Both men had signed contracts on Nurmi's behalf, and both were banned by the Polish Athletics Federation for it.

Despite his earlier promises, Nurmi did not travel to Italy, because he was aware of the IAAF's ongoing investigations about his amateur status. This caused unfortunate consequences not only for his middlemen and meet organizers; the Finnish consulate in Rome complained about Nurmi to the Foreign Ministry of Finland, pointing out that his last-minute default would weaken Finland's reputation in Italy.[38]

SVUL's official explanation for Nurmi's absence was that he had been denied permit to compete, because he had already competed twenty-one days abroad, the maximum limit set by the amateur rules. The explanation appears comical in view of Nurmi's earlier tours; for example, in both 1925 and 1929 he had competed continuously in the United States for about six months.[39]

The Shamateur Controversy of 1933 – A Case Study

Paavo Nurmi's suspension in 1932 has been thoroughly covered by researchers, but less has been written about the following year's shamateur controversy in

---

[35] "Stanislau Petkievicz julistettu kilpailukelvottomaksi koko eliniäkseen," [Stanislau Petkievicz banned for life], *Saarijärven Paavo*, December 31, 1931.

[36] "Petkievicz yritti lyödä mynttiä Nurmen kustannuksella," [Petkievicz tried to cash in on Nurmi's expense], *Uudenmaan Sanomat*, December 31, 1931.

[37] Virtapohja, *Mies josta tehtiin patsas*, 160; Karikko and Koski, *Legendary Runner*, 121.

[38] *Ibid.*

[39] Virtapohja, *Mies josta tehtiin patsas*, 79–80, 138.

Finland. On October 6, 1933, a rare written proof of shamateurism surfaced when Helsinki-based *Svenska Pressen* published a facsimile of a warranty [*takuusitoumus* in Finnish] signed on July 14, 1931 by Ossian Roschier, an official of a major sports club *Helsingin Kisa-Veikot* (HKV). According to the document, HKV would guarantee payment to Paavo Nurmi of 50% of the revenues of a two-day meet organized by HKV on August 3 and 4, 1931, provided he runs once on both days. If the Swede Edvin Wide also participated, two thirds of the revenues would be paid jointly to Nurmi and Wide. Transaction would take place during the meet's second day, after which the warranty would be given back to HKV to be destroyed.[40]

The document and the scandal it caused have gained some attention from Finnish researchers, but its context has not been hitherto properly understood. The role of Nicolaus von Bell has been especially neglected. Von Bell's actions in the 1930s add further insights into how under-the-table network in Finnish athletics functioned.

A Finnish-Swedish official employed in the police service of Helsinki, von Bell had since at least the late 1920s worked as an unofficial manager of Finnish athletes, which had given him a controversial reputation. "Sports has its parasites like plants, and as cows have flies. Such a fly must mister von Bell be considered," described *Turun Sanomat* in 1929.[41] Occasionally, von Bell was also linked to Paavo Nurmi, as his Helsinki-based "agent" [*asiamies* in Finnish].[42]

In March 1930, von Bell was prohibited to act in any role under SVUL because he had offered Finnish athletes for Swedish meets with excessive demands for return payments. After he was seen next summer with three Finnish athletes in Sweden and Denmark, SVUL decided to decline all competition permits to Sweden for the rest of the autumn. Athletes were also prohibited to collaborate with anyone apart from the officials of SVUL when organizing trips abroad.[43]

Late in 1932, von Bell petitioned SVUL to overturn his ban. If SVUL would not do this, he threatened to release documents that would prove that SVUL's officials had also been involved in breaking the amateur rules. In preparation

---

[40] "Document avslöjar vårt idrottsstyre!," [Document reveals our sports conduct], *Svenska Pressen*, October 6, 1933.

[41] "Juttuja ja kuulumisia," [Things and tidings], *Turun Sanomat*, July 16, 1929.

[42] "Paavo Nurmi kilpailukelvoton," [Paavo Nurmi banned], *Uusimaa*, April 5, 1932.

[43] "Urheilijamme eivät pääse eroon von Bellistä," [Our athletes can not get rid of von Bell], *Turun Sanomat*, 20 April, 1930; "Suomalaisille ei Ruotsiin kilpailulupia," [No competition permits for Finns to Sweden], *Länsi-Suomi*, August 30, 1930.

for countering this threat, SVUL founded a temporary amateur committee to oversee all investigations about amateur breaches in 1933. Von Bell's ban was upheld.[44] When the document signed by Roschier was published, it was assumed in SVUL that von Bell had acted on his earlier threats and leaked the document to Finnish-Swedish reporter Carl Adam Nycop, who had written the article.[45]

Nycop had a reputation similar to von Bell. On July 24, 1931, the Swedish *Idrottsbladet* had published the rewards of Nurmi and other Finnish runners from a two-mile World Record attempt in Helsinki that same night.[46] Nycop was later revealed as *Idrottsbladet*'s source. Yrjö Reijonen, who was the president of the organizing club *Helsingin Toverit*, denied *Idrottsbladet*'s claims on the spot, and assured that Nurmi and the others were not paid "a single mark."[47] Nycop explained later that the information had been meant for Stockholm's sports clubs, and he had given it only after being asked about Nurmi's fee in a telephone call.[48]

The claims of *Idrottsbladet* were labeled as fictional, but a facsimile of a signed offer could not be dismissed as easily. Interestingly, the meet referred to in Roschier's offer was supposed to take place ten days after the two-mile World Record attempt, but did not eventually go ahead, in all likelihood explaining why the document was not destroyed.

Nurmi and Wide denied knowing anything about Roschier's offer. Roschier could do little else than admit that he had made the offer, and explained that it had been based on the proposal of von Bell, and that after meeting Nurmi personally, he decided to cancel it when "noticing that Nurmi had no information about von Bell's actions."[49]

---

[44] "Piikkarit hyllyllä – pykälät pöydällä Urheiluliitto ja v. Bell keskustelevat 'amatöörikysymyksestä'," [The Athletics Federation and v. Bell discuss the 'amateur question'], *Suomen Urheilulehti*, October 12, 1933; Minutes of the SVUL's board, January 22, 1933, SVUL's archive, Sports Museum of Finland's archive.

[45] "Paljastukset urheilumaailmassa," [Revelations in sports world], *Ilta-Sanomat*, October 7, 1933.

[46] Nurmi would have received 50% of the meet's total revenue that was estimated to be over FIM 200,000 if at least 15,000 spectators showed up. Additionally, before the meet, Nurmi received a sum of FIM 25,000, and his fellow competitors Lauri Lehtinen FIM 15,000, Volmari Iso-Hollo FIM 14,000, and Lauri Virtanen FIM 10,000. "100,000 markkaa!" [100,000 marks!], *Sosialisti*, July 27, 1931.

[47] "Världsrekord av Nurmi, Lehtinen o. Virtanen på 2 eng. mil," [World Record of Nurmi, Lehtinen and Virtanen in the English two mile], *Hufvudstadsbladet*, July 25, 1931.

[48] Laine, "Sala-ammattilaisuus," 317; Karikko and Koski, *Legendary Runner*, 117.

[49] "Urheiluliitto vaatii v. Belliä esittämään kaikki kompromettoivat asiapaperit," [The Athletics Federation demands von Bell to present all documents], *Uusi Suomi*, October 12, 1933.

The case displays similarities with later drug scandals.[50] Roschier put the blame solely on himself, assuring that the rest of the HKV's board, on an organizational level, knew nothing about the offer. Roschier, who was also a member of the coaching committee of the Finnish Athletics Federation (FAF, founded under SVUL in 1932 as the national governing body of athletics), was promptly banned by the FAF for two years from having any role in the federation or its clubs.[51]

In the bourgeois press, von Bell's motive was explained as revenge. He had a difficult history with SVUL and the FAF, and with Paavo Nurmi, who had reportedly turned his back on his promise to run in Jules Ladoumèque's professional meet in Paris in autumn 1933, in which von Bell had been involved as a middleman.[52] While this cannot be verified, it would go a long way in explaining the timing of the publication.

Von Bell denied being the one to leak the document – of which four copies had been made, he stated – while presenting correspondence that showed that all of Nurmi, Wide and Roschier had been well aware of his arrangements regarding HKV's meet, and that the shares of revenues were suggested by Roschier rather than him. Von Bell had been in correspondence with both Wide's agent and Nurmi, the latter of whom had claimed in a letter to have discussed the proposition personally with Wide. Von Bell stated that he wished that "officials of sports clubs would leave him alone from their offers and enquiries."[53]

The media discourse about the controversy displays the fact that shamateurism had ramifications that reached beyond sport. Working-class newspapers relished the opportunity to attack bourgeoisie for the "dirty business" that had been uncovered and criticized that only von Bell was blamed of shamateurism in Finland.[54] Bourgeois newspapers presented von Bell as a villain, whose working in the police should be questioned based on his character,[55] and complained that his revelations only served the purposes of Finnish-Swedish and

---

[50] On the connections between anti-doping and amateurism, see, John Gleaves and Matthew Llewellyn, "Sport, Drugs and Amateurism: Tracing the Real Cultural Origins of Anti-Doping Rules in International Sport," *The International Journal of the History of Sport* 31, no. 8 (2014): 839–853. https://doi.org/10.1080/09523367.2013.831838.

[51] Laine, "Sala-ammattilaisuus," 318.

[52] "Urheilu – Mistä puhutaan," [Sports – what is talked about], *Vaasa*, October 10, 1933.

[53] "Porvarillisen urheilun surkea tila," [The poor state of bourgeois sports], *Kansan Työ*, October 15, 1933.

[54] *Ibid.*

[55] "Juttuja ja kuulumisia," [Things and tidings], *Turun Sanomat*, October 14, 1933.

working-class newspapers in Finland, as well as Sweden.[56]

An additional aspect was language politics – a perennial feature of domestic sports politics in the bilingual Finland during the interwar period.[57] By publishing a document that incriminated Paavo Nurmi, *Svenska Pressen* was accused of deliberately causing harm to Finnish sports. According to *Vaasa*, the entire Finnish-Swedish press had embraced a "fighting mentality" towards the FAF, because "it is led by a Finnish man [Urho Kekkonen], who has taken the right attitude in our relations with Sweden."[58]

The scandal served to further increase tensions between sporting relations between Finland and Sweden. After Swedish *Idrottsbladet* had also published Roschier's document with the usual accusations of shamateurism, *Suomen Urheilulehti* retaliated by publishing letters and telegrams that contained monetary offers to Finnish athletes from Swedish officials and managers – the earliest of which were from 1921.[59]

The authenticity of the document itself was not questioned by anyone. Nor was it denied that a star of Nurmi's caliber could receive as much as 50% of an athletics meet's revenue. The case displays that sometimes the same people who were supposed to monitor the amateur rules were involved in secret transactions to athletes, who also collaborated among themselves when arranging meets. The risks that delving into the black-market of athletics contained were outweighed by mutual financial interests. Working-class newspaper *Vapaus* estimated that events such as the two-day meet in Roschier's document usually generated between around FIM 200,000 to 300,000.[60] Depending on Wide's participation, Nurmi's reward would thus have secured between FIM 66,700 to 150,000 (EUR 26,285 to 59,111 in 2022).

The Roschier controversy was entangled with an issue that had ramifications for international athletics as a whole: Jules Ladoumègue's running federation (usually "*Ladoumèque-liitto*" in Finnish sources). Late in 1932, Ladoumègue

---

[56] "Urheilu – mistä puhutaan," [Sports – what is talked about], *Vaasa*, October 17, 1933.

[57] Jouko Kokkonen, "Kansakunta kilpasilla: urheilu nationalismin kanavana ja lähteenä Suomessa 1900–1952," [A competing nation: sports as channel and source of nationalism in Finland 1900–1952], (PhD diss., University of Jyväskylä, 2008), 171–174.

[58] "Amatööripulma käy yhä vaikeammaksi," [Amateur problem becomes even more difficult], *Vaasa*, October 7, 1933. In the previous autumn, the FAF had terminated sports relations with Sweden due to the perceived role of the IAAF's Swedish board members in the suspension of Nurmi.

[59] "Ruotsin urheilun johtomiehet tehneet ammattilaistarjouksia ainakin vuodesta 1921 alkaen," [Swedish sports leaders have made professional offers at least since 1921], *Suomen Urheilulehti*, October 19, 1933.

[60] "Juoksijan palkka," [Runner's pay], *Vapaus*, 10 October, 1933.

had founded a sports association named after him with an ambitious purpose: to openly pay athletes compensation. In the spring of 1933, rumors emerged in Finland that more than fifty Finnish athletes were prepared to join Ladoumèque's revolution against the IAAF.[61] Nicolaus von Bell and Carl A. Nycop – who seem to have been close associates – were involved in the project as Finnish liaisons.[62]

Interestingly, Kyösti Ojansuu, one of the organizers of the Ladoumèque federation's Finnish branch, asserted in *Suomen Urheilulehti* that the new federation did "not accept professionalism" and "vehemently opposes shamateurism," and claimed that only compensations for lost earnings were paid to athletes.[63] This rhetoric and the assurances that the federation "much appreciates youth education and patriotism" were probably targeted to Finnish readers, who had for decades been told of the individualistic and degenerated nature of professional sports by most of the media and sports organizations.

Even if the number of interested athletes would have been exaggerated, there was genuine interest in Finland. For example, influential journalist Martti Jukola voiced his sympathies for attempts to create a more honest system of payments than the one that the IAAF had unintentionally managed to create. Jukola was even rumored to be involved in the Finnish branch of the federation, which he denied.[64]

By many accounts, Ladoumèque tried actively to get Finnish runners to join his venture with the help of von Bell and Nycop. Eventually only experienced middle-distance runner Eino Purje (formerly Borg) accepted the offer. Purje travelled to France in September 1933 and competed in four meets organized by the Ladoumèque federation.[65] During his trip, the FAF banned him from competing in athletics meets in Finland and working in the clubs of FAF in any capacity.[66]

Purje's "professional career" proved to a be case in point for the proponents of amateur athletics. Soon after running in France, he sued Nicolaus von Bell

---

[61] "Mitä kuuluu?" [How are you?], *Suomen Sosialidemokraatti*, May 12, 1933.

[62] "Uusi urheiluliittoko?" [New sports federation?], *Lahti*, May 13, 1933.

[63] Kyösti M. Ojanen: "Totuus Ladoumèque -liitosta ja nykyisestä urheilukriisistä," [Truth about Ladoumèque federation and current sports crisis], *Suomen Urheilulehti*, September 18, 1933.

[64] "Ketkä Latomäki liiton johdossa Suomessa?" [Who are leading the Ladoumeque federation in Finland?], *Pohjois-Savo*, October 19, 1933.

[65] "Eino Purje latomäkiläinen," [Eino Purje one of Ladoumeque's runners], *Aamulehti*, September 3, 1933.

[66] "Piikkarit hyllyllä – pykälät pöydällä Urheiluliitto ja v. Bell keskustelevat 'amatöörikysymyksestä," [The Athletics Federation and v. Bell discuss the 'amateur question'], *Suomen Urheilulehti*, October 12, 1933.

for taking FIM 9,700 from him.[67] Whether the law suit was caused by Purje's poor knowledge of professional sports, in which managers were entitled to commissions – as opined a columnist of *Hufvudstadsbladet*[68] – or by von Bell's cheating, is impossible to ascertain from newspaper sources, but the loser was Purje: the district court of Helsinki ruled the case in von Bell's favor.[69]

By next autumn, von Bell was back working in amateur athletics, reportedly by offering the Dane Henry Nielsen and the Pole Janusz Kusociński to Finnish meet organizers.[70] His continuous collaboration with elite athletes and meet organizers – despite being publicly branded as a cheater and been banned by SVUL – is a proof in itself of his usefulness: people with good connections were needed by those who wanted to secure additional earnings in a nominally amateur sport.

Ladoumèque's federation quickly faded away, but the threat posed by shamateurism remained. The FAF responded to this by changing its rules in 1932 to enable canceling athletics meets until forty-eight hours before the meet if there were suspicions that under-the-table payments were being paid, with this action exercised once that summer.[71] In June 1934, the FAF canceled all athletics meets in Finland for a month because of alleged under-the-table payments.[72] The FAF president Urho Kekkonen commented on the strict decision as follows:

> This is a question that is related to the development of all our sports life. If shamateurism becomes a dominant practice, and our athletes are nurtured into dishonesty, then we must give up what we call amateur sports. It should also be remembered that promoting shamateurism will result in the abolition of state subsidies [for sport] – If shamateurism is to be ended, it should be done even if we would lose some gold-medal chance as a result. – It must be

---

[67] "Purjeen Ranskan matkan jälkinäytös," [Sequel to Purje's France trip], *Warkauden Lehti*, November 18, 1933.

[68] "Lilla Ronden av Bebe," [Little set of Bebe], *Hufvudstadsbladet*, January 17, 1934.

[69] "Purje-Bell. Manageri voitti juoksijan oikeudessa," [Purje-Bell Manager won the runner in court], *Turun Sanomat*, January 17, 1934.

[70] "Hra von Bell urakoi yhä urheiluelämässä," [Mr von Bell still working in sports], *Turun Sanomat*, September 14, 1934. Soon after, von Bell moved from amateur athletics to professional boxing. "Suomen Ammattinyrkkeilyliitto perustettu," [Finnish Professional Boxing Federation founded], *Helsingin Sanomat*, November 25, 1935.

[71] "Urheiluliitto kurittaa Kiffeniä ja kummallakin on kannattajansa," [The Athletics Federation chastises Kiffen and both have their supporters], *Suomen Urheilulehti*, June 6, 1932; Karikko and Koski, *Legendary Runner*, 124.

[72] "Urheiluliitto on kieltänyt nyt kaikki kilpailut," [The Athletics Federation has now banned all meets], *Warkauden Lehti*, June 7, 1934.

remembered that the amateur rules have not been devised here. But on the other hand: as long as the international federation upholds the current amateur rules and does not agree to repair them, based on suggestions made by for example the Finnish federation, we have no other option but to follow the rules. That is that![73]

Kekkonen's comment highlights that Finnish sports leaders saw dishonest black-market dealings between athletes, sports clubs, and middlemen as a threat to the integrity of sport in Finland, and even more threatening was the possibility that shamateurism would negatively impact on the public funding for sport generally. It was thought that allowing costs compensations would result in more honest sport in the future. Since that time, the rules had to be followed – but not to the degree where Finland would lose its best athletes.

Shamateurism in Post-war Finland

The logic of shamateurism remained in place for decades after the Second World War. Due to the stranglehold of the small coterie of the IOC's leaders on the amateur rules, elite athletes of the post-war era had to partake in similar practices to their predecessors in the interwar era.

In Sweden, shamateurism of track and field athletes was tackled with drastic measures in 1946 and 1947, when the Swedish Athletics Federation banned star runners Arne Andersson, Gunder Hägg, and many others for under-the-table payments. What made the Swedish shamateur cull unprecedented in international athletics was the sheer scale of the investigations and verdicts: more than 200 leaders and twenty-five athletes were given sentences of various severities.[74]

The Finnish sports authorities never went to these lengths to enforce amateurism, which is best evidenced by the treatment of long-distance runner Viljo Heino, a close rival of the suspended Swedish runners. When the IAAF investigated Heino for similar under-the-table payments in 1946, the FAF decided to suspend his manager, who had allegedly received the funds.

---

[73] "Jos sala-ammattilaisuus on lopetettava, on se suoritettava, vaikkapa joku kultamitalimahdolli-suus meiltä menisikin," [If shamateurism is to be ended, it should be done even if we would lose some gold-medal chance], *Sisä-Suomi*, June 27, 1934.

[74] Wikberg, "Amatör eller professionist," 198–239.

This decision satisfied also the IAAF, and enabled Heino to continue his career.[75]

Even still, the athletes' position was ambivalent in Finland. The perspective of athletes was summarized by Finnish athletes such as the 400m Olympic medalist Voitto Hellsten and former 1500m World Record holders Olavi Salsola and Olavi Vuorisalo in a rare public critique of the amateur rules, which was published in an extensive article of the magazine *Viikkosanomat* in December 1960.[76] According to Hellsten, the best Finnish sprinter of the 1950s, amateurism effectively forced athletes to break the rules:

> Many athletes had to get unsalaried leaves from their work or find a substitute because of taking part in the last autumn's international meets against France and Hungary. I was on unsalaried leave and had to pay 8,800 marks to my substitute. It was not enough that I did not get wages, I had to pay to be able to participate. – No one can serve two masters. If one does that, both suffer. And the one that suffers more is – usually work.[77]

Included in the article was information that exhibited under-the-table rewards paid in Finnish meets in different athletics disciplines. The interviewed athletes denied having provided material for the article themselves, and assured that under-the-table rewards did not make anyone rich. The latter remark is common in athletes' contemporary and post-career comments about shamateurism: athletes had to be careful when talking about the amateur rules in public.

Even if athletes were only rarely declared professionals, exceptions proved that the rule existed. In 1960, Swedish middle-distance runner Dan Waern, a rival of Olavi Salsola and Olavi Vuorisalo, gave an interview to a Swedish magazine, claiming that he could not afford to be an amateur, and had taken under-the-table rewards as a result. The article of *Viikkosanomat* and investigative journalism preceding its publication had clearly been inspired by Waern's comments.

Finnish sports authorities reacted to the revelations with criticism of those who received rewards and those who paid them, and with defense of amateurism as a principle of elite sport.[78] What was also similar was how the au-

---

[75] Jörg Krieger, *Power and Politics in World Athletics. A Critical History*, (New York: Routledge, 2021), 115–116.

[76] "Meidän ei kannata olla amatöörejä," [We cannot afford to be amateurs], *Viikkosanomat*, December 9, 1960.

[77] *Ibid.*

[78] "Amatööriurheilumme pyykinpesu jatkuu," [The laundering of our amateur sport continues],

thorities tried to tackle the problem later; in 1963, the FAF devised a short-lived license system in which athletes received five competition licenses monthly, the purpose of which was to prevent athletes from competing as much as they wanted.[79]

As for Dan Waern, the Swedish Athletics Federation decided to only warn him, after which the IAAF intervened, banning him for life. A new feature in the case was that also tax officials took an interest in Waern's earnings,[80] an additional threat that also applied to Finnish athletes.[81]

Yet, post-war amateur conflicts did not lessen the potential for earnings in the Nordic countries. Because all of Finland's annual athletics meets, approximately 400 in the mid-1950s,[82] were organized during a short Nordic summer, athletes could fill their calendars even on short tours. In 1961, retired Trinidadian sprinter Mike Agostini claimed in *Sports Illustrated* that the best rewards in athletics could be found in the Nordic countries. In the late 1950s, he had one year competed eighteen times in nineteen days in Finland and Sweden, earning $1,200 dollars after expenses. Agostini claimed that during the 1960 Olympics in Rome, there were meet organizers bartering with athletes for their services, many of them from the Nordic countries, towards which "a mass trek of athletes" was directed after the Olympics.[83]

Competing extensively on short tours could obviously lead to injuries, but it was a risk not only Agostini was willing to take. Finnish javelin thrower Hannu Siitonen, for example, competed some years nearly fifty times in the 1970s, precisely because of the availability of under-the-table rewards. Based on the recollections of Siitonen, the Finnish Championships in athletics (*Kalevan kisat*) had a similar role in Finland as the Olympics had internationally – as a marketplace, in which athletes and meet organizers could negotiate about rewards in future meets.[84]

Viikkosanomat, December 16, 1960; "Urheilunjohtajat ja sala-ammattilaisuus," [Sports leaders and shamateurism], *Viikkosanomat*, December 30, 1960.

[79] "Paljon melua mollissa," [Much ado in a minor key], *Suomen Urheilulehti*, June 6, 1963; Pentti Vuorio, "Hajahuomioita alkukesän yleisurheilusta," [Notions about early summer's athletics], *Urheilun Kuva-aitta* no. 5, 1963.

[80] Wikberg, "Amatör eller professionist," 247–250.

[81] Jouni Lavikainen, "'If the IOC Finds Out about This, All of You Will Be Declared Professionals': The Professionalization of Finnish Track Athletes from the 1960s to 1980s," *The International Journal of the History of Sport* 38, no. 10–11 (2021): 1054. https://doi.org/10.1080/09523367.2021.1984233.

[82] Kokkonen, *Suomalainen liikuntakulttuuri*, 141.

[83] Mike Agostini, "My take-home pay as an amateur sprinter," *Sports Illustrated*, January 30, 1961.

[84] Lavikainen, "If the IOC Finds Out about This," 1052–1054.

The IOC's decision to finally allow broken-time payments in 1962,[85] and the development of the FAF's stipend system in 1970 did not end shamateurism in Finnish athletics. There is ample evidence that shows that in the 1960s and 1970s, the culture of under-the-table payments continued, and provided good earnings at least to those star athletes who actively sought to realize their market value. In the 1970s, Olympic medalists could expect to earn FIM 3,000 to 6,000 in the biggest meets in Finland, such as the World Games in Helsinki and Saarijärvi Midsummer Games, which exceeded average national monthly salary. Well-known national level athletes could also generate decent incomes, depending on their willingness to partake in covert negotiations.[86]

Athletes with sports-minded employers were supported with similar means as in the interwar era – by enabling training in work time, and with salaried leaves to partake in competitions. These were complemented by the FAF's stipend system that improved the possibility of financing off-season training.[87] All of this official and unofficial support made the position of elite Finnish track and field athletes comparably favorable by international standards in the 1970s. For star runners such as the Olympic champions Lasse Virén and Pekka Vasala, there was little reason to join professional circuits such as the International Track Association (ITA) in the United States, in much the same way that there had been little reason for the likes of Paavo Nurmi and Volmari Iso-Hollo to join Ladoumeque's federation in the 1930s.

Transition to professional athletics

In Finnish research, the IOC's congress in Baden-Baden in 1981 has often been seen as the watershed moment in terms of the professionalization of the Olympic Games, with the IOC president Juan Antonio Samaranch, elected in 1980, its *primus motor*. Baden-Baden's congress allegedly started the process that paved the way for the end of amateurism in the Olympic movement in general, and athletics in particular.[88]

---

[85] Llewellyn and Gleaves, *The Rise and Fall of Olympic Amateurism*, 121–131.

[86] Lavikainen, "If the IOC Finds Out about This," 1052–1055.

[87] *Ibid.*, 1053, 1055–1057.

[88] For example, Juha Kanerva, "Virén riemastutti, Vainio itketti," [Virén delighted, Vainio caused grief], in *Sadan vuoden olympiadi. Suomalaisen olympialiikkeen historia,* [History of the Finnish Olympic movement], ed. Vesa Tikander, Ossi Viita and Merja Vilén (Helsinki: WSOY, 2007), 240–243; Kokkonen, *Suomalainen liikuntakulttuuri,* 237.

Based on more recent research, the importance of Baden-Baden's congress has been overstated in Finnish literature. During the congress, British world-record miler and Olympic champion Sebastian Coe spoke emphatically for open money prizes, which Samaranch's predecessors would not have tolerated. However, Samaranch's wish to moderately liberalize the eligibility code and Rule 26 – that contained amateur definitions in the Olympic Charter – was not fulfilled. To the contrary, the federations could only agree that the Olympic Games were essentially to remain the domain of amateur athletes. International sports federations were given license to fashion their own eligibility codes on the condition that they were approved by the IOC, but this only revived an initiative passed at the IOC session in Vienna in 1974.[89]

According to Llewellyn and Gleaves, the resistance to Samaranch' visions can be interpreted either as "continued fealty to amateurism or, perhaps, more cynically as a way in which to preserve a system of free labor that best served their [the federations'] own financial interests."[90] An example of this is provided by the IOC Athletes' Commission that was founded after Baden-Baden's congress in December 1981. Initially, the Commission did not promote or even support professionalism of athletes in the Olympic movement. In 1982, the first chairman of the Commission, a former Olympic sailor, the Finn Peter Tallberg gave his support for amateurism, writing that "no athlete should use participation to the Olympic Games for personal [financial] gain."[91] Tallberg's views were shared by many in the IOC, and at the IOC session in Berlin in 1985, the IOC member Will Daume called once more on modernizing the amateur rules without going so far as towards an "open Olympics."[92]

Researchers have found various explanations for why amateurism in international athletics came to an end when it did. Turrini has argued that rather than due to the decision-makers of the international sports federations, track and field's transition to a professionalized and commercialized sport was caused by collaboration between American elite runners and shoe giants Adidas, Puma and Nike. By gaining foothold in The Athletics Congress (TAC, formerly the

---

[89] Llewellyn and Gleaves, *The Rise and Fall of Olympic Amateurism*, 177.

[90] *Ibid.*

[91] Risto Tallberg, "Amatörismin umpisolmu," [Dilemma of amateurism], in *Citius Altius Fortius Suomen Olympiayhdistys ry 1907–1982*, ed. Helge Nygrén (Helsinki: Suomen Olympiayhdistys ry, 1982), 49–53.

[92] Llewellyn and Gleaves, *The Rise and Fall of Olympic Amateurism*, 183.

AAU) and forming financially strong athlete organizations, athletes were able to force the TAC and then the IAAF to accept reforms like trust funds. According to Turrini, athlete activism also motivated the United States federal government into passing the Amateur Sports Act (ASA) in 1978.[93]

Duckworth, Hunt and Todd have challenged Turrini's argument about the key role of athletes, emphasizing instead a distinct combination of economic, social and political factors. According to the researchers, athlete activism would have been insufficient without "the financial muscle" of Adidas and Nike, and rather than "altruistic motive to aid athletes in their struggle," ASA was passed because the federal government sought advantage in the Cold War's sports contest against the Soviet Union.[94]

What Turrini and Duckworth, Hunt and Todd agree on, is that the commercialization of road running in the United States in the 1970s played a crucial part in transition towards over-the-table rewards. According to Krieger, the change was brewing also inside the IAAF. During the progressive presidency of Adriaan Paulen (from 1976 to 1981), the IAAF prepared the ground for the coming of professionalism and adopted a new commercial strategy to capitalize on the financial potential of athletics. Much like in the IOC, the transition required political maneuvering, as there was still support for amateurism inside the federation.[95]

After trust funds, in which athletes could deposit their appearance fees and sponsor revenues, were approved by the IAAF and the IOC, the FAF established a trust fund for Finnish athletes in 1983. Especially for female athletes, the change was significant. Women's marginalized position in athletics had been reflected in comparatively lower levels of under-the-table payments.[96] In Finland, even international star athletes such as sprinters Riitta Salin and Pirjo Wilmi (later Häggman) in the 1970s were closer to genuine amateurs than shamateurs of any sort.[97] Conversely in the 1980s, managers such as Tor Westerberg had both male and female athletes as clients, which enabled new and better income streams from meets and corporate sponsors.[98]

---

[93] Turrini, *End of Amateurism*, 154–159, 181.

[94] Austin Duckworth, Thomas M. Hunt and Jan Todd, "Cold hard cash: commercialization, politics, and amateurism in United States track and field," *Sport in History* 38, no. 2 (2018): 158–159. https://doi.org/10.1080/17460263.2018.1460275.

[95] Krieger, *Power and Politics*, 152–153.

[96] Turrini, *End of Amateurism*, 90–92; Duckworth, Hunt and Todd, "Cold hard cash," 150.

[97] Lavikainen, "If the IOC Finds Out about This," 1056.

[98] *Ibid.*, 1059–1061.

The rampant commercialization of athletics in the 1980s pitted athletes and federations on different sides in terms of the division of the newly founded streams of money from sponsors. Adriaan Paulen's successor as the IAAF president, Primo Nebiolo, in particular, endeavored to commercialize athletics without securing athletes their share from the revenues.[99] This was evidenced by the attitude of the IAAF towards managers such as Tor Westerberg. The IAAF warned its member federations in April 1985 about agents who negotiated deals between athletes and meet organizers, "a practice which the IAAF Council is determined shall not become a feature of International Athletics."[100] As I have demonstrated, such a practice was already commonplace in the interwar period. Because the agents were still considered as an unwanted by-product of the commercialization of sport, they had to operate in a "grey area" of elite sports. This did not promote transparency in sports and left athletes vulnerable to betrayals by dishonest fixers.

From the mid-1980s to early 1990s, amateurism in athletics gradually came to an end, in a shift which mirrored that of the wider Olympic movement. Samaranch' project to eradicate amateurism from the Olympic Games took over a decade, but was finally completed in 1991 when the revised eligibility code was published, without reference to the Olympians' amateur or professional status.[101]

In Finland, the FAF allowed athletes to negotiate their own appearance fees in 1988 and started to give monetary rewards to athletes based on results in major international competitions. These had to be paid to the trust fund of the FAF until 1993 when the IAAF changed its rules to allow direct prize payments – after being forced to do so by the agents of star athletes.[102] Athletes could obviously still use trust funds, and many of them did, but tended to do so because it was beneficial with regards to taxation and not because it was obligatory. The start of a professional era did not mean that disagreements between athletes, managers, and federations came to a sudden halt, but these were now dealt with without ideological edict that denied athletes from earning a living from sport.

---

[99] Krieger, *Power and Politics*, 167.

[100] Lavikainen, "If the IOC Finds Out about This," 1060.

[101] Llewellyn and Gleaves, *The Rise and Fall of Olympic Amateurism*, 190.

[102] Turrini, *End of Amateurism*, 166; Krieger, *Power and Politics*, 168.

Conclusions

In this chapter, I have displayed the effects of amateurism on Finnish athletics in a period spanning most of the twentieth century. One of the purposes of focusing on such a long time period was to explore the dynamics of shamateurism in terms of historic change and continuity. One of the findings here deals with the latter. Finnish athletes, who grew up in different societal settings throughout the twentieth century, faced similar problems as they developed towards the international elite level of sport. Requirements of elite sport grew, but the means to finance sport remained limited because of the amateur rules, safeguarded by a small group of privileged decision-makers in both the IOC and the IAAF.

Finnish sports authorities were ready to allow compensation to athletes decades before most of the IOC's members. In the interwar era, SVUL and the FAF constructed support systems that were blatantly against the amateur rules, which significantly improved the possibilities for Finnish athletes to train full-time before major international events. At the same time, SVUL and the FAF opposed shamateurism and the gradual transition of athletics towards an openly professional context. Full-time training for international events was acceptable, but individualistic competition tours to pursue profits was not.

SVUL and the FAF tried with different means to control athletes' competing, as well as the people who athletes collaborated with, but did not achieve long-term results. "Under-ground labor-relations" between athletes, meet organizers and unofficial managers functioned in a fairly similar way when comparing the 1920s and 1970s, for example, despite the large-scale change in Finland's society during this period. After the establishment of trust funds and increasing tax investigations, the shamateur system gradually deteriorated in the 1980s.

Notwithstanding the views of working-class newspapers in the turbulent interwar era, the media discourse about shamateurism tended to be in favor of athletes. This produced headlines such as "Petkievicz tried to cash in on Nurmi's expense" and "Our athletes can not get rid of von Bell." In reality, as much as middlemen sought to cash in on athletes, athletes also used middlemen for their own benefit. In the post-war decades, the political aspect of shamateurism utilized as a weapon of the working-class media diminished, as did the conflicts related to language politics. What endured was the ambivalent position of athletes. Because all earnings from sports were categorically prohibited, and under-the-table payments were paid without taxes, athletes were on the wrong side of both the laws of sport and the state, and as such had to act accordingly.

The social control of the amateur enforcers and the resistance of the shamateur athletes provides a fascinating insight into a dynamic of sport that was
partially hidden for nearly a century. Because the source material most readily available to researchers has been produced by the governing organizations
of sport and by media professionals, historical and sociological research on
questions of amateurism and professionalism has inevitably tended to focus
on their perspective. Further research is required in order to understand the dynamics of shamateurism from the perspective of athletes and their associates,
by using primary source material produced by they themselves, such as letters,
diaries, and oral history.

CHAPTER 5

1946, Year One? Prospects from the European Athletics Championships in Oslo on Gender, Amateurism and Politics

Matti Goksøyr and Jörg Krieger

Introduction

As 1945, according to Dutch historian Ian Buruma, was year zero, 1946 marked a new beginning.[1] The Allied nations had won the war. The Nazi dictatorship had been crushed. Antagonists had worked together. New relations emerged. In sports, even the old schism between the socialist workers sport and IOC- "bourgeois" sports was set aside. And in 1946, the first major sport event after the Second World War took place in the shape of the 1946 European Athletics Championships in Oslo. But what could the first international championships in athletics after the war promise? Was 1946 really the first year of a new era?

In hindsight many of the things that followed are relatively straightforward to explain; the Cold War, the Iron Curtain, and the extreme sports rivalry between East and West. But how did developments pan out at the European Athletics Championships in 1946, so quickly after years of death and destruction? What did the first major international meet after the war signal in terms of gender, amateurism, and politics? Did sports present openings before the establishment of the Cold War with NATO and the Warsaw Pact; openings and signals that soon would be forgotten and deemed unrealistic? Did the emerging cold war "truths" already exist? Or were there other observations?

This chapter explores the 1946 European Athletics Championships by working out how the event became a platform for the emergence of new developments in sport. A particular focus lies on the media reports of the event, in par-

---

[1] Ian Buruma, *Year Zero: A History of 1945*. (New York: Penguin Books, 2014).

ticular the Norwegian press. In addition, archive materials have been valuable sources since primary sources on the event itself are scarce.[2]

European Championships

The 1946 European Athletics Championships in Oslo, Norway, attracted 353 athletes of both genders and from most European nations, in all 20, including, for the first time, the Union of Soviet Socialist Republics (USSR, also Soviet Union). It was the third European Athletics Championships, organized under the auspices of the International Association of Athletics Federations (IAAF). The first had been staged in Torino, Italy, in 1934, with the intention to raise funds for the IAAF administration.[3] The second event took place in Paris in 1938.

The IAAF's arguments for giving its first post-war event to Norway, not exactly a powerhouse in athletics, remain unclear. In 1945, the IAAF held its meetings in Stockholm, where its President Sigfrid Edström resided, and the administration was located. Although there is not much to suggest that very suspicious things were going on in the IAAF circles, the build-up to the Championships in 1946 included rumours, secrecy, and confidentiality. In early September 1945, the leader of the Norwegian Athletics Federation (NFIF), Mogens Oppegard, "became familiar with information" saying that the IAAF before long was going to hold their first Council meeting after the war in Stockholm. He received private and confidential information that one of the cases up for debate was a European Championships in 1946. By his own judgment, there was no time or possibility to inform or gather the board of the Norwegian Federation. Oppegard then, on his own initiative, travelled to Stockholm to "investigate the chances of an eventual assignment."[4] Uninvited, he managed to

---

[2] Today's IAAF (World Athletics) do not possess archive materials directly from the event, probably because of problems linked to change of administration address in 1946 from Sweden to England, a familiar peril for all sorts of archive survival. Perhaps also because the international administration of the event was not done by the IAAF itself, but by a committee the IAAF had established to organize the European Championships, the "IAAF European Committee," but nor from this body archives exist. (Email information from the IAAF 15. Oct. 2020). The Norwegian federation organised the event through a separate body, from which no archives exist. Some files are available here, though: Norges Friidrettsforbund [Norwegian Athletics Federation] archives: Riksarkivet (RA) [National Archives]: DA-0014-Norges Friidrettsforbund; RA: 0008 – G31-B1/46 Europamesterskapet I friidrett 1946 (S-1718 Legasjonen/ambassaden i København).

[3] Jörg Krieger, *Power and Politics in World Athletics. A Critical History.* (London: Routledge, 2021).

[4] NFIF, 'Reports from the board, 1933-49' [Beretninger, 1933-49], RA, 6-7.

gain access to the IAAF Council and after a couple of days' negotiations, struck a deal on behalf of the NFIF saying that they were interested in holding the Championships.

On what grounds the International Federation operated with Oppegard we do not know with certainty. The IAAF Minutes report that the organization first had to debate whether championships should be organized at all in 1946. After having concluded that the event should be realized, the IAAF Council empowered IAAF President Edström to choose between Sweden and Norway as organizers. What had really made an impression on the IAAF Council were the Norwegian sporting youth's efforts during the war. Their organising experience from hosting the so-called Oslo Games in 1938 and 1945 was also in their favour.[5] So, the NFIF representatives went home and propagated for an idea they had so brilliantly negotiated. In their mind this was an offer that would never materialise again in their lifetimes. Almost immediately, through official channels, the somewhat accidental proposers from Norway received "a proposition of holding the European Champion-ships 1946" from the IAAF.[6] The Norwegian board, without much hesita-tion, followed up.

Initially, the NFIF board at its post-war re-start summer 1945 had voted "to postpone" international cooperation, probably awaiting the international organizations' own decisions.[7] Nevertheless, after initial doubts and discus-sions, the NFIF began to show a keen interest as 1946 marked their fifty years anniversary. The board of the Norwegian Federation accepted the offer and sought to arrange it in a "proper and dignified way."[8] In the words of the com-ing organizers, the assignment was a just reward for their efforts during the war. The sole reason had to be an appreciation of "Norwegian sport's youth's efforts, struggles and sacrifices during the war."[9] Such an interpretation pro-

---

[5] The Oslo Games [Oslo-lekene] were athletics events taking place at the Bislett stadium with broad international participation; *Bergens Aftenblad*, September 21, 1938, 6.; *Norges Handels og Sjøfartstidende*, September 11, 1945, 6.

[6] NFIF, 'Reports from the board, 1933-49' [Beretninger, 1933-49], gives an impression of a some-what accidental meet up in Stockholm between the IAAF board members and representatives from Norway where an un-official offer seems to have been given. The Norwegians found that this was a chance that "probably never would come back" and decided to follow up.

[7] NFIF, Board protocol July-August 1945, RA – DA 0014.

[8] NFIF, Board protocol October 1, 1945, RA – DA 0014.

[9] *Norsk Idrett*, no. 10, vol. 14 (August 15, 1946). According to *Aftenposten*, August 22, 1946, the Times (of London) in an editorial supported such an interpretation, ("English tribute to Norwe-gian organizers") and the decision to give the event to a Scandinavian country.

vided opportunity of emphasizing the peace-loving and friendship-building character of the event.

In post-war austerity, competition among willing organizers was neither high nor was the Norwegian interest self-evident. Much of the sports infrastructure, especially outdoor stadiums, had been damaged due to the war. Some had been used for German military purposes, as parking lots for vehicles and other equipment, while others again in times of rationing had been converted to potato fields.[10] When it came to the Winter Olympics Games – an event more in line with Norwegian sporting tradition – the nation's interest had been put on hold. Even if the desire was unquestionable, the Olympics had to wait until 1952. The immediate post-war years in Norway were dominated by austerity, certainly not big spending. There was no room for prioritizing play and sports. After war and Nazi occupation, top priority was re-building, and not building sports facilities, but living houses, factories, and production halls. There were no funds for sports on the state budget.[11] Hence, the allocation of Oslo for the 1946 European Athletics Championships is one event in history where a full explanation is lacking.

Norway, the Soviet Union, and Sport

The year 1946 presented a new and different world, though not yet in the shape that would soon become its foremost distinction. Although the United Nations had been founded and the Soviets had found their place in the Security Council, the Cold War had not started, at least not "officially."[12] The North Atlantic Treaty Organization (NATO) and the Warsaw Pact were still on the drawing board. The "Eastern Bloc" was waiting to establish itself. The Norwegians were discussing different geopolitical strategies and alliances, among them a Scandinavian/Nordic alternative. Nonetheless, the links westwards across the North Sea and the Atlantic Ocean had been strengthened by the war. At the same time, the USSR had emerged as victorious, but had not

---

[10] In 1944 161 sports grounds had been taken for military purposes. Matti Goksøyr & Finn Olstad, *Skjebnekamp. Norsk idrett under okkupasjonen 1940-1945* (Oslo: Aschehoug, 2017), 123.

[11] Instead a stately controlled football pools company was established to cover sports expenditures. M.Goksøyr et.al, *Kropp, kultur, tippekamp* (Oslo: KD, 1996).

[12] Even though e.g. Winston Churchill in his twelve volume work on the 2. World War ("The 2.World War" Norwegian version in 12 volumes, 1946) gives a clear impression that it for long had been ready to break out.

yet taken up its new role in the world. Clearly, it had changed its status; it was no longer a "pariah state."[13] Based upon military and political strength, the Soviets and Stalin had to be counted.

Norway had been one of the Nazi occupied, Allied nations during the war. However, unlike the other nations ending up with a NATO affiliation, Norway experienced Soviet troops on their lands, similar to many Central and East European nations. Towards the end of the Second World War in 1944-45, the Red Army had driven the German Nazi troops out of the northernmost part of Norway; Finnmark. Shortly after military victory was fulfilled, the Soviets troops retreated to USSR soil. Thus, they were allies *and* liberators. During the war more Russians died on Norwegian territory than Norwegians.[14] All this added to the Russians enhanced reputation and a solid standing in the immediate postwar years in Norway.

But what about sport? The international federations before the war acted as private-run enterprises with relatively clear amateur and anti-Soviet agendas. The Soviets on their side had the workers' sport, organized in the RSI (Red Sports Internationale) and the Spartakiades. However, after the war, the RSI was phased out and the USSR expressed an increasing will to take part in the international sports world.[15]

In fact, the first "post-war" sports competitions in Norway were held in liberated Finnmark in the spring of 1945. Soldier-athletes from the Soviet Red Army met the locals in skiing races and the skiers of the Red Army brought back the much longed for normality in the form of sports competitions, with "tobacco, ladies and dancing."[16] For the majority of organised Norwegian sports, normality had been on hold for five years due to a successful boycott of the Nazified Norwegian sport.[17]

During the winter 1945/46 Soviet speed skaters demonstrated their capacities at Norwegian ice tracks. Without being a member of the International Skating Union (ISU), the Soviets took part in the unofficial 1946 European Championships. While in Norway they also took part in an international

---

[13] Tony Judt, *Postwar. A History of Europe since 1945* (London: Vintage Books, 2005)

[14] Counting Russian prisoners of war being kept in Norwegian prison camps. "100 000 russerfanger i Norge," University of Oslo, Department of History, last modified October 21, 2020, https://www.norgeshistorie.no/andre-verdenskrig/1741-100000-russerfanger-i-norge.html

[15] James Riordan, *Sport under Communism* (London: Hurst, 1978).

[16] Matti Goksøyr and Finn Olstad, *Skjebnekamp. Norsk idrett under okkupasjonen 1940-1945* (Oslo: Aschehoug, 2017), 308-311.

[17] Matti Goksøyr, "How can you play when your house is on fire? The Norwegian sports strike during the Second World War," *Scandinavian Journal of History* 43, no. 3 (2018), 433-356.

"duel" meet between Soviet and Norway and therewith upheld a long Russian tradition. Pre-revolution Russians had also competed in Norway. Before World War II, Soviet speed skaters visited as members of the workers sports organisation, RSI, and were contenders at the Spartakiades. It was hardly a coincidence when former ice skater Platon Ippolitov's book on sport in the Soviet Union was translated to Norwegian and published in 1946.[18]

However, according to American historian Robert Edelman, the Soviets were interested in all forms of sport and strove to become members of the separate sports federations and the Olympic Movement. The slow development of the Olympic connection, due to political resistance in both camps, may have dominated the perception of the situation. From the Soviet side, real tempo did not occur until their political leaders, the Politburo and Stalin, had changed strategy and decided that Soviet sports should compete with Western powers. Regarding the Olympic Games, the Soviet Union have often been regarded as going into a politically decided sports isolation (by some also called 'training camp') to prepare for the coming meets, which seemed unavoidable.[19] Thus they were forced to wait for Olympic participation until the summer of 1952. However, and this is Edelman's point, they did participate in numerous other international sports encounters. One of these was the European Athletics Championships in 1946.

The IAAF and its International Connections

While athletes representing the Russian Empire participated in athletics at the 1912 Olympic Games, the Soviet Union had not been a member of the International Athletics Movements prior to the Second World War. Instead, Soviet sport officials created a communist sport movement after the Russian Revolution. Brief exchanges with IAAF officials during the interwar period existed, but the Russians had no intentions of joining the IAAF at the time.[20] This changed when future IAAF President Lord David Burghley

---

[18] Platon Ippolitov, *Russiske idrettsstjerner. Sport i Sovjetsamveldet før og nå* (Oslo: Tiden Norsk Forlag, 1946). The translator was none other than the football hero from the Berlin Olympics, Jørgen Juve. In his preface he writes that "the war brought us closer to the Russians. [...] We learned that the youth that advanced over the fronts came from the sports movement, all of them."

[19] Riordan, *Sport under Communism*, 30.

[20] Krieger, *Power and Politics*.

entered the scene.[21] At the 1945 IAAF Congress – the same meeting during which the Norwegians persuaded the IAAF to entrust them with the Euro 1946 – Burghley persuaded the participating members to invite the USSR to the same event as well as inviting them to join the IAAF.[22] Burghley was politically conservative, but pro-Soviet participation in all sports including the Olympics, unlike his more sceptical colleague, and later IOC President, the American Avery Brundage. The next year Burghley would travel to Moscow to receive the USSR's formal application to join the International Athletics Federation.[23]

Neither the IAAF, the local organisers nor the press could say for sure whether "the Russians" were going to compete in Oslo. There was no reply. The newspapers wrote about the mystery of the Soviet participation: Would they show up or not? Norwegian papers reported that the air, at home and abroad, was thick with rumours.[24] All this allowed for an anticipated show of Soviet athletes to the European world. As one might expect, the newspapers' political stand became more visible when they spoke about sports political matters. Only one week ahead of the scheduled start of the event, rumours of an announcement from Radio Moscow, saying that the Russians had joined the IAAF, were reported. If that was the case, the *Manchester Guardian* followed up, they were "more than welcome."[25]

It turned out not to be the case, the Russians did not join the IAAF. But on August 18, 1946, a major part of their delegation showed up.[26] The Norwegian press gave the "Russians" a warm welcome, however mixed with some cultural reservation on the otherness of the guests: even if they have proven

---

[21] Jörg Krieger and Austin Duckworth, "'Vodka and caviar among friends' – Lord David Burghley and the Soviet Union's entry into the International Association of Athletic Federations," *Sport in History* 41, no. 2 (2021), 260-279.

[22] Minutes, IAAF Meeting of the Council in Stockholm, September 6-8, 1945, IAAF Archives, 55; Also: Krieger and Duckworth, "Vodka and caviar among friends."

[23] Letter, IAAF President J. S. Edström to the athletic representatives from Soviet Russia, Oslo, August 5, 1946, in "Pages from correspondence with USSR 1947-1981," IAAF/World Athletics archives; Robert Edelman, *The shifting Olympic front* (Forthcoming); Sigurd Beldo, "Alliert, fiende og konkurrent. Hvordan ble sovjetrussiske idrettsutøvere omtalt i norsk presse i tiden etter 2.verdenskrig" (Master thesis, NIH, Oslo, 2006).

[24] *Arbeiderbladet*, August 9, 1946. Aftenposten (conservative) is negative to allowing the Soviets to compete (since they are not members of the IAAF, yet). Verdens Gang August 10, 1946 disagrees and hints to Aftenposten's collaborationist views during the war.

[25] *Arbeiderbladet*, August 15, 1946, quoting Manchester Guardian August 14, 1946. Also, *Arbeiderbladet*, August 9, 1946.

[26] *Arbeiderbladet*, August 19, 1946.

to be our friends at war, they are in some ways different. However, it was also positively reported that" Those who expected to meet masculine power-women went home disappointed. Here were grace and charm, and some real beauties in between," the conservative *Aftenposten* reported after the arrival of the Soviet team.[27] It became increasingly clearer that the athletes of the USSR, especially their female representatives, had to be taken seriously in all respects.

As an international sports event where the Soviet Union took part for the first time, the 1946 European Athletics Championships was bound to be a political happening. The IAAF called it "a unique exception," mainly due to the fact that the USSR was not a member of the organisation, something they hoped would change after this successful and friendly display of goodwill.[28] The Soviets held a low profile, politically, at the event, preferring to display their female athletes as ambassadors. However, as is common knowledge from literature and research, there probably were KGB agents among the athletes.

The opening ceremony mainly consisted of an entry march from all twenty teams and opening speeches, one by the Norwegian King, Haakon VII. "Sportsmen and -women long for a spirit of comradeship between all peoples," the King is quoted as saying. In that sense he joined the underlying sentiment of promises in the air in 1946, while at the same time describing sport's foremost outspoken value; the creation of a spirit of comradeship. There was little "othering" in the speeches of the "year one" European Athletics Championships.[29] Comradery had to be present "between *all* peoples."[30]

"The marching-past of the participators was a remarkable and fascinating sight. Several of those who now met at the stadium, during the war stood on opposite sides of the battle front," the Norwegian newspaper *Arbeiderbladet* wrote.[31] This seemed to become the most common of observations.[32] Former

---

[27] *Aftenposten*, August 19, 1946.

[28] Minutes, IAAF, 1946.

[29] Otherness here will be taken to describe a term that "encompasses the many expressions of prejudice on the basis of group identities" and group-based inequality. E.g. John A. Powell and Stephen Menendian, "The Problem of Othering: Towards Inclusiveness and Belonging," *Othering and Belonging*, downloaded 1.11.2020, https://www.otheringandbelonging.org/the-problem-of-othering/.

[30] Speech, *Arbeiderbladet*, August 23, 1946.

[31] *Arbeiderbladet*, August 23, 1946.

[32] E.g. *New York Times*, August 26, 1946.

foes were now meeting on friendly terms, except for Germany. To invite the real enemy was unthinkable in 1946, and Germany was kept out of international sports world till 1952. Thus, former foes were Finland and the Soviet Union, wartime adversaries in the periods 1939-1940 and 1941-1944. Finland was an athletics powerhouse, but only among the males, and mostly in long distance running and javelin. The Soviets, although freshmen on the IAAF scene, had strength on the female side. Women were not allowed to run longer distances than 200 meters, but the Soviet athletes excelled in sprint and throwing events. Thus, their friendly meets were mostly indirect, as the Finns and the Soviets rarely met eye to eye.[33]

A rare moment from a sporting view, however, was the finish of the marathon and the 10,000 meters during the first main day of the event. Due to organizational delays, the 10,000 meters had not finished when the marathon runners approached their stadium finish, leading to the rare sight of the final crossings of the finish lines occurring almost simultaneously. When athletes from Finland won a double victory in both events, the evening truly was memorable for the Finns, but also noteworthy to non-Finnish spectators. The sympathy for Finland and her cause had increased immensely in 1939 after the "Finnish Winter War." Scandinavian young men volunteered to unite forces with the Finns, and tales of the Winter War created an image of the brave, enduring capacities of the neighbours in the north. The Finnish word "Sisu" became a household term.[34][35] The achievements in Oslo then contributed to an already high self-esteem and external admiration when it came to long-distance running.[36]

A nation that did not show and thus became invisible, was Austria, although defined as victims of the war. As their athletics federation had been completely overtaken by Nazi Germany in 1938 and as other Austrian institutions ended its existence, a new national federation had to be re-built after the war. For the "first victim of National Socialism," year one came too early. Austria's new athletics federation had not yet been re-established.[37]

Except from an incident at the opening day of the IAAF Congress, when the present Italians had to declare their cleansing from fascism, the presence of ath-

---

[33] There were exceptions: e.g. at the medals podium for the men's shot put, where the Finnish bronze medalist and the Soviet silver medalist had the winner, Huseby from Iceland, between them.

[34] Meaning a combination of force, endurance and resilience, though with parts lost in translation.

[35] Goksøyr and Olstad, *Skjebnekamp.*

[36] Matti Hannus, *Flying Finns* (Jyväskylä: Tietosanoma, 1990).

[37] Rudolf Müllner, personal e-mail information, November 30, 2020; Tony Judt, *Postwar.*

letes from "New Italy" did not stir much commotion. However, the incident caused IAAF President Edström to strongly declare that he would "allow no political debates" at this congress.[38] Otherwise the presence of the Italians was only mentioned when some journalists spotted a slight uncertainty about how to interpret spectator behavior. Uncertainty as to whether the plaudits were meant for them did, according to scrutinizing reporters, fluster some of the Italian athletes. However, journalists noticed that although the spectators had their favorites, like the "Finns on the opening day," the "dashing Russian girls," Gunnar Huseby, the "shotput Viking from Iceland" and the English long-distance runner, Sidney Wooderson, the spectators behaved "exemplary," giving athletes from "new Italy" their due amount of applause, equally to what was handed athletes from "allied or neutral" nations.[39]

Easier to notice was the relationship and the expressed attitudes from the Norwegian spectators towards Swedish athletes. At the end of the day, Sweden, who had been favourites, became the most successful nation, with a total of eleven gold medals, far ahead of the USSR and Finland, with six and four wins, respectively. Yet, the geographically and culturally close neighbour to the organizers, was not entirely popular in 1946. Results count, especially in sports. But the way they are achieved definitely plays a part as well. Some reporters commented on the occasional Swedish misfortunes: "On the terraces a widespread and genuine Norwegian *schadenfreude* prevails."[40] Two days later the same paper, while trying to build an argument that athletics' spectators were more cultured and civil than football crowds, had to admit that "the somewhat mean feeling of joy over the fact that the Swedes had been beaten, could clearly be sensed the first day." What a relief then when the commentators could come up with the following observation: "Yesterday it [the mean feeling of joy] had disappeared completely."[41]

If this "disappearance" was true, it might have shed some light on and encouraged the idea of a year one with fresh beginnings. In 1946, most of Europe had strong wishes and incentives to "start a new beginning" and to "have the strength to forget."[42] However, history is sometimes difficult to shrug off. The history of the Swedish-Norwegian interrelationship shows a multitude of uneven relations between the former "brothers." In that sense it had established a reservoir of am-

[38] *Friheten*, August 22, 1946.

[39] *Aftenposten*, August 24, 1946.

[40] [«skadefryd»] *Arbeiderbladet*, August 24, 1946.

[41] ["Den litt lumpne fryden over at svenskene ble slått var sterkest første dagen. ... Igår forsvant den helt"]. *Arbeiderbladet*, August 26, 1946.

[42] Tony Judt, *Postwar*, 61.

munition that could be picked up and used perhaps particularly in presumedly 'innocent' situations of which sports was an outstanding example.[43] Seen from the Norwegian side, Sweden was the "relevant other" and Swedish actions and arrogance during the first part of the war had provoked and magnified just and understandable reactions.[44] Particularly the Swedish policy in the International Ski Federation with the staging of a "World Championships" in Cortina, Italy in 1941 (later rendered null and void) when a majority of Norwegian sportsmen was boycotting wartime's nazified sport and hence was unable to participate had created harsh feelings.[45] Remnants of this could be expressed by Norwegian spectators in various sports encounters immediately after the war and later.[46]

The presentation of the Soviet women: Exoticism and Heroism while Patronizing

The first European Athletics Championships, 1934 in Torino, had been for men only. By the time of the next Championships, in 1938, the idea of including women had gained ground – after all the IOC had opened competition for female athletes ten years before, in Amsterdam 1928, only to reduce it for subsequent occasions. While the men's 1938 European meet took place in Paris, the women gathered in Vienna, which through 'Anschluss' by the time of the event had become a part of the German Reich. Eighty women from fourteen nations took part. The women representing the Reich dominated by winning the fair part (fifteen) of the twenty-seven medals.

When it came to gender issues, the 1946 European Athletics Championships was a gate-opener.[47] That goes for both the host country and the federation

---

[43] Matti Goksøyr, "Søte bror, storebror – læremester og likeverdig rival?" in *Studier i idrott, historia och samhälle*, ed. Johan R.Norberg (Stockholm: HLS Förlag, 2000).

[44] Leif Yttergren, *I och ur spår. Konflikter och hjältar i svensk skidsports historia under 1900-talet* (Lund: KFS, 2006), 100.

[45] Matti Goksøyr, "The Rings and the Swastika: Political Ambiguity in Sport before and during Second World War," *The International Journal of the History of Sport* 36, no. 11(2019), 998-1012.

[46] Matti Goksøyr, "'Og så ein svensk-norsk landskamp! Ein blir så patriotisk i slike stunder': Norsk-svenske idrettsforbindelser etter 1905," in *Norsk-svenske relasjoner i 200 år*, ed. Ø. Sørensen and T. Nilsson (Oslo: Aschehoug, 2005).

[47] In the official minutes from the only IAAF Council meeting before the event, it is added in handwriting that the president was empowered to decide "whether women's Championships shall be held." Minutes, IAAF, 1945, art. 10.

behind the event, as well as for women athletes in general. The event was the first to include both sexes, with men and women competing at the same event following the IAAF's takeover of the women's events in athletics in 1936.[48] However, there were no more events for women than there had been in 1938. Women runners were still trapped in the aftermath of the "scandal" of the 800 meters at the 1928 Olympics. Nor were they allowed to run longer distances than the 200 meters until the 1960 Rome Olympic Games.

Women from both the USSR and the host country, Norway, participated for the first time at the European Athletics Championships. While the USSR women had stayed away from the 1938 event for (sports) political reasons, the Norwegian women competitors had been kept away for more traditional gender reasons. The Norwegian sports federation ("Norges Landsforbund for idrett," NLFI) led what could be described as a traditional, conservative non-inclusive gender policy, meaning that female athletics was encouraged to a very small degree. The rivalling workers sports federation, "Arbeidernes Idrettsforbund" (AIF), from a basis of a sport for all philosophy in the 1930s included women's athletics to a much larger degree – as was generally the case with the international workers' sport movement. In fact, the disapproving attitudes of the NLFI made it possible for the Nazi sports organization of the occupiers during the Second World War to claim that they were the ones who made female athletics in Norway possible.[49] The validity of this would have the presumption of not counting the workers' sport. However, it is a fact that the historically approved national sports federations, NLFI, most importantly the national Athletics Federation, did not organize national championships for women until 1947, the year after the European Championships in Oslo.

When American commentators reported that "Red team puzzles Oslo track meet," they were referencing to the Red Army; its male soldiers.[50] However, the connotations and content of Red Team quickly changed. It was the women's achievements that brought reactions from the Norwegian media. The presence of women, and especially the presence of female athletes who performed at a high level, was a relatively new phenomenon in 1946. Male journalists admit-

---

[48] Jörg Krieger, Michele Krech, and Lindsay Parks Piper, "'Our Sport': The Fight for Control of Women's International Athletics," *The International Journal of the History of Sport* 37, no. 5-6 (2020): 451-72, https://doi.org/10.1080/09523367.2020.1754201

[49] Goksøyr and Olstad, *Skjebnekamp*, 140.

[50] *New York Times*, August 21, 1946.

ted being positively surprised and impressed. They openly laid bare their attitudes to a degree that makes them grateful objects for 21st century historians.

At their first show the USSR dominated the women's events. The dominance
called for comments and explanations. Since the aforementioned 'scandal' at
the 1928 Amsterdam Olympic Games, women were not allowed to run even
middle distances in international athletics' meets, while the men ran all distances up to a marathon. Still there were nine events deemed suitable for women,
and the USSR won five of them. Altogether the USSR won six gold medals.
Hence, the female Soviet athletes attracted attention, however, not solely by
their sports abilities.

The Soviet women's participation also must be considered a successful charm
offensive that impressed the Norwegian press. Their presentations varied from
open admiration, "phenomenal Russian sports women" on the front pages, to
male chauvinism, while straightforward ironically patronizing.[51] Some of them,
mostly the conservatives, openly led bare that they had problems of accepting
for instance a female shot-putter, writing: "may I introduce my fiancée, the
European shot put champion," meant as excessive irony.[52] There was also open
admiration and newfound conviction about the femininity of the Soviet female
athletes. Jevgenia Tsjetsenova, presented as an unmarried twenty-four-year-old
clerk at the Moscow City Council won both the 100 and 200 meter sprint.[53]
However, in the next sentences she was represented as "charming" and "pretty and enchanting" and as a person you (as a man) wouldn't want to run for
the bus with as they admitted they would have no chance against the "little,
adorable Tsjetsenova."[54] This was in stark opposition to other Western accounts
of Soviet women, in which they were portrayed as manly and muscular.[55] In
contrast, Norwegian journalists were impressed by the Soviet women's combination of athletic skill and elegance, though some of them still needed to be
convinced that women sports had a right to exist. "More and more are starting
to open their eyes for its [women's athletics'] advantages."[56] Also the more
conservative of male sports journalists held such views towards the end of the

---

[51] *Arbeiderbladet*, August 23, 1946.

[52] *Morgenbladet*, August 23, 1946.

[53] *Ibid.*

[54] *Verdens Gang*, August 23, 1946.

[55] Lindsay Pieper, *Sex Testing: Gender Policing in Women's Sports.* (Champaign: University of
Illinois Press, 2016).

[56] *Arbeiderbladet*, August 24, 1946.

Championships.[57] Still, there were clear differences between the ways in which male and female athletes where described.

Initially it was the men who were placed in traditional heroic roles. In year one such heroes were not hard to find. Even when presenting the Soviet athletes who did not show up, the press could for example include a sentence about "[h]is brother…also one of the Soviet Union's most renowned sportsmen, was killed outside Moscow in 1941."[58] Heroism in the post-war context was described through sacrifices, killed husbands, hardships, soldiers' duties, and more. Background information was very much about this, for males and females: How had they managed through the war?

Still, the press was pleased and seemingly happy when they could describe the athletic women with accepted female values and interests. They revelled in descriptions of women in traditional roles, combined with athletic prowess, heroism, and exoticism. For instance, Tatjana Sevrjukova; the winner of the women's shot-put, "who with her 14 meters puts demonstrated that a mother can be capable of more than cooking porridge."[59] However, in the press script she had been presented as a student of architecture in Moscow with an earlier degree from the Academy of Music in Tasjkent, for the time being making a living as a musician. Her husband was "killed during the war," when she worked as an un-specified "instructor" for troops.[60]

However, in other reports, the emphasis was even more traditional. Simultaneously, the press' cultivation of exoticism seemed to grow with geographical distance. An American report came up with coarse stereotypes: "the Cossacks of the cinder lane" and "(a) team cloaked in mystery."[61] While a local report before the start of the event from the athletes' camp was more concrete. In a re-assuring way – even if they belonged to the exotic others, they had recognisable, safe interests – it revealed for those who were waiting to hear and see what the Red Team consisted of: "Coquettish Russian women chewing confectionery candy and talking about fashions." Their relaxation is by the female interpreter described like this, perhaps to assure the world: "Women take care of their clothes by sewing and ironing. They also mend the clothes of the 'boys.'" "What do the women look like?" the same interpreter is asked (this is before the event had started) – and she

---

[57] *Morgenbladet*, August 26, 1946.

[58] *Arbeiderbladet*, August 21, 1946.

[59] *Verdens Gang*, August 23, 1946.

[60] *Arbeiderbladet*, August 23, 1946.

[61] *New York Times*, August 21, 1946.

answers: "Very sweet. Pure beauties many of them. They seem small and very feminine […] Extremely occupied with fashion for example."[62]

Among the newspapers that represented the whole spectrum of political affiliation from the Conservatives to the Communists, the Soviet women had more in common than differences. All papers praised the elegance of the Soviet women and their sporting superiority.

When the discus thrower Nina Dumbadze set a new world record, a few days after the Championships – registered as the first approved world record by a Soviet athlete – she and her compatriots were praised for their technical and systematic training. In the conservative Aftenposten, "Mrs. Dumbadze," was described as "sympathetic, stately and beautiful," was congratulated with her "wonderful" technique, after all a world record on a Norwegian field was not an everyday occurrence. The Social Democratic *Arbeiderbladet* described her as an athlete who can "convince that women's sports have its right."[63] In other words, a 'right' that was not self-evident.

To make women invisible has been one way of exerting power in gender relations.[64] One evident example of invisibility was the article by the conservative Aftenposten on who to look out for at the 1946 Championships. It mentioned more than thirty possible favourites among the men and zero women.[65] Another obvious example from the ice-skating track was the conservative press arguing that women's results should not be counted in international meets between Norway and the USSR. The reason offered by male journalists was that the Soviet women were far superior, making the counting of the joint national team results less exciting. At the same time this of course gave the Norwegian team a better chance of winning while making the Norwegian women even more invisible. The Soviets rejected the idea, although without giving any reasoning that would resonate with more modern feminist views, struggling for the idea that women's achievements should be counted as equal to men's achievements to create equality of status.[66]

---

[62] ["Kokette russerinner som knasker konfekt og snakker om moter"]. ["Kvinnene steller klærne sine. De syr og stryker. De steller klærne til guttene også"] *Arbeiderbladet*, August 22, 1946.

[63] *Aftenposten*, evening issue, August 30, 1946; *Arbeiderbladet*, August 31, 1946.

[64] Berit Ås developed a theory of suppression techniques in Norwegian, 1979. "Made invisible" means "forgotten, overlooked and/or ignored." "The five master suppression techniques," Kilden, Kjønnsforskning.no, downloaded November 25, 2020, The five master suppression techniques | Kilden (kjonnsforskning.no).

[65] *Aftenposten*, evening issue, August 17, 1946.

[66] Beldo, "Alliert, fiende og konkurrent."

Nevertheless, the presence and presentation of the USSR can be interpreted as the opposite of this particular suppression technique. The female athletes became very visible in the press. To a perhaps surprising degree they were praised for their abilities and capacities, and even their feminine elegance. If there were reservations, it would be on the cultural side, where reservations were still felt. However, the year one impression of the USSR athletic woman was one of praise and admiration.

If there were small differences among the newspapers on the gender issue, they became more visible when they directly or indirectly touched upon the amateur question. For instance, the English women were excused for not being as elegant as the Soviet women in the way of dressing – they perhaps did not have the same support of state, some newspapers suggested – hence they could be excused for wearing paper or cardboard flags on their uniforms instead of a flag made of cloth.[67]

Amateurism

The impression the women made led to the question of amateurism and state support. While the Soviet women were praised for their elegant clothing, the English, in a distinct post-war context, were excused for not having the same standard.

Commenting on reportedly well-paid Soviet athletes who wanted to join the IAAF, the *New York Times* informed that "Professionalism is scheduled to be the hottest topic" at the meeting in Oslo.[68] The Oslo meet involved both Championships and an IAAF congress. The set of problems caused by amateur principles was in the forefront of media coverage before the event opened. They also dominated the debates at the congress, in many cases without reaching agreements, so that quite a few cases had to be postponed or sent over to the new commission "for the purpose of studying the amateur question," which the congress felt necessary to establish.[69]

The European Championships would demonstrate contemporary aspects of amateurism. The proponents of the traditional – described by some as the aristocratic, amateur ideal – emphasized the moral standards of the athlete. The consequences of this were demonstrated in 1946. There were the traditional amateurs represented by the IAAF and the British, home of the gentleman amateur, who mainly aimed at continuing down the traditional

[67] *Arbeiderbladet*, August 23, 1946.

[68] *New York Times*, August 21, 1946.

[69] Minutes, IAAF 15th Congress in Oslo, August 1946, IAAF/World Athletics archives.

road and more or less did, or at least pretended to, play by the rules. Nevertheless, events and discussions before and around the contest had shown the world new strategies to deal with or to overcome the amateur rules, while still both providing income to the athlete and pretending to play by the book. Two versions of the new world were visible, symbolized by images of the Swedes and the Soviets.

One was the western 'market amateurism' where money could come from event organizers and promotors who paid much coveted athletes so-called 'under-the-counter' money. Athletics contests were popular and attracted large crowds, which generated income to event organizers. In the days of amateurism when no open payment to the athletes could be made, this created a pool of money that nobody seemed to have the legal and moral right to administer except when the organizer was a local sports club whose income could be poured into new sports activities.

However, before this moral and philosophical problem had been solved, inventive event organizers saw the opportunity to exploit them. To attract the best and the most popular athletes to come to an event, organizers had started to pay them 'start money'. The economic market forces in competitive sports made sure that only the best profited from this. This seem to have been in operation in most places where sports were popular, not only in Sweden. For example, the Finnish winner of the 10,000 meters, Viljo Heino, could return to the track only on the eve of the Oslo event, as he had to sit out a suspension for alleged breach of the amateur rules. In the popular vernacular he was said to have taken "too much start money."[70] Swedish newspapers published reports that Heino had received large sums for running at events in Sweden, something that he himself denied. The case was sent to the Finnish federation for investigation who suspended him from international competitions for the time it took to investigate his case.[71] The Finnish federation concluded that although Heino's manager had received money, it could not be proven that Heino himself had received any of it. Additionally, instead of sentencing the athlete, which seems to have been common practice in Sweden, they excluded the manager, forever.[72]

---

[70] Hannus, *The Flying Finns*. Story of the great tradition of Finnish distance running.

[71] Investigation led by Urho Kekkonen, then president of Suomen Urheiloliito [Finnish Sports Federation], later president of the Republic of Finland. Minutes, IAAF 15th Congress in Oslo, August 1946, IAAF/World Athletics archives.

[72] Minutes, IAAF 15th Congress in Oslo, August 1946, IAAF/World Athletics archives, 16; Karin Wikberg, *Amatør eller professionist? Studier rörande amatörfrågan i svensk tävlingsidrott 1903–1967* (Stockholm: SISU, 2005), 211.

His return did not go uncommented though, as the Swedish delegate Bo Lindman at the opening day of the IAAF Congress raised a critical question as to
whether Heino should be allowed to start. None other than Urho Kekkonen,
then President of Suomen Urheiloliito [Finnish Sports Federation], later President of the Republic of Finland, successfully intervened on the side of Heino.
Surprisingly perhaps, it was the amateur prophet Avery Brundage, as leader of
the event jury, who concluded that Heino was indeed an amateur. The jury had
simply addressed the Finnish Athletics Federation who notified that they could
find "no evidence" of Heino having received any salary. Instead, the Finnish
delegate at the congress expressed astonishment that the case had been raised,
since it did not occur on the official agenda. According to Norwegian newspapers, Heino had travelled to Oslo at random, though officially listed "assistant
coach" in the Finnish team, hoping to obtain a start permit.[73]

Undoubtedly, the most sensational case or the biggest scandal over breach of
amateur rules in the 1940s, and a backdrop for the Heino case, was the Gunder Hägg affair.[74] Sweden, with an official status and practice as a neutral nation
during the war, had turned up as the leading athletics nation in a period when
much of the organized international sporting life was closed down. Nevertheless,
their middle-distance runners Gunder Hägg and Arne Andersson impressed the
track world. Hägg, particularly, made an impact. During the summer of 1942 he
broke no less than ten world records. He was also accused of breaking the amateur rules.

The Gunder Hägg story developed as a dramatic Second World War side
show.[75] Named "Gunder, the wonder" by British reporters, he ran at the
mentioned Oslo Games in September 1945 as one of the "world stars." Before his career was over, he managed to set sixteen world records. However,
for a substantial amount of his career he, according to his Swedish federation, seemed to live on the edge of the amateur rules, which makes his 1946

---

[73] Minutes, IAAF 15th Congress in Oslo, August 1946, IAAF/World Athletics archives;
Verdens Gang, August 22, 1946; *Arbeiderbladet*, August 20, 1946. They compared him
to Paavo Nurmi before the LA Olympics 1932, which did not turn out well for Nurmi.
Chris Turner, Viljo Heino 1914–1998: Flying Finn – floating Finn. 16–17.

[74] It was only ten days since the sentence against Hägg that Heino was accused of approximately
the same misdeeds (March 17 and March 27, 1946). In early June of the same year the Finnish
Sports Federation penalized him with a competition ban for as long as the investigation of his
case lasted. In early August his ban was lifted for domestic competitions, so he in fact could qualify for international competitions through convincing running at the Finnish Championships,
which he did. (Vesa Tikander and Kenth Sjöblom, personal information, December 14, 2020).

[75] E.g. *New York Times*, November 10, 1945, January 15, March 16, March 18, March 25, 1946.

case not so sensational. Already in 1942, he had to sit out a suspension for violating the amateur rules. He then came back after obviously a good training session to break all the mentioned world records. The big scandal started a couple of years later, in March 1946, when the Swedish Athletics Federation took his amateur status away and banned him for life, or "for ever," as the rules said.[76]

The Hägg case happened less than half a year before the Championships in Oslo. Compared to – and in contrast to – the Heino case, it demonstrates differences in the practice of the amateur rules and the strength of the amateur ideology. National sports leaders were inclined to eradicate their best athletes if they found them morally lacking and judicially guilty; pulling them literally out of the track made the leaders shine morally.[77] At the same time, Swedish athletics would continue to shine since the records Hägg had accomplished were not withdrawn. According to the Swedish historian Karin Wikberg, some of them were even reported to the IAAF after the verdict. In this way, Sweden kept its world records.[78] Hägg and Andersson could therefore not compete in Oslo, where they would have been favourites to win. Norwegian newspapers, as other media in the western world, were careful to express any direct signs of loss by their absence. However, the Hägg case had involved a considerable number of persons and charges were brought against forty-four athletes with twenty-five convicted. Hence, it raised questions about the reasonableness of the amateur rules.[79] The rules' focus solely on the athlete, while the provider of the money, in most cases sports leaders, went free, was disputed. This led people from many nations to question the fairness of the rules.[80] In the Swedish debate also the question of the organizers' responsibilities, especially when the organizer was a sports leader, was problematized. Even the very pro-amateur Swedish IAAF General Secretary Bo Ekelund was very critical of event organizers who, in effect, contributed to athletes changing "from nice Swedish boys [into] lying, deceitful criminals."[81]

---

[76] Karin Wikberg, *Amatør eller professionist? Studier rörande amatörfrågan i svensk täflingsidrott 1903–1967*, (Stockholm: SISU, 2005).

[77] By the prevailing rules, leaders and entrepreneurs who had tempted and paid off athletes with money were not sentenced at all. The legendary Finnish runner, Paavo Nurmi, himself also barred by similar circumstances just before the LA Olympics in 1932, criticized this, commenting on the Hägg case, and arguing for more fair rules. *New York Times*, April 24, 1946.

[78] Wikberg, *Amatør eller professionist?*, 211.

[79] Wikberg, *Amatør eller professionist?*, 211.

[80] Edelman, *The shifting Olympic front*; Wikberg, *Amatør eller professionist?*

[81] Wikberg, *Amatør eller professionist?*, 201.

The amateur question had been predicted to be the "hottest" subject of the Congress in 1946.[82] And, even if other themes were listed higher up on its agenda, the temperature of the amateur debate reached the expected heights. The Congress rejected a Scandinavian proposal to increase day money during international representation from £10 to £15. The existing IAAF amateur commission had been "unanimous" in their rejection to allow any form of compensation for lost earnings ("broken time"). At the congress, a majority, while keeping to their principle, was only willing to legalize that "in occasional hardship cases [...] it will be permitted [...] for a payment to be made directly to the employer, of compensation for loss of salaries or wages, to the wife, the children, the mother or the father of the athlete during his absence..." Avery Brundage emphasized that for an athlete "duties... towards his family and his employer should come first and sport should come only in the second place."[83]

The decision to (still) reject broken time compensation led the Swedish representative Lindman to state that he could take no responsibility that such payments would not be made in Sweden, making the Swedish IAAF President Edström react strongly and "very much regret" such statements. Edström was followed up by several others, among them Avery Brundage, who asked whether Lindman would be willing to withdraw his assertions.[84] The whole debate could easily be interpreted as a demonstration and a confirmation of where athletics leaders were coming from regarding social class as well as their continued loyalty to Victorian, aristocratic ideas.

The Norwegian press, across class and political divides, were on moral grounds negative to the idea of money in sports, and thus, in general negative to professional sport. In 1946, Norwegian sport had remained built upon and around the principle of amateur sport, but with a growing positivity for receiving compensation for lost earnings. The repugnance for "the ghost of professionalism" was visible throughout, whether the issue was American or Scandinavian wrongdoers.[85] The "Hägg case" – although discussed as a parallel or a contrast to the Heino case – was gradually less mentioned. It was hard to find sports persons who flagged a defence for

---

[82] *Verdens Gang*, August 22, 1946; *Arbeiderbladet* August 22, 1946.

[83] Minutes, IAAF 15th Congress in Oslo, August 1946, IAAF/World Athletics archives, 27.

[84] *Ibid.*

[85] Matti Goksøyr and Finn Olstad, *Fotball! Norges Fotballforbund 100 år* (Oslo: Norges Fotballforbund, 2002).

Hägg. Hence, when the amateur debate turned up again it was related to athletes representing the USSR.

Stories of Soviet sportsmen receiving salaries had reached the Norwegian sports pages. The stories were challenging both on moral and political grounds. Commenting on the reports that assumedly well-paid Soviet athletes wanted to join the IAAF most parts of the press agreed that: "professionalism is scheduled to be the hottest topic," at the IAAF meeting in Oslo.[86] The other significant way of coping with amateur rules was the system that the USSR preferred: "amateur" athletes with a favourable labour contract or fictitious jobs. While Soviet sportsmen and women before World War II had been openly professional, not disguising that they received money for sports achievements, after the war they changed strategy, and hence status. In order to compete with Westerners, they, while still denouncing the 'capitalist way,' had to abide by their rules, in this case their amateur rules.[87] They could no longer be paid for sports achievements. Acknowledging that athletes needed an income to be able to train properly, the solution was to give athletes fictitious jobs, often linked to the military system. This became the favoured system for Soviet sports for many decades.

The way this was represented at the European event of 1946 is interesting because it demonstrates a clear gender difference. The women, who in the competitions were far superior to their male colleagues, often were presented as students, musicians, clerks, or other feminine occupations. The men on the other side usually held masculine occupations, like soldiers or officers, perhaps illustrating an existing gender bias in the Communist state.

Even though it was flagged as the "hottest" issue, the media did not seem to expect any clear solution of the problem of the amateur rules. It was "too complicated," and inside the IAAF it seemed to be England versus the rest. This seemed to have been the case especially regarding the question of "compensation for lost earnings" presumably pointing to differences in the class base of the sport.[88] Consequently, the socialist leaning part of the press, if they were pushed, would express sympathy to the idea that open, honest professionalism (the Soviet pre-war type) was preferable in comparison to the "camouflaged" professionalism that was in operation in the Western world, with athletes only pretending to be amateurs.[89]

---

[86] *New York Times*, August 21, 1946.

[87] Edelman, *The shifting Olympic front*, chapter 2.

[88] *Arbeiderbladet*, August 20, 1946.

[89] *Ibid.*

Conclusion: Prospects Taken; Prospects lost

What did the IAAF Championships of 1946 announce? Perhaps the first gasp of oxygen after a near death experience and hopes of a rapid return of an uncertain normality, whatever that would be. Nevertheless, the happiness resulting from meeting up peacefully with former and new friends was unmistakable.

The context of post-war was there, unavoidable, from the Norwegian organizers who excused the state of the welcoming city, the Polish and their lacking preparations and the not-so-elegant clothing of the English. It was there, regarding who were *not* present.

The Championships also demonstrated and confirmed differences between the Scandinavian countries. The Norwegians were the happy organizers, proud to have been trusted with the first big international athletic meeting after the war, and content with a sole gold medal (in decathlon). Sweden, neutral during the war, managed to maintain its position as an athletics powerhouse, even without their disqualified "star runners." They were the undisputable Scandinavian big brother, superior on and off the field, winning a total of eleven gold medals while still being dominant in the board room. The Finns, heavily marked by war, proved their worth in endurance running and became the third best nation with four gold medals. The championship did, however, demonstrate a fierce athletic rivalry with neighboring Sweden, not only on the field, but even more when it came to be practicing amateur rules. The post-war context seems to have meant insecurity in general regarding which directions to take. Conservatism had been a part of the IAAF for long. Even though new nations and new interests had entered the scene, the old, by some called aristocratic culture or mentality, was still strongly present. This was also in part due to the leadership in international athletics which had changed little. The same old men who had led the federation throughout the interwar period remained at the helm for much of the second half of the 20th century.[90]

Even though women had demonstrated capacities by some thought impossible, the Championships did not immediately, or even on a short-term basis, open up in terms of provision for female athletes. Regarding the ever-present amateur question, the pressure was mounting for a change. This would be far from revolutionary, representing only minor revisions. It is revealing for the strength of the aristocratic amateur ideal that not even the idea of compensation

---

[90] Krieger, *Power and Politics.*

for lost earnings gained support. Regarding politics, the 1946 event signaled inclusion and new friendships, after all the USSR could participate and compete in a congress and a Championships, organized by a body of which they were not a member. Yet, the question of politics was an even more context related problem. Even if optimistic feelings of grasping the opportunity of a peaceful meetings was in the air, the insecurity as to which direction this would take was also there.

From the view of the IAAF Congress, which took place simultaneously, amateurism was the most important athletic problem. The sixty-four delegates representing twenty-two nations, plus two "guest representatives for the Soviet athletes," gave the subject a thorough and passionate treatment, while the gender subject apparently did not exist, and attempts to raise political questions were resolutely clubbed down by the IAAF president.[91] Even if the IAAF Congress through its decisions held on to its traditional convictions, it could be argued that athletics in year one in the fields of gender and amateurism signaled new developments. Through "the others" who now participated, athletics sent signals of opening its gender line. The sport was still embedded in traditional beliefs about women's capacities, now mostly visible in the events and running distances allowed for women. Nonetheless, regarding how women's athletics was viewed and commented upon, the Championships presented acceptance of women's capacities. However, running distances did not change until the Rome Olympics of 1960 and praiseworthy achievements had a tendency of being presented with otherness as an explanatory factor.

When it comes to amateur rules, the signals from the event in 1946 are mixed. The rules and their intentions survived, mainly because they were protected by the old school leaders of sports, both in athletics and in the Olympic movement. Avery Brundage, crucially, is the name not to be missed here. Thus, the same old mismanagement of the rules could go on. The Soviet type of evasion of the rules by reporting fictitious jobs was thriving along with the Western way of ensuring that gifted athletes were provided with the income they arguably deserved. Even if the aperture to the Championships, by the examples of Heino and Hägg, displayed open problems connected to the amateur rules, many years would pass until they were done with and the problems resolved.

Political comments were what the IAAF president least wanted in 1946. In retrospect however, we know that exactly in these years started the processes

---

[91] It should be mentioned though that Avery Brundage successfully "moved that a special commission for Women's sports be elected." Minutes, IAAF, 1946, 22–23.

of the world growing apart. From the end of the war there had been high hopes of peace and goodwill. The Germans were out of sight, and the Soviet women had become the spectators' new darlings, what could possibly go wrong? As we have seen, the Soviets mainly went for their version of soft diplomacy through their successful female athletes. As a strategy it seemed to work, at least in the short term. Then came the deterioration of East-West relations, de-Nazification gave way to anti-communism and cold war, and new geo-political blocs emerged.

Was a new sports era that simply reflected a "meetings on sports' terms," realistic? To keep sports free from politics, like in the good old days when the supposed family feeling, free from class differences, created a cozy atmosphere, still seemed to be the most important thing. In such a perspective, the pretty Soviet sports women as un-political ambassadors – though political through their national affiliation – became a disturbance. Better then, as Tony Judt has described in his book *Post-war*, to run a policy of conscious amnesia.[92]Although not totally, the Germans had to sit out for some years. Soon, new antagonisms took over for the old, while at the same time making it possible to propagate the old school recipe for sports: sports and politics should not mix.

---

[92] Judt, *Postwar*, 61.

CHAPTER 6

Women in Norwegian Athletics in the 1960s and 1970s

Gerd von der Lippe and Bieke Gils[1]

Introduction

In May 2022, newspapers and sport enthusiasts in Norway celebrated the fiftieth anniversary of female participation in the Holmenkollen relay, an annual iconic race in the city of Oslo organized since 1923 and initially open to male participants only.[2] This was still the case on the legendary Sunday in May 1972 when two female runners, Ingrid Ellingsen and Gerd von der Lippe, appeared at the start under the respective pseudonyms of I. Ellingsen and Øyvind Foss. While the race organizers were less than pleased with their bold initiative, as with their well-organized activism on behalf of women's inclusion in the years to follow, it would force them to open the race to female participants from 1975 onwards. Gerd and Ingrid were not alone, however, in their attempts to gain legitimacy as athletes at the time. American Roberta Gibb ran the male-only Boston Marathon already in 1966 as an unregistered participant, to be followed by American Kathrine Switzer in 1967 who registered under a male pseudonym, sparking controversy and international outcry while pushing the envelope for women's sport in the West. As we illustrate in this chapter, also Ingrid and Gerd's activism in the 1970s was both inspired by, and indicative of, much larger demands for women's rights and social justice inside and outside of sport, nationally and globally.

---

[1] It needs to be noted that, academically speaking, both authors contributed equally to this chapter. Since the chapter not only details much of Gerd's personal experiences, but also aims to be a tribute to women's collective fight against discrimination in sport, in which fight Gerd played a prominent role, it is only appropriate that Gerd figures as first author.

[2] See Mette Bugge, "Én stafett og to «falske» menn," *Aftenposten*, May 13, 2022. Øyvind Nordli & Wenche Fuglehaug Fallsen, "Jentene som står opp," *Aftenposten A Magasinet*, Juni 30, 2022. Marte-Ericsson Ryste, "Tidsvitne: Kvinneopprør i Holmenkollstafetten: Gerd von der Lippe forteller," *kvinnehistorie.no*, 2003.

Our chapter seeks to piece together the rather fragmented and much under-researched history of women in Norwegian athletics during the 1960s and 1970s, with a specific emphasis on the Holmenkollen relay in 1972 in relation to the first author's political activism in the years before and after this event. The chapter is based on the first author's rich anecdotal accounts of her experiences and her recollection of people and events, in addition to existing literature on the topic, and a considerable number of newspaper articles. The second author's role, in conversational and written collaboration with the first author, has been to interpret and verify the first author's writings and personal narratives and to help formulate and contextualize them. The piece can best be placed in the (auto)biographical history genre; it uses and unveils the first author's personal narratives and experiences to describe and contextualize the process of women moving from the margins of Norwegian athletics' history to its center.[3] The chapter does not pretend to be 'complete' or impartial in any way, as it is narrated mostly through the first author's lens. It does, however, aim to contribute to continuing to tell, and re-tell, the often fragmented but important *her*stories of athletes and pioneering women more generally. Even in 2023, the need for writing women into the largely male-dominated field of sport historiography has not dissipated.[4] This piece must also be read as a tribute to female athletes in athletics, as well as to women's collective efforts to fight discrimination across the board.

Our chapter starts with a short introduction to, and contextualization of, the Norwegian Athletics Federation, followed by an overview of Berit Berthelsen's (1944–2022) groundbreaking sport performances in the 1960s. It then addresses Gerd von der Lippe's early athletics career and activism in 1963 when she and several other women on the Norwegian national athletics team made demands to compete internationally, against the will of the Athletics Federation's leaders. They partially succeeded; their team did compete abroad, but the competition was never officially registered, and their efforts went largely unnoticed.

In later years, our chapter goes on, Gerd continued her activism and political engagement and would become one of the front figures of the women's equal rights movement in Norwegian sport by participating in the Holmenkollen relay under a male pseudonym in 1972. Together with a group of university

---

[3] See for example Jaume Aurell, "Making history by contextualizing oneself: autobiography as historiographical intervention," *History and Theory* 54(2) (2015): 244–68.

[4] See for example Hege Duckert's recently published popular book on women's firsts & forgotten women's stories in the Norwegian context: Hege Duckert, *Norsk kvinnehistorie* (Oslo: Kagge Forlag, 2021).

student and athlete peers, a Sport Action Committee (*Idrettsaksjonen-73*) was formed in 1973, alongside an *Action Committee for Female Participation in the Holmenkollen Relay*. The concerted efforts of these committees would push the race organizers to include women in 1975 and help pave the way for successful athletes like Norwegian Grete Waitz (1953–2011) to participate and excel in athletics competitions not previously organized for women.

While individually successful athletes like Berit Berthelsen in the 1960s and Grete Waitz in the 1970s, as we conclude, set important examples for generations of athletes to come by means of their excellent sporting performances, it was not without the continued and well-orchestrated political action of women like Gerd von der Lippe and Ingrid Ellingsen in the Norwegian context, and Roberta Gibb and Kathrine Switzer in the United States for example – among many other examples of female athletes and their allies – that Western sport's male hegemony became questioned more widely and profoundly, and that significant changes for women in sport began to happen.

Traditional Views and Berit Berthelsen's Pioneering Role in the 1960s

The Norwegian National Athletics Federation (NFIF) was established in 1896 though it was not until 1947 that it opened up to female membership and women were allowed to participate in Norwegian athletics championships. Women initially made up about 17% of the membership,[5] which increased to 39% by 1980.[6] The reason for women's late admission was the federation's traditional views on competition for women. According to the federation's national coach, Helge Løvland, women should not engage in any systematic workouts or participate in competition, but exercise in playful, non-exerting ways instead.[7] This sentiment was particularly strong in and outside the NFIF in the 1940s and '50s.

From 1947 to 1950, the Norwegian championships for men and women were held in separate locations every year. From 1951 on, both sexes competed together in the same location and the winners were handed their trophy by the Norwegian king. The women's national team had its first international competition in 1953 against Denmark, together with the Norwegian male team. The

---

[5] Norges Friidretts Forbund (NFIF). Report: 1.8.1946-1.10.1947, 1947, 20.

[6] Norges Friidretts Forbund (NFIF). Report: 1.8.1979-1.10.1980, 1980.

[7] Helge Løvland, *Treningslære* (Oslo: Norges Landsforbund for idrett, 1938), 90–93.

men won with 118 points versus 94 for Denmark, while the women lost with 38 to Denmark's 57 points.[8] At that time, men competed in a much larger number of distances than their female counterparts. From 1964 on, the women's national team competed at least once a year internationally, while the men competed more frequently and against a larger number of different teams from European countries.

It was not until the 1960s that Norwegian female track and field athletes made headlines nationally, and internationally as news media coverage for women's sport at the time was minimal. It was Berit Berthelsen (1944–2022), a farmer's daughter, born at the end of World War II in Hakadal in Akershus near Oslo, who would dominate Norwegian athletics in the 1960s. Berit won a total of thirty-five national medals and three European medals in long jump, of which two were gold and one bronze. She made her breakthrough in 1961, at the early age of seventeen, in an international competition against Denmark. It was then that Berit set her first national record in long jump with 5.79m. Her athletic performances would very much contribute to helping Norwegian women's athletics up out of the shadows and increasingly into the public eye.[9]

Berit's first competition in the Norwegian Championships was in 1962, in which she won three disciplines, the 100m, 200m and the long jump. At that time women competed in eleven distances in contrast to their male counterparts who competed in nineteen. There was usually only one annual international competition for women, whereas five were organized for men. The women's athletics team lost all competitions in the 1960s, while men ended up just about even with their competitors. Berit was one of the very few who was considered good enough to be allowed to lift weights together with the men, and she improved gradually. In 1963, she set her first Norwegian record on the 400m. She would improve this record six times in the years to come.[10] That same year she also broke the Norwegian record in long jump, which she would improve seventeen times.

In 1964 Berit participated in long jump during the Olympic Games in Tokyo. She managed to qualify for the final, in which she ended ninth. Newspapers reported that:

---

[8] Aage Møst, *Raskest, Høyest, Lengst i 100 år: norsk friidrett 1896–1996* (Oslo: Norges fri-idretts-forbund/Universitetsforlaget, 1995), 204.

[9] Møst, *Raskest, Høyest, Lengst i 100 år*, 236.

[10] *Ibid.*, 368.

> [o]ur track and field girls have been used to stand in the shadows of the boys, but
> our superb long-jumper Berit Tøien Berthelsen and Oddrun Lange Hokland (both
> married during the season) have raised the media's interest in women's events…
> Berit is one of the 10 best long-jumpers in the world (Munthe-Kaas,1964).[11]

In 1965 she was elected the best Nordic female athlete during the Nordic Championship, in which she won five gold medals:

> Berit Berthelsen was the champions' Prima Ballerina with nothing less than five
> wins: 100m-12.0, 200m-24.4, 400m-54.4, long jump-6.37 and Norwegian gold
> on 4 x 100m relay – 47.0 with Berit as final runner. We do not exaggerate when
> we say that her effort was the best a Norwegian and Nordic female track and
> fielder has ever made in the course of three days (Munthe-Kaas, 1965, p. 242).[12]

In 1967 Berit won the unofficial European Championship in Praha in long
jump. It earned her *Morgenbladet*'s Gold Medal. Shortly after she got injured,
however, and was unable to compete in the long jump, though she did participate successfully in other disciplines:

> Later in the season Berit did not compete in long jump out of necessity though fo-
> cused on running distances, including the 800m. … She was bold enough, how-
> ever, to leave for Denmark (…), and to return as Nordic Champion in pentathlon
> [5 events in 1967: 80m hurdles, high jump, long jump, 200m and shot put]. Yes,
> this new teacher at Bolteløkka school can manage lots of things [running, travel-
> ling and teaching]. Now we are wondering what she wants to focus on in Mexico
> City – would there be more injuries preventing her entry there? Will there be a
> 400m? 800m? Long jump? Or pentathlon? (Munthe-Kaas,1967, p.186).[13]

Berit carried the Norwegian flag during the opening parade in the 1968 Mexi-
co Olympics.[14] She participated in long jump and qualified second with 6.48 m.
During the final, however, she ended up in seventh position. It was also that year
on the tenth of September in Oslo that Berit set her last and longest-standing
Norwegian long jump record with 6.56m. This record stood for forty-one years
until 2009.[15] In 1969, during the European Championships in Athens she earned

[11] Einar Munthe-Kaas, *Sportsboken 1964* (Norsk Kunstforlag. A/S., 1964). Note that the reporter
deemed it necessary to state that both women were married during the season, potentially to reassure audiences that though these women performed exceptionally athletically, they still adhered
to traditional societal heteronormative prescriptions.

[12] Einar Munthe-Kaas, *Sportsboken 1965* (Norsk Kunstforlag. A/S., 1965), 242.

[13] Einar Munthe-Kaas, *Sportsboken 1967* (Norsk Kunstforlag. A/S., 1967), 186.

[14] Einar Munthe-Kaas, *Sportsboken 1968* (Norsk Kunstforlag. A/S., 1968), 155.

[15] Møst, *Raskest, Høyest, Lengst i 100 år*, 369.

a bronze medal in long jump with 6.44m, just one cm short of silver and five short of gold. She managed all of this despite an injury.[16] During the Norwegian championships that same year she won five distances: 100m, 200m, 400m, 100m hurdle, and long jump. In other words, she won almost half of the eleven different distances.[17] Berit won her last Norwegian Championship in 1974.

Berit was by far the most successful Norwegian female track and fielder in the 1960s. Between 1962 and 1974 she set twenty new Norwegian records in long jump. She was the only Norwegian who achieved that. What made her even more special, were her records in a variety of other events: 100m hurdles (twice), 400m (eight times), 200m and 100m (both three times). No other Nordic athlete had set so many records during fourteen active years. Gerd recalls:

> Those of us who travelled together with Berit to national and international com-petitions experienced her as immensely helpful and kind. I remember well a happening on the boat from Denmark to Norway in 1961 with the national women's team and the junior men from Norway. Berit and I wanted to have some fun before we entered Norway. Together with some of the men we orga-nized competitions in 10 m running, long jump and hand stands on the boat, inspiring much laughter and smiles. Berit encouraged many of us to join. We were young and happy. On that journey we had many interesting conversations. I never forgot when she told me that I had to train harder and more seriously to be able to compete in the Olympic Games in Tokyo in 1964. She made it, and I did not. I will not easily forget this kind and humble woman's smile.[18]

Norwegian Athletes' Demand for International Competitions

While the NFIF had admitted women in 1947, the federation's view that wom-en should not participate in competitions became a particularly contentious point in 1963. That year the NFIF decided that women should not compete in-ternationally because they had not won any of the previously held international athletics competitions for women as a national team. Men, on the other hand, could participate in nine international competitions that year.

---

[16] Einar Munthe-Kaas, *Sportsboken 1969* (Norsk Kunstforlag. A/S., 1969), 139.

[17] Møst, *Raskest, Høyest, Lengst i 100 år*, 263.

[18] Berit had accepted to be interviewed by this paper's authors, but unfortunately she passed away in January 2022 before we were able to speak to her.

The different treatment of male and female athletes and their competitions by the NFIF at the time becomes especially apparent in Gerd von der Lippe's recollection of her negotiations with the federation's leaders. Gerd was then at the beginning of her athletic career. As a representative of Kristiansand Sport Club (KIF) she had set the junior record on the 100 m with a time of 12.1 in 1960 and had won three individual gold medals on the 100m, 200m and 400m during the Norwegian Championship in 1961 and 1962.

"I was so angry when I was told that the board of the NFIF did not want us to compete internationally in 1963," Gerd said, continuing:

> Some of us on the national team were inspired by the Women's movements in the United States and Western-Europe, and we saw our exclusion as an act of discrimination. I persuaded my friend, Reidun Corneliussen, on the national team to go talk to our male leaders about this issue. We were both students in Oslo at the time. The men reacted with astonishment when we asked them to facilitate an international competition for the women's team. It was probably the first time that the NFIF female athletes had dared to complain about anything. In the past they had just shown themselves happy and thankful to be included.
>
> Not surprisingly, the first part of our conversation revolved around how 'bad' they thought the women's team was because we had been losing all competitions thus far. There was no country who would want to compete against us, we were told. Then I suggested that we could just compete against a foreign team. The two leaders looked at each other and ended up with a clear 'no' because there were no male officials who were able to travel with us. Then I replied, while looking at Reidun: if you find a place for us to compete, we could lead the women's team ourselves. This they accepted and appointed Reidun as leader of our women's team. They found us a place, a town called Itzehoe in Schleswig-Holstein in the north of Germany. Reidun and I were very happy, while the leaders looked a little worried.
>
> What a travel and competition! Our fellow athletes on the national team were impressed with our efforts, and everyone was in a good mood. Berit Berthelsen was unfortunately not able to travel with us because of the very short notice; under regular circumstances we would have known at least two months ahead where and when we would be travelling. We arrived the day before the competition and stayed in a hotel. In the evening we went into town with some of the mayor's son's male friends and we had a very good time. When our fellow athletes on the team asked us when we had to return to our hotel, we answered smilingly: "Stay as long as you want. Just be ready tomorrow on the track one hour before the start of the competition." Under normal circumstances, female athletes would not have been allowed to be out late and would have had to return to their hotels early. The day of the competition, my teammates appointed me to give the speech in front of Itzehoe's

mayor as I was one of the only ones who spoke a little German. I opened with "Lieber Herr Burgermeister" and was much more nervous doing this speech than for my race later that day. Among the audience was also the mayor's son and some of his friends.

Gerd remembers well how the competition did not go without some unexpected events:

All of us were shocked when Berit Dønnum Brekke suddenly collapsed during her 800 m competition. She was hurriedly brought to the hospital but recovered quickly and was able to return to Norway together with us after the competition. She had fainted because she pushed so hard with only one functional lung. She had not told any of us about this and to our surprise, there had been no NFIF doctors who had asked her about her health. This was quite indicative of how little resources and importance the women's team was given at the time! Berit, however, was in a good mood on our way back and so were we.

However successful and pleasant this international competition had been for many of its participants, to Gerd and her teammates' frustration, the event had to remain unregistered and thus unofficial as there had been no male officials accompanying the team. It was also a way for the NFIF to avoid criticism in the aftermath of Berit Dønnum Brekke's collapse. The NFIF's efforts in keeping the competition invisible and its participants unacknowledged, were not surprising and underscore, once again, the NFIF's leaders patronizing attitude at the time.

The inclusion of women in sport, let alone discussions around gender balance, would stay outside of the political responsibility of Norwegian sport organizations until the 1970s. Women's underrepresentation was seen as an individual "women's problem" or a "time-lag problem."[19] Men in positions of power who supported women's inclusion in sport – especially in higher positions – were regarded as overly generous and kind.[20] It was also not until 1968, that the NFIF's board recruited its first female member, in addition to sixteen men. It took ten more years until 1978 for the board to recruit a second woman in addition to fifteen men. Though still greatly outnumbered by their male counterparts, this would put women in a slightly better position to leverage concerns together and to demand collective change for female athletes.[21]

---

[19] Jorid Hovden, "The Gender order as a Political Issue in sport: A Study of Norwegian Sports Organizations," *NORA - Nordic Journal of Feminist and Gender research*, vol.14, Issue 1 (2006).

[20] Gerd von der Lippe, Conversations with two male leaders of NFIF for an international competition in Itzehoe, 1973.

[21] See Elin Kvande & Bente Rasmussen, *Nye kvinneliv. Kvinner i menns organisasjoner* (Oslo: Ad Notam Gyldendal, 1993).

The 1970s: Women's movements & women's sport in Norway

Women's liberation movements in Western Europe and the United States brought the question of feminism and equal rights decisively to the political agenda at the end of the 1960s.[22] In Norway three different women's movements were created: *Nyfeministene* (radical feminists) in 1970, *Kvinnefronten* (Marxist and socialist feminists) in 1972, and *Brød og Roser* in 1976. These groups quicky gained considerable membership and popular traction; in 1973 *Nyfeministene* counted 1000 members and *Kvinnefronten* 3500, in a country of nearly four million inhabitants.[23] The Norwegian women's movement was most prominent and active in and around universities, and tightly connected to wider radical student protests in the 1960s: demonstrations against the formation of the European Union in the early 1970s, as well as the global movement against the war in Vietnam.[24] The movement behind women's inclusion in the Holmenkollen relay, as we will describe in more detail below, also consisted of supporters from these overlapping groups.

According to Anne-Mette Vibe, the Norwegian women's movement and the demand for women's inclusion in sport were initially two distinct causes as many believed that "good feminists do not participate in sport."[25] This attitude would change in the years to come, thanks to the successes of several Norwegian sportswomen, and Gerd and her entourage's political activism more specifically. In her description of what she calls "the women's sport revolution of the '70s," Vibe points to four milestones that advanced Norwegian women in sport between 1968 and 1978. These include: the Norwegian women's cross-country team victory in the Olympic relay in Grenoble, France in 1968; the inclusion of women in the Holmenkollen relay in 1975; the inclusion of women in the legendary *Birkebeiner* long distance cross-country ski-race in 1976; and the approval of football as an official sport for women in 1976.[26]

---

[22] Also extensive discussions of feminist literature like Betty Fridan's bestseller *The Feminine Mystique* (1963), the revival of Simone de Beauvoir's *Second Sex* (1949) in the '60s, Germaine Greer's *The Female Eunuch* (1970) and several of Marilyn French's books including *The Women's Room* (1977), contributed to significant wind in the sails of both local and global women's movements at the time.

[23] Birgit Wiig, *Kvinner selv* (Oslo: Cappelen, 1984), 326. See also Elisabeth Lønnå, "Den nye kvinnebevegelsen i 1970-årene," *kvinnehistorie.no*, 2019.

[24] See Lønnå, "Den nye kvinnebevegelsen i 1970-årene."

[25] Anne Mette Vibe, "Kvinneidrettrevolusjonen på 1970-tallet," *kvinnehistorie.no*, 1998

[26] *Ibid.*

The demand for Norwegian women's participation in cross-country skiing, an activity that historically had been practiced by both men and women as a way of transport, was made during the same years as the fight for women's inclusion in the Holmenkollen relay. The Norwegian championships for males in cross-country skiing had been established in 1938, while the first women's championships was held in 1954.[27] The breakthrough for the acceptance of women in cross-country skiing came later, in 1968, when the women's team *Jentut'n* won gold in the Olympic relay in Grenoble, France. In subsequent years, one of the women from the winning team, Berit Mørdre-Lammedal, would play a key role in the demand for women's participation in the *Birkebeiner* long distance cross-country ski-race (54 km), established in 1932, which was viewed as too strenuous for women. Before an official women's category was finally established in 1976, Berit had already shown that women were fully capable of finishing the race successfully by participating several times unofficially in the early 1970s.[28] In other words, and in line with Gerd von der Lippe and others' pioneering work in those same years, Berit Mørdre Lammedal's persistent unofficial participation as a form of resistance and activism helped challenge the Norwegian Ski Federation's traditional attitudes and open up the *Birkebeiner* race for women also.

With regard to changes in organized sport at the time, female membership increased slowly until its "take off" in the 1970s. From 1951 to 1959, women's membership was about 23–24%, which increased to 29% in 1969, and to 35% in 1979. Similar trends were seen in athletics. The 1970s were also characterized by the "Sport for All" movement, an initiative of the Norwegian Confederation of Sport, and advertised widely in newspapers, on radio and TV. The 1970s and '80s also witnessed a fitness and jogging boom, in which all citizens were encouraged to participate and for which many clubs all over the country arranged large numbers of low-cost, easily accessible recreational activities and competitions like jogging, orientation and hiking.

In 1973 the Equal Status Act, a key pillar of the later official equal-status policy in Norway, was introduced as one of the ten major promises in the Labour Party's election program.[29] That same year *Idrettsaksjonen-73*, a sports political action

---

[27] See Gerd von der Lippe, "Endring og motstand mot endring av feminiteter og maskuliniteter i idrett og kroppskultur i Norge 1890–1950 – med et sideblikk på Tyskland, Sverige og Danmark: en feministisk analyse av et empirisk materiale" (Doctoral dissertation, Telemark College, Bø, 1997), 207–8.

[28] Vibe, "Kvinneidrettrevolusjonen på 1970-tallet."

[29] Hege Skjeie, *Den politiske betydningen av kjønn. En studie av norsk topp-politikk*. Rapport 92 (Oslo: Institute for Social Research, 1992), 77.

group, was formed with radical students on its board, including this chapter's first author. News about this group was reported in several newspapers including the national paper *Dagbladet*, in which the director of the Norwegian School of Sport Sciences (NIH) expressed his support for the initiative.[30] Also the left-wing socialist newspaper *Klassekampen*, produced several articles about *Idrettsaksjonen-73* and in 1975 wrote that "[m]ore people should join the Action Sport Group" and that an action week would be organized to recruit people interested in sport politics.[31] Also *Fædrelandsvennen*, the primary newspaper in the Southern part of Norway, published several articles in support of *Idrettsaksjonen-73*.

In December 1973, *Dagbladet* announced, in a piece entitled "Focus on sport," that members of *Idrettsaksjonen-73* would be engaging themselves in advocating for increased governmental funding for local Norwegian sport clubs.[32] Kjell Odd Trystad, president of the Speed-skating Federation; Hans B. Skaset, the vice-president of The Norwegian Confederation of Sport; Lasse Efskind, the former world champion in speed skating for men; and this chapter's first author discussed and debated sport politics in front of a large audience with Parliament member, Einar Førde as chair. The aim of *Idrettsaksjonen-73* was "Sport for All." This was a reaction against the funding of elite sport at the expense of grassroots sport, the increasing commercialization of sport, and the discrimination against women.

Alongside *Idrettsaksjonen-73* operated *The Action Committee for Female Participation in the Holmenkollen-Relay*, already established in 1972 primarily by students from the University of Oslo who were also members of *Idrettsaksjonen-73*. These overlapping memberships underscore how both representatives of the women's movement and sport movement were tightly connected to one another. The Holmenkollen relay was already in the early 1970s considered instrumental for the diffusion and popularization of running in Norway,[33] and regarded as an institution in itself.[34] The fight for women's participation in the relay those same years, to which we now turn, was according to Vibe, one of the best orchestrated campaigns in the history of women's sport in Norway.[35]

---

[30] "Idrettsaksjonen 1973," *Dagbladet*, May 26, 1973.

[31] J.T. Jensen, "Bli med i idrettsaksjonen," *Klassekampen*, 1975, 38. See also "Idrettsaksjonen skal vekke politikerne," *Klassekampen*, June 22, 1973.

[32] "Søkelys på idrett," *Dagbladet*, December 4, 1973.

[33] J.F. Löchen, *Friidrett 5*, 1973, 231.

[34] Sofie Hvitsten Harnes, "Apropos – Holmenkollstafetten 1972," *Friidrett (NFIF) 23*, 1972, 263.

[35] Vibe, "Kvinneidrettrevolusjonen på 1970-tallet."

The fight for women's participation
in the Holmenkollen relay

The Holmenkollen relay was started in 1923 by the all-male athletics club, *Tjalve*. In the first editions of the event there were about 100 male runners, each running ten legs. In 1972, 2985 male participants from 199 teams were registered to run fifteen legs. The sponsor of the event was the conservative newspaper, *Aftenposten. Tjalve*'s leader, Egil Gulliksen, was at the same time the president of the NFIF. In northern mythology, notably, the god Tjalve is the ruler of the world.

Both the start and finish of the relay were in Bislett Stadion in Oslo. In 1967, women were allowed to run a relay in that stadium during the men's interval. The first author of this paper took part in this competition and recalled that she and her teammates were satisfied at that time with that marginal role. Before 1972 there had been no discussions, either in organized athletics or in the media, about whether women ought to take part in this relay of fifteen legs. It seemed so 'natural' that this was a competition for men. The legs were from 390m up to 2800m long, while the longest official distance for women at that time was 1500m. The Holmenkollen relay organizers were regarded as generous when they included female runners to entertain the audience during the interval. However, Gerd recalls how – encouraged by the new women's movements – her experiences forced a change in attitude by 1972. These included demonstrations against the Vietnam War and the politics of the European Common Market (today EU) in the 1970s, in addition to her candidature for membership on the students' board for *Green Grass* in 1971 (a green-red coalition close to the People's Movement against the European Common Market). Male sporting traditions and the sidelining of female athletes, which for long had been taken for granted by both men and women, now came under pressure from women's movements and political activists who demanded change.

That the Holmenkollen relay was an all-male event was seen as self-evident in a tradition where men were considered participants and women the sideline figures who would watch and applaud. This was taken for granted for forty-nine years, from 1923 until 1972. In addition, in 1968 women were also not allowed to run during the men's interval, as had been the case in 1967. Gerd recalls that this made her very angry and that it was difficult for her and other women and athletes at the time to see themselves as active agents who could change their conditions.

In 1972 Ingrid Ellingsen and Gerd von der Lippe took part in the Holmen-
kollen relay illegally. Gerd used the male pseudonym, Øyvind Foss because
her correct name was too easily linked to the women's national team, while
Ingrid used the first letter of her first name and her own last name. One of
Gerd and Ingrid's student peers, Sigurd Haga, from their own close network
and private field of opinion, was one of the main protagonists and supporters.
The slogans they used read "Yes to women in the Holmenkollen relay" and
"No sex tests in the Holmenkollen relay." Ingrid and Gerd were both pun-
ished by the NFIF, with Gerd being banned from qualifying for the Norwe-
gian national team that year.

This women's sporting protest received major media attention, particularly
because Gerd had been a national champion and a member of Norway's national team since 1960. Besides, and in Gerd's words: "we were young and fearless
like several other feminists in the 1970s. And it was not just us protesting.
There were also eleven men on our team. Most of us were running with slogans
against the European Common Market, and some for the Market. Even Pravda
in the USSR ran a short media report on our protest."

In support of the protesters' actions, the sport editor of *Dagbladet* (a national
paper against the European Common Market) wrote:

> I do not believe in the idea of not integrating sport and politics, because it is
> impossible. ... We do not find any rules or paragraphs, either in the laws of the
> Norwegian Confederation of Sport or in the Norwegian Athletics Federation
> that state that such innocent actions (to run with slogans in the Holmenkollen
> relay) are against the laws of sport (Isdal, 1972).[36]

The protests – especially Ingrid and Gerd's actions – were considered as heresy
by the male athletics establishment. Not only had Ingrid and Gerd broken two
different paragraphs of sport rules; they had run in a male-only event, and as
representatives of a club they were not members of. Additionally, Gerd had
broken three rules by running under a false name.

Shortly after the protest Ingrid and Gerd were called into a meeting with three
members of the NFIF board and the male leaders of their club *Tyrving*. The
leaders' main issue was the disrespect the women had shown for the established
gender order. Gerd followed up with an article in *Friidrett*, the journal of the
NFIF with the heading: "Serious discrimination in athletics." Her main concerns were the low numbers of women's competitions and the very low budget

---

[36] Leif Isdal, "Vårens hysteriske eventyr," *Dagbladet*, May 15, 1972.

allocated to girls and women's sport. The article also referred to a letter written by *Tjalve*'s leader (the leader of the club that organized the Holmenkollen relay) to the newspaper *Dagbladet*. In the letter he wrote that if the number of participating men in the Holmenkollen relay decreased significantly, they could consider changing the rules to allow women. At that very moment, however, the Holmenkollen relay was not able to include more runners, he said.[37]

From 1973 until May 1975 *The Action Committee for Female Participation in the Holmenkollen Relay* lobbied and worked hard for women's participation in the Holmenkollen relay. Gerd and her supporters sent in a formal application to demand the right to run in the competition and started a petition to show their adversaries that they had widespread support. The signatures in support of their initiative were sent by post to Gerd's home address in Oslo. *Aftenposten,* the sponsor of the relay, announced as part of the growing antagonism to their fight:

> I want to state at once that there is no chance of including women in the Holmenkollen-relay. It is technically impossible. (...) We do not want to take the risk of reducing or destroying an event which for the time being is running well and is a success (*Aftenposten*, 1973).[38]

Aftenposten's statement goes to the core of the issue: what is taken for granted must not be discussed. It could be read as a dogmatic statement in defense of a tradition where male athleticism was the norm with women at its margins. The Action Committee would go on to use this statement as an example of extreme orthodoxy on the part of their antagonists. They would use the statement in their campaigns, in media, in meetings with sport organizations and officials, as well as when speaking with students about the event, in several towns in the Southern part of Norway. The real reason, as more and more people began to understand, was that *Tjalve* simply did not want to include women in the event. The argument that the race was full and that there was no space for more, as *Tjalve*'s leader had written in his letter to *Dagbladet*, was clearly a non-argument. *Tjalve* considered the Holmenkollen relay as its property; it was their arrangement and their members worked in their leisure time to suit the needs of male competitors only.

The Action Committee also tried to get the case on the agenda of the *General Assembly* in the NFIF on November 11, but was unsuccessful. There

---

[37] Gerd von der Lippe, "Grov diskriminering I norsk friidrett," *Friidrett 23 (10)*, 1972, 387-388.

[38] "Tjalves formann: Ikke snakk om kvinner i Holmenkollstafetten," *Aftenposten*, November 8, 1973.

was, however, growing support for women's participation in the Holmenkollen relay among many of the NFIF's male and female members, as well as
among the members of other organized sports as indicated by the petition's
signatures.[39] Additionally, popular papers like *Dagbladet, Arbeiderbladet*
(later *Dagsavisen*) and *Fædrelandsvennen* sided with the Action Committee
– though not all male journalists supported them. Under the heading "Women
(without a smart strategy) in the Holmenkolen-relay?" one of *VG*'s journalists
wrote: "Honestly, is it really that important [for women] to take part in the
Holmenkollen relay, which for many years has had too many participants?
Do they not grasp the organizers' justification for why they should not run?"[40]
Three members of the Action Committee served the journalist a reply a few
days later in an article entitled "How to support women's sport." In their answer they quoted him from an article he had written in *Friidrett* in 1971[41]: "A
woman's place is in the kitchen by the stove. She needs to cook and give birth
to children. This has always been the case, and this is how it should continue.
But now women want to run 3000m."[42] After a while, however, *Aftenposten*
became isolated as the only paper that did not support women's participation in the Holmenkollen relay. Even the Norwegian queen (at that time the
crown-princess) expressed her support when a journalist on the national Norwegian TV Channel (NRK) asked her for her opinion. In 1974, more than
one hundred men from various student clubs had slogans against discrimination of women written on their tracksuits during the official opening of the
Holmenkollen relay. Various members of the women's movement, including
Nyfeministene and *Kvinnefronten* also supported the cause.[43]

The next year, 1975, was the Women's Year of the United Nations, which
the Action Committee used to give weight to their campaign. They had built
a strong base of support over the last three years. In support of women's participation, for example, was the former leader (1973–1984) of the Norwegian
Confederation of Sport, Ole Jacob Bangstad. Bangstad had earned a military
Defense Medal after World War II for his efforts against the Nazis. He wrote

---

[39] The list with supportive signatures was published in *Dagbladet*: "Annonse – Ja til kvinnelig
deltakelse i Holmenkollstafetten. Nei til kvinnediskriminering I idretten," *Dagbladet*, November
8, 1973.

[40] Jan Hedenstad, "Kvinner (uten list) i Holmenkollstafetten," *VG*, May 15, 1973.

[41] Jan Hedenstad, *Friidrett 12*, 1971.

[42] Sofie Hvidsten Harnes, Kari Hogseth & Gerd von der Lippe, "Hvordan støtte kvinneidretten?,"
VG Debatt, May, 1973.

[43] Vibe, "Kvinneidrettrevolusjonen på 1970-tallet."

a letter to Gerd in 1975, saying "congratulations with the double victory."[44] That year, Gerd's team not only won their race in the Holmenkollen relay, but women also gained official access as participants. Other supporters included the former leader of the Norwegian Sport Federation, Torfinn Bentzen, who in a letter to Gerd expressed his regret that he had not been able to support the women in his position as leader. He assured Gerd, however, that he was not against women's participation in the relay.[45] The leader of the Socialist Party of Norway, professor of social psychology, Berit Ås, also expressed her support, among many others.

The pressure on *Tjalve* was now so strong that the organizers simply could not ignore women. The women's deadline to respond was, however, set much shorter than the men's. Women were formally invited on April second, with a deadline on April seventh, in contrast to the men's deadline on April twenty-first. The Action Committee wrote to all women's clubs to remind them of the short response time.

To the great surprise of the Holmenkollen relay's organizers, thirty women's teams started and finished the run, encouraged and applauded by large numbers of enthusiastic spectators. Contrary to *Aftenposten*'s reassurance some days before the race that women did not know what they were doing in thinking they could participate, the women clearly *did* know what they were doing and had organized themselves very well. The day before this incredible triumph, the editor of *Dagbladet* wrote:

> Tomorrow the ladies are invited to take part in the Holmenkollen-relay for the first time after a couple of years of intense fighting with the equally stubborn organizers of the event. The fact that 30 women's teams are ready to run in this tough competition is a great victory for women's sports on its own. The work carried out by the Holmenkollen-relay Action Committee has been phenomenal. This group not only managed to wipe the floor with the organizers, but they also made them open the temple gate for women (Isdal, 1975).[46]

The final irony was that Ingrid and Gerd – the two women who had started the battle to run in the Holmenkollen relay by taking part illegally in 1972 by pretending they were men – were members of *Tyrving* and not *Tjalve*. Their club won the first legitimate women's race with Gerd on the team in 1975. Even *Af-*

---

[44] Ole Jacob Bangstad, "Gratulerer med dobbelt seier," letter to Gerd von der Lippe, May 12, 1975.

[45] Torfinn Bentzen, "Kjære Gerd," letter to Gerd von der Lippe, October 10, 1973.

[46] Leif Isdal, "De visste hva de gjorde," *Dagbladet – Sport*, May, 1975.

tenposten could not but call this "A new success in the Holmenkollen-relay."[47]

In 1978, the Norwegian leftwing newspaper *Klassekampen* invited people to "[m]arch at ease on the 8th of March," meaning that it had become easier to join the women's march and walk in solidarity on National Women's Day. Large numbers of people participated all over the country. As a result of the media coverage the Holmenkollen relay victory in 1975 had received, Gerd was asked to hold the main appeal in Oslo just before the start of the march and slogans like "Sport for all" and "no to discrimination in sport" were carried high on banners and placards in the air during the event. In other words, while the women's movement and sport in the early 1960s had often been considered distinct entities pursuing two separate causes, the fight for women's inclusion in sport had during the 1970s become an integral part of the women's movement agenda.

Without the fight for equal rights in the 1970s and demands for women's increased inclusion in sport, Norway might not have had a successful long-distance runner like Grete Waitz (1953-2011). Grete won her first Norwegian championship in 1971 in both the 800m and the 1500m. She also won the first ever held 3000m Norwegian championship run in 1973. Between 1971 and 1983 she would collect one victory after the other on the 800m, 1500m, 3000m, as well as in various cross-country running distances nationally and internationally. She probably became most well-known internationally by winning nine editions of the New York Marathon between 1978 and 1988 – which no other runner in history has accomplished – earning her the name "Queen of New York,"[48] and "first lady of the marathon." While men had been running the Olympic marathon since 1896, Grete's accomplishments as successful long distance and marathon runner helped to finally open up Olympic marathon running for women – as late as 1984. Grete won silver on that occasion.

---

[47] Breim, "Suksess – også med jentene," *Aftenposten*, May 12, 1975. It needs to be noted that while Gerd's political activism in Norway had opened the door for women's participation in the Holmenkollen relay and increased the pressure on Norwegian sport more generally on behalf of women's continued inclusion, she herself lost her researcher and teacher positions at the Norwegian School of Sport because she had broken three of the NFIF's rules. She was, however, recruited to help start a new study of sport and outdoor life in the small rural village in Bø, Telemark. Today that college is the University of South-East Norway, where Gerd is Professor Emerita.

[48] Gerd von der Lippe, *Idrett som kulturelle drama* (Oslo: Cappelen Damm, 2001), 214.

Conclusion

May 2022 marked exactly fifty years since Gerd von der Lippe and Ingrid El-lingsen participated illegally in the Holmenkollen relay. To celebrate this an-niversary, several Norwegian newspapers including *Aftenposten* and *Bergens Tidende* reminded its readers of this iconic moment, and the courage it took these women and their supporters to try and change stereotypical gender roles in Norwegian sport and society.[49]

In this chapter we have addressed these pioneering women in the recent his-tory of Norwegian athletics, with a particular focus on the first author's vivid recollections of the Holmenkollen relay in 1972 and her political activism lead-ing up to women's inclusion in the race, from 1975 onwards. In tandem with political shifts and social justice activism in Western Europe and the United States in the 1960s and 1970s, activist groups in Norway also demanded change for various social causes, with a particular focus on women's rights.

Women's rights and sport in the early 1960s in Norway were initially consid-ered two separate causes. However, spurred on by global activism inside and outside of sport in the years that followed, alongside significant political shifts such as Title IX in 1972 in the United States, the struggle for women's rights in sport became more visible and part of a larger global feminist agenda. In this paper we have argued that the political activism of women like Gerd von der Lippe, Ingrid Ellingsen, Berit Mørdre Lammedal in Norway, and Roberta Gibb, Kathrine Switzer in the United States – among many others – has been instrumental in this accomplishment.

What the abovementioned newspaper reports from 2022 also emphasize, is the need for continued conversations about equal opportunities for female ath-letes in the Norwegian context, supported by concrete action. While Gerd (who celebrated her eightieth birthday on 16 November 2022[50]) and her contempo-raries' activism paved and continue to pave the way for younger generations of female athletes to come, much work remains left to be done.

Another area that remains wanting is historical research on women's sport in Norway. Aside from Gerd von der Lippe's work, there are few scholarly his-

---

[49] See Nordli & Fuglehaug Fallsen, "Jentene som står opp." Also published in *Bergens Tidene* on July 1, 2022.

[50] Gerd also tells her story in a Norwegian podcast (ed. Solfrid Bratland-Sanda) around her 80th birthday. See/listen to "E16: Gerd von der Lippe 80 år: Et liv med idrett og kvinnekamp," Tre-nerstudenten – PODash.

torical writings or accounts describing, analyzing, and synthesizing twentieth century Norwegian women's sport history critically and in depth. It is our hope that this chapter might inspire researchers to engage more with women's sport history in academically rigorous ways, and for students in sport institutions and beyond to be curious about, and attentive to the existing but infrequently told *her*stories past and present in sport.

CHAPTER 7

Premiere at a Crossroads: The 1983 Helsinki World Championships in Athletics

Jörg Krieger

Introduction

Studies on sports mega-events have grown immensely over the past decades. Scholars have produced in-depth research on the most economically and politically impactful individual sporting events, such as the Olympic Games or the FIFA World Cup. Others have attempted to conceptualize this continuously changing field of research.[1]

However, those single-sport events that do not meet the defined criteria to be considered mega-events, have escaped academic scrutiny. For example, a recent special issue entitled "The Sport Mega-Events of the 2020s: Governance, Impacts & Controversies" in *Sport in Society* features research articles of conceptual nature and focus on the Olympic Games and the FIFA World Cup only.[2] However, other major sporting events that do not feature multi-sports or football, such as the World Championships in Athletics, are also exceptional happenings worthy of similar academic attention.

There is little doubt that the 1983 World Championships in Athletics, held in the Finnish capital Helsinki, was a unique occasion. Sandwiched between two highly politicized editions of the Olympic Games in 1980 (Moscow, Soviet Union) and 1984 (Los Angeles, USA), it featured athletes from both sides of the Iron Curtain in the core Olympic sport for the first time since 1976. Moreover, the event in Helsinki was the first time that individual athletics world champi-

---

[1] John Horne and Wolfram Manzenreiter, "An Introduction to the Sociology of Sports Mega-Events," *The Sociological Review* 54, no. 2 (2006): 1–24.

[2] Jan Andre Lee Ludvigsen, Joel Rookwood and Daniel Parnell, "The sport mega-events of the 2020s: governance, impacts and controversies," *Sport in Society* 25, no. 4 (2022): 705-711.

onships were held outside the Olympic Games.[3] However, with the political impact of the Olympic Games significantly higher than of single-sport world championships, academics have largely ignored the event. This chapter aims to fill this research gap by exploring the organization of the event and highlighting its multi-faceted significance. Archival sources were collected from the TAHTO Center for Finnish Sports Culture in Helsinki and the World Athletics Archive in Monaco. I argue that the 1983 World Championships in Athletics was a landmark event due to the turbulent times in international athletics and the diversity of new challenges the organizing committee had to navigate. Athletes, sport officials, judges, spectators (in the stadium and in front of television) and investors encountered firsts that left a long-lasting legacy of the 1983 World Championships in Athletics that has escaped the attention of international scholars until now.

The Deal with the IOC

The history of the World Championships in Athletics begins with a deal that prevented the occurrence of such an event for more than seven decades. Pierre de Coubertin, founder of the modern Olympic Movement and the International Olympic Committee (IOC), had opposed the foundation of an independent governing body for the sport of athletics for several years. Coubertin did not want to lose control over the core sports of the Olympic Games, as he considered international sport federations as "instruments of tyranny."[4] Coubertin was concerned that national interests would influence the decision-making within individual governing bodies of sports as he favored a strict division between politics and sport.[5] His opposition led to multiple interpretations of the rules set, culminating in disputes between British and American sport officials at the 1908 London Olympic Games.[6] The Swedish organizers of the 1912 Stockholm

---

[3] Jörg Krieger, "Born on the Wings of Commerce: The World Championships of the International Association of Athletics Federations," *The International Journal of the History of Sport* 33, no. 4 (2016): 418-43.

[4] Quoted in Jörg Krieger, *Power and Politics in World Athletics. A Critical History* (London: Routledge, 2021), 17.

[5] For a critical discussion on the relationship between sport and politics see: John Hoberman, "The Myth of Sport as a Peace-Promoting Political Force," *The SAIS Review of International Affairs* 31, no. 1 (2011), 17–29.

[6] Matthew P. Llewellyn, "The Battle of Shepherd's Bush," *The International Journal of the History of Sport* 28, no. 5 (2011): 688–710.

Olympic Games wanted to avoid any such controversies and pushed for the establishment of what became later known as the International Amateur Athletics Federation (IAAF, since 2020 known as *World Athletics*).[7] The IAAF's founding President Sigfrid Edström convinced Coubertin about the necessity of the federation and found a compromise. The two men agreed that whilst the IAAF should oversee the governance of athletics, the Olympic Games would remain the "world championships" in the sport.[8] In 1913, the year of the IAAF's official foundation, Edström wrote to Coubertin that the IAAF would "acknowledge the Olympic winners as champions of the world and that no other championship-meetings may be held anywhere else."[9]

The IOC-IAAF deal meant that the IAAF's hands were tied when world championships in individual sports started to emerge during the 1920s and 1930s, with interest in spectator sport growing. A small number of traditional Olympic sports such as fencing (foil) in 1926, cycling (road) in 1927, or archery in 1931 introduced world championships outside the Olympic Games. Bound to the agreement with Coubertin and due to Edström's close links to the IOC – he became IOC vice-president in 1931 and IOC president in 1946 – the IAAF did not initiate own global athletics events during the interwar period. The IAAF's leaders kept a tight grip on the amateur character of athletics and defended the sport from potential commercial influences. However, in need of generating more income, the federation did create European Championships in Athletics that were first held in Torino, Italy, in 1934. Thus, when the IAAF decided to stage its European Championships in Oslo in 1946, less than a year after the end of the Second World War, the event saw challenges to amateurism, politics, and gender (see Chapter 5 in this book).

Discussions on independent world championships emerged again in 1956 when the IAAF had run into financial difficulties. However, the IAAF Council, the federation's executive body that was now presided by Lord Exeter David Burghley, opted against the possibility. The Council members considered it too costly for member federations to participate in another international event at the time. Instead, Burghley decided to propose to the IOC to share potential

---

[7] Hans Bolling, *The Beginning of the IAAF. A Study of its Background and Foundation* (Monaco: IAAF, 2007), 8. See also Chapter 1 in this book.

[8] Guy Schultz, The IAAF and the IOC: Their Relationship and its Impact on Women's Participation in Track and Field at the Olympic Games, 1912–1932, unpublished M.A. thesis, International Centre for Olympic Studies, University of Western Ontario, London, ON, Canada, 2000), 23.

[9] Letter, Sigfrid Edström to Pierre de Coubertin, 30 January 1913, Correspondence 1913, J. Sigfrid Edström Collection (hereafter JSEC), Riksarkivet Stockholm (hereafter RAS).

income from television sales – first generated at the 1956 Melbourne Olympic Games – with the international sport federations. Moreover, just like Edström had been, IAAF President Burghley was interwoven in a complex web of personal and institutional interdependencies that prevented him from independent decision-making. He held a position as IOC vice-president and consequently had an interest in maintaining the agreement with the IOC in maintaining the Olympic Games' unique status. Furthermore, Burghley strongly fought for the preservation of amateurism within the Olympic Movement and therefore rejected any potential commercial "distractions" infiltrating athletics. The international press criticized Burghley heavily for his conflict over interest and conservative ruling over the sport. For example, the French newspaper *L'Équipe* accused Burghley of the implementation of a "dictatorship."[10] Yet, Burghley's double role proved to be beneficial for the IAAF as he secured the federation a higher share of the IOC's television revenues compared to the other international sport federations. He later also used the potential organization of world championships as a threat to the IOC when the IAAF pushed for more athletics events for women.[11]

In summary, the conditions that led to the foundation of the IAAF and the personal connections of the federation's first two presidents Edström and Burghley hindered the establishment of world championships in athletics. Whilst prior the to Second World War, few Olympic sports had their own world championships, this changed in the 1950s and 1960s when an increasing number of federations recognized the economic potential of such an event. With the introduction of the World Championships of the International Swimming Federation (FINA) in 1973, the IAAF became the only Olympic sports federation without independent world championships. However, the rise of capitalism also began to affect athletics and those fighting to preserve the idealistic and amateur character of the sport began to come under threat.

---

[10] Letter, Gaston Meyer to David Burghley, n.d., Folder Correspondence David Burghley, IAAF Archive Monaco (hereafter IAAFA).

[11] Letter, David Burghley to Avery Brundage, 27 July 1956, Film 32, Folder 20, Avery Brundage Collection (hereafter ABC).

Turn Towards Commerce

The turn towards the organization of world championships in athletics came in the 1970s when the international amateur sport movement shifted towards commerce. Private broadcasters became increasingly prepared to spend large sums for exclusive television rights. These developments led to the creation of distribution schemes amongst Olympic sports' main stakeholders: the IOC, the NOCs, and the IFs.[12] In parallel, sport marketers entered the scene, trying to convince athletes to wear their brands. German shoe manufacturers *Puma* and *Adidas* battled for the superstars in athletics.[13] The third group was composed of high-profile sponsors which signed long-term deals with sport federations that boosted financial accounts in the sports industry. Significantly, Olympic athletes could still not profit from the commercialization of their sport directly. The amateur regulation remained in place until the mid-1980s with prize money only introduced a decade later.

From the 1970s onwards, wary about the agreement with the IOC and any potential frictions, the IAAF took a two-tiered approach to explore the possibility of staging an independent international athletics event. The first step was the organization of a World Cup for continental teams at which national teams – rather than individuals – competed against each other from 1977 onwards. The element kept the event distinct from individual world championships, i.e. the Olympic Games, for the time being.[14] The new IAAF President Adriaan Paulen, who succeeded Burghley, in 1976 strongly supported the initiative. Paulen was convinced that the IAAF had to organize independent international events to expand the the federation's financial possibilities. Like the IOC and FIFA, sport marketers consulted the IAAF in its attempt to realize its financial potential. In early 1977, the IAAF signed an agreement with sport marketing firm *West Nally* to seek commercial sponsorships for the federation.[15]

Following the success of the first 1977 World Cup, held in Düsseldorf, Paulen, with the support of *West Nally*, pushed for the second step in the process and the implementation of world championships. The IAAF's marketing advisors

---

[12] Stephen R. Wenn and Robert K. Barney, *The Gold in the Rings* (Champaign: University of Illinois Press, 2020).

[13] Krieger, *Power and Politics.*

[14] Krieger, "Born on the Wings."

[15] Minutes, IAAF Council Meeting in Düsseldorf, 5–6 September 1977, Folder IAAF Council Minutes, IAAFA, 12.

were confident that the IAAF could now generate more income than the shares the federation received from the IOC from the Olympic broadcasting revenues. Moreover, the IAAF's larger share of those revenues was under threat from the other sport federations who continuously fought for a more equal distribution scheme. At the 1978 IAAF Congress in Puerto Rico, the IAAF finally decided to break with the IOC-agreement and stage own world championships from 1983 onwards. The IAAF strategically selected that year to avoid any clashes with the FIFA World Cup and the Olympic Games in an attempt to generate greater income from sponsors and broadcasters.[16] In contrast to the Olympic Games, the IAAF and *West Nally* further decided that on-site advertisements were to be allowed for the world championships to increase the revenues from potential sponsors. To be clear, the world championships were not the only event the IAAF initiated in the late 1970s and early 1980s. World Junior Championships, a "Golden Series" and indoor athletics events were created and sold to sponsors in packages. However, the IAAF considered that the world championships would become the crown jewel in its competition calendar.

Other Winds of Change

Athletics' commercialization was not the only change within the sport. Other developments impacted the experiences of administrators, officials, coaches, athletes, and spectators of future world championships, alike.

In the late 1960s, international governing bodies of sport had introduced doping controls. The IOC tested for the first time at the 1968 Winter Olympic Games, in Grenoble, and the IAAF implemented doping controls at the 1971 European Athletics Championships. The doping regulations within athletics were overseen by a newly introduced IAAF Medical Committee. This group of leading international doping scientists became influential in the development of a test for anabolic steroids – without catching a significant number of athletes. Like the IOC Medical Commission that coordinated the doping controls at Olympic Games,[17] the IAAF Medical Committee became responsible for the controls at IAAF events, including the new world championships.

---

[16] Minutes, IAAF Congress in San Juan, 5–6 October 1978, Folder IAAF Congress Minutes, IAA-FA, 54.

[17] Jörg Krieger, *Dope Hunters. The Influence of Scientists on the Global Fight Against Doping in Sport, 1967–1992* (Champaign: Common Ground, 2016).

In parallel, the IAAF continued its dichotomization of gender and required female athletes to undergo sex testing before they could participate in international athletics' competitions.[18] In 1970, the IAAF introduced a standard certificate for all women who had "passed" the IAAF's sex test. Like with anti-doping, no "cheaters" were detected, but instead athletes who did not fall into the gender binary were disqualified. As with the doping controls, the scientists of the IAAF Medical Committee oversaw the collection of all competitors registered for the women's events in athletics.

The sex testing regime paralleled the increase of female participation in international athletics. In the 1920s and 1930s, the IAAF enforced the integration of women's athletics into its federation and the male-only leadership had restricted women to participate only in a few events.[19] This was particularly the case in the longer running disciplines after the IAAF had taken off the 800-metre race following a sensationalized incident of female runners collapsing after the race at the 1928 Olympic Games. The 800-metre run was re-introduced in 1960 and the 1500-metre race added at the 1972 Olympic Games.[20] Most importantly though, women began to campaign for the introduction of the women's marathon from the late 1960s onwards when Kathrine Switzer famously ran and finished the Boston marathon. In 1974, the first international women's marathon was staged in Waldniel, Germany.[21] Towards the end of the 1970s, the women activists had successfully demonstrated to the IAAF that the women's marathon event had global participation and found an advocate in IAAF President Paulen. In 1979, the IAAF sanctioned the first women-only marathon and Paulen successfully began to lobby for the inclusion of the event at the Olympic Games from 1984 onwards.[22] This development directly impacted the organization of the 1983 Athletics World Championships.

---

[18] Lindsay Pieper, *Sex Testing. Gender Policing in Women's Sports* (Champaign: University of Illinois Press, 2016); Jörg Krieger, Lindsay Parks Pieper and Ian Ritchie, "Sex, Drugs and Science: The IOC's and IAAF's Attempts to Control Fairness in Sport," *Sport in Society* 22, no. 9 (2019): 1555–1573.

[19] Jörg Krieger, Michele Krech and Lindsay Parks Pieper, "'Our Sport': The Fight for Control of Women's International Athletics," *The International Journal of the History of Sport* 37, no. 5–6 (2020): 451–472.

[20] Jaime Schultz, "Going the Distance: The Road to the 1984 Olympic Women's Marathon," *The International Journal of the History of Sport* 32, no. 1 (2015): 72–88.

[21] Annemarie Jutel, "'Thou dost run as in flotation', Femininity, reassurance and the emergence of the Women's marathon," *The International Journal of the History of Sport* 20, no. 3 (2003): 17–36.

[22] Schultz, "Going the Distance."

On the administrative level, women also began to push for changes and increased involvement in decision-making by the end of the 1970s. In 1976, two women ran for a seat on the IAAF Council for the first time, but both missed out. It took until the mid-1990s before two women were elected for positions on the federation's executive body with the IAAF Women's Committee pushing hard for more focus on women's athletics and female leadership.[23] The most impactful change on the administrative level came in the election of the Italian sport official Primo Nebiolo to IAAF President in 1981. The eccentric Nebiolo would become the major driving force to accelerate athletics' commercialization. With his controversial method to aid smaller member federations via a newly created technical development programme in exchange for support of his polices, he established an organizational culture that made him practically unchallengeable.[24]

Whilst the developments listed above all concerned politics of sport, wider political issues also heavily impacted international sport by the beginning of the 1980s.[25] After decades of absence, international sport organizations had found a way to include the People's Republic of China (PRC) by altering the name of the sport organizations based in Taiwan. The PRC had stayed away from international sport competitions because it considers Taiwan part of its own territory. By altering Taiwan's official name to "Chinese Taipei," the IOC and the IAAF had forced Taiwan to accept a compromise that allowed the PRC to keep face.[26] Thus, the PRC participated for the first time at the 1984 Los Angeles Olympic Games. Arguably, the biggest political challenge came in the form of the Cold War rivalry between the USA and the Soviet Union that continued to impact sport events throughout the 1980s. Following the Soviet Union's invasion of Afghanistan in December 1979, the USA led a boycott of the 1980 Moscow Olympic Games. In total, sixty-five invited countries did not participate at the Games. Four years later, Eastern bloc countries organized a counter-boycott at

[23] Michele Krech, Jörg Krieger and Lindsay Parks Pieper, "A 'token gesture' in World Athletics governance? The IAAF Women's Committee under Ilse Bechthold, 1990–2005," *Sport in Society* (2022, ahead of print).

[24] Jörg Krieger, "'The Sole Anti-Democratic Federation in the Entire Olympic Movement': Early International Association of Athletics Federations Development Initiatives Between Commercialization and Democratization, 1974–1987," *The International Journal of the History of Sport* 33, no. 12 (2016): 1341–1360.

[25] For a differentiation between politics in sport and politics and sport see: Hans Bonde, "Danish Sport and the Nazi Seizure of Power: Indoctrination, Propaganda and Confrontation," *The International Journal of the History of Sport* 26, no. 10 (2009): 1458–1480.

[26] Yi-Ling Huang and Chen-Huei Wang, "Chinese Question in the Olympic Movement: From the Perspective of Taiwan," *The International Journal of the History of Sport* 30, no. 17 (2013): 2052–2068.

the 1984 Los Angeles Olympic Games. Thus, the major sporting superpowers did not meet each other on the biggest global stage for more than a decade between the 1976 and the 1988 Olympic Games. In athletics the first international clash was to be the newly inaugurated world championships in Helsinki.

The Success of the Finnish Bid

In view of the multitude of challenges the organizers of the first World Athletics Championships were expected to face, the selection of the host city was of paramount importance to the IAAF. Following the decision at the 1978 Congress to stage world championships, the IAAF sent a circular letter to all member federations informing about the decision and asking for bids to host the event. Federations were given more than a year to apply with the bidding process closing on January 1, 1980.[27] Two bids reached the IAAF: one from the Finnish member federation with the host city of Helsinki and one from the West German member federation with the host city of Stuttgart.

Finland seemed to be a natural choice for the IAAF due to the country's athletics tradition. The country had produced numerous successful athletes prior to the First World War and during the interwar years. Following sixteen years without a gold medal in the Olympic Games, the 1970s saw a revival of Finnish success in athletics that the Finnish Athletics Federation wanted to carry into the first world championships, ideally on home soil. The bidding committee highlighted Finland's vast athletics history in the bidding documents, especially the country's long list of middle- and long-distance runners: ranging from Hannes Kolehmainen to Paavo Nurmi and Lasse Viren.[28] The Finnish bid emphasized the organization of previous international athletics events staged in Helsinki. The city was host to the 1971 European Championships in athletics and had staged the European Cup Final in athletics in 1977.[29] At both events, the organizers could rely on a large number of volunteers, and it was outlined in the bidding documents that the volunteering culture in Finland would significantly

---

[27] Minutes, IAAF Congress in San Juan, 57.

[28] Letter, Suomen Urheiluliitto to IAAF, 17 December 1979, Folder "Suomen Urheiluliitto – Hbb21-MM-83 Application Process," TAHTO Center for Finnish Sports Culture (hereafter TAHTO), 1.

[29] Letter, Lord Major of the City of Helsinki Teuvo Aura to IAAF, 5 December 1979, Folder "Suomen Urheiluliitto – Hbb21-MM-83 Application Process," TAHTO Center for Finnish Sports Culture (hereafter TAHTO).

contribute to a modest overall budget.[30] Helsinki's Olympic Stadium, site of the 1952 Olympic Games, was foreseen as the main site for the championships.

The bid from Stuttgart differed little from the Finnish application. West German IAAF Council member August Kirsch claimed that Stuttgart's bid was superior because it entered the bid with a stadium of higher capacity allied with a higher overall budget due to projected ticket sales. The West German Athletics Federation had already successfully hosted the 1977 World Cup in Düsseldorf and considering that the World Cup was regarded as the run-up event to world championships, the German bidding committee had hoped that the IAAF Council would award the event to Germany again. They were proven to be mistaken, however. In March 1980, the majority of the IAAF Council members followed Helsinki's arguments and voted eleven to six votes in favor of the Finnish capital.

Kirsch argued that the Finnish bid succeeded as it convinced the IAAF Council member about Finland's long athletics tradition and the interest of the Finnish public in the sport.[31] This was also suspected by the Finns in the official report of the world championships.[32] However, the political circumstances surrounding the bidding process appeared to have been a more decisive factor. This fact was also noted by German media.[33] Should West Germany, a close ally of the United States, have been selected as host, the IAAF would have had a significantly higher risk of a potential boycott from the Eastern bloc. Finland, on the contrary, remained outside the conflict between the great powers and did not join the North Atlantic Treaty Organization (NATO) as it tried to avoid conflicts with the Soviet Union. Such neutrality was highlighted in Helsinki's bid, emphasizing that "our good relations to all the IAAF member countries guarantee that every guests [sic] will feel most welcome in Finland."[34] This was reiterated in Helsinki's presentation to the IAAF Council in March 1980 when the bidding committee argued: "the neutral standpoint of Finland and the stable political scene would ensure that there was little chance of a disturbance of a political nature."[35] Clearly, the West German athletics' officials were aware of

---

[30] Letter, Suomen Urheiluliitto to IAAF, 17 December 1979, 2.

[31] August Kirsch, "Zum Geleit," in *Leichathletik WM 1983*, ed. Robert Hartmann and Michael Genandt (Munich: Copress, 1984), 2.

[32] Report, "The Official Report of the World Championships in Athletics 1983," Folder "Suomen Urheiluliitto – Hbb53-MM-83 Correspondence with IAAF, B 1983," TAHTO, 2.

[33] "Helsinki stiehlt selbst Olympia die Show," *Leichtathletik* 31 (1983), 1073.

[34] Letter, Suomen Urheiluliitto to IAAF, 17 December 1979, 1.

[35] Minutes, IAAF Council Meeting in Paris, 10–12 March 1980, Folder IAAF Council Minutes,

this advantage and pointed out to the IAAF Council members "that they were voting here for a City[sic] and not for a country."[36] However, their attempts to negate the political connotations did not have the desired effect.

Following the success of their bid, the Finns put together an organizing committee under the leadership of Carl-Olaf Homén, who resigned from his post as President of the Finnish Athletics Federation to focus entirely on the organization of the world championships. The organizing committee was composed of fifteen individuals from different branches and oversaw the preparations of the event. Thirteen committees were established with different focus areas ranging from security to liaison.[37] The focus on volunteering and the modest approach towards the organization can be seen in the fact that for the first two years of operation, only one person was full-time employed for the preparation of the event. This number grew to eleven at the end of 1982 and peaked at 34 for the time of the event.[38]

In a somewhat ironic turn of events, the first athletics world championships – an event with the expressed purpose to make athletics more commercial and the IAAF more profitable – were thus due to take place in a stadium with a statue of Finnish running legend Paavo Nurmi outside. The Swedish-led IAAF had made Nurmi a scapegoat in 1932, when it had banned the runner for life following questions over his amateur status.[39] Now, Helsinki and Nurmi stood symbolically for the departure into a new, economically-driven era of athletics – and the organizing committee did not fall short of highlighting that Nurmi's (and other former athletics' stars) popularity in Finland was at the heart of the upcoming championships. For example, Homén informed the international athletics community in 1982 that "Finland is the country of Paavo Nurmi and Lasse Viren and that is why the atmosphere in the country is extremely favorable towards the First World Championships in Athletics."[40]

IAAFA, 10.

[36] *Ibid.*, 11.

[37] Report, "The Official Report of the World Championships in Athletics 1983," 4ff.

[38] *Ibid.*, 13.

[39] Leif Yttergren, "J. Sigfrid Edström and the Nurmi Affair of 1932: The struggle of the amateur fundamentalists against professionalism in the Olympic movement," *Journal of Olympic History* 15, no. 3 (2007): 21–31

[40] Letter, Carl-Olaf Homén and Lauri Tarasti to Head of Sports Division, 15 March 1982, Folder "Suomen Urheiluliitto – Hbb53-MM-83 Press Release, B 1982," TAHTO.

Pioneering in the Organization of
World Championships in Athletics

Political Maneuvering

Despite the political symbolism of competition between athletes from the Eastern and the Western bloc, the Organizing Committee had to deal with relatively
few political furors. The most severe issue arose in July 1983, a few weeks
before the beginning of the event. The USSR Light Athletic Federation had
complained to IAAF President Primo Nebiolo about the accreditation of representatives from the radio station *Free Europe*.[41] *Free Europe* had received open
support from the US government since its foundation in the late 1940s and
from the Central Intelligence Agency (CIA) since the 1970s to provide information and political commentary to the people of communist Eastern Europe.[42]
Characterized as "subversive slanderous radio station," the Soviet federation
objected the accreditation. Rather than rejecting the demand outright, Nebiolo
forwarded the letter to Helsinki asking for clarification. The IAAF President
did not want to risk a potential boycott. The organizers, however, explained
that there was no legal basis for a rejection of *Free Europe*'s application for
accreditations due to the freedom of press principles in Finland. Thus, *Free
Europe*'s reporters were allowed at the world championships, but the Soviets
did not complain again. The initial saber-rattling appears to have sufficed, but
such approach foreshadowed Soviet complaints about security concerns and accreditations for Soviet citizens ahead of the 1984 Los Angeles Olympic Games.
This, of course, eventually led to the USSR boycott of the Games.

   In another political matter, the organizing committee followed national politics. In what appears to have been the most delicate political decision of the
world championships, the organizers banned the Palestinian Athletics Federation from using the Palestinian flag during the opening ceremony. Palestine
had been granted IAAF membership in 1978 under the name of "Gaza Amateur
Athletic Association" after the international governing body had sided with Israel for decades when it was impossible to grant a membership to a federation
which did not govern athletics in a clearly defined geographical territory. How-

---

[41] Fax, USSR Light Athletic Federation to Lauri Tarasti, 28 July 1983, Folder "Suomen Urheiluliitto – Hbb53-MM-83 Correspondence with IAAF, B 1983," TAHTO.

[42] Stacey Cone, "Presuming A Right to Deceive," *Journalism History* 24, no. 4 (1999): 148–156.

ever, by the late 1970s, most Asian member federations supported a Palestinian application to the IAAF, and the Palestinian federation highlighted that it represented the area of Gaza.[43] In 1981, the IAAF Congress allowed the federation, again on suggestion by Arab-led Asian member federations, to change its name to "Palestine Amateur Athletic Federation" after intense debates, which effectively enabled participation at the world championships in 1983.[44] This was a significant step considering that the IOC and other major governing bodies of sport continued to reject Palestinian membership applications.[45]

However, whilst Palestinian athletes could as a result compete on the track and on the field – the organizing committee was not challenged on sporting matters – the situation differed for political matters. Even though the Finnish bid for the world championships propagated the idea that Finland had friendly relations with all countries, exceptions existed. In concrete terms, Finland held close diplomatic ties to Israel and did not recognize Palestine as an independent country. Consequently, the Finnish government denied the Palestinian Athletics Federation to march into the stadium with the Palestinian flag during the opening and the closing ceremonies. After the event, the Palestinian federation complained vigorously about this "political fleecing" and highlighted that it had provided a flag on demand of the organizing committee, but the decision was reverted due to political pressure.[46] Importantly, the IAAF sided with the Palestinians and reprimanded the organizing committee for denying the Palestinian federation the right to use their flag. However, the IAAF, in the response letter to the federation, also highlighted that:

> The Organizing Committee, the IAAF and the Palestine AAF were put in a most difficult position at the last minute when the matter was taken out of our hands and taken up at Government level, and whilst we deplored the fact that the World Championship Rules were disregarded, nevertheless we could not alter the stand taken by the Government of Finland.[47]

---

[43] Minutes, IAAF Congress in San Juan, 27.

[44] Minutes, IAAF Congress in Rome, 1–2 September 1981, Folder IAAF Congress Minutes, IAA-FA, 12f.

[45] Issam Khalidi, "Palestine Goes International: On Palestinian Achievements in Sports throughout the Decades," The Palestine Chronicle, 8 October 2021, https://www.palestinechronicle.com/palestine-goes-international-on-palestinian-achievements-in-sports-throughout-the-decades/.

[46] Letter, Zuhair Abu Al-Kheir to IAAF, 22 September 1983, Folder "Suomen Urheiluliitto – Hbb53-MM-83 Correspondence with IAAF, A 1982-83," TAHTO.

[47] Letter, IAAF General Secretary John Holt to Zuhair Abu Al-Kheir, 6 October 1983, Folder "Suomen Urheiluliitto – Hbb53-MM-83 Correspondence with IAAF, A 1982-83," TAHTO.

With no prior experience in overseeing such a high-caliber sporting event as the world championships before, it appears that the IAAF had naively underestimated the political realities in hosting countries. The Finnish government's intervention concerning the Palestinian flag brutally demonstrated to the IAAF that it could not act outside national laws, however. The IOC had learned similar lessons previously, when the Canadian government denied Taiwanese athletes visas to compete at the 1976 Montreal Olympic Games.[48]

Despite some smaller incidents, the 1983 World Championships in Athletics came to be generally characterized by its unpolitical nature, during a time when international sport regularly became the battle ground for ideological differences. Even though this success cannot be directly attributed to the IAAF or the organizing committee, the selection of Helsinki as a rather neutral political ground seems to have been a wise move. As he had done during the bidding process, Homén regularly emphasized that the Finnish athletics federation and the organizing committee held good relationships to all member federations. This situation had contributed to separate politics from sport in the run up and during the championships.[49] In fact, this was not simply reduced to rhetoric. Due to the IAAF's compromise on the question of the "two Chinas," athletes from the PRC and from Chinese Taipei participated at a major international sport events for the first time.[50] The fact that this happened in Helsinki was symbolic, as the IOC's invitation to the National Olympic Committees from both regions had marked the beginning of the "two Chinas" conflict within global sport.[51] Zhu Jinhua became the first the athlete from the PRC to win a gold medal at an international athletics event, a year prior to becoming the first to do so in an athletics competition at the Olympic Games. Similarly, the United States and the Soviet Union sent large delegations of athletes and officials to the championships. Both camps saw the emergence of future athletics' stars in Carl Lewis (USA) and Sergey Bubka (Soviet Union), who both won gold medals in Helsinki. West- and East-Germany also met each other on the track and on the field, even though

---

[48] Donald Macintosh, Donna Greenhorn and Michael Hawes, "Trudeau, Taiwan, and the 1976 Montreal Olympics," *American Review of Canadian Studies* 21, no. 4 (1999): 423–448.

[49] Brochure, "Helsinki. The City of Athletics," Folder "Suomen Urheiluliitto – Hbb53-MM-83 Correspondence with IAAF, A 1982-83," TAHTO, 6.

[50] Only two athletes from Chinese Taipei participated in the world championships.

[51] Yuxiang Hao, "A Political History of Chinese Elite Sport During the Great Proletariat Cultural Revolution, 1966–1976," unpublished Ph.D. thesis (The University of Texas at Austin, 2020), 222.

those two rivals competed more regularly with each other – but more on a continental than on an international level.

In total, competitors from 152 nations participated in the first world championships, making it the most universal sporting event at the time, outperforming the Olympic Games.[52] In comparison, the 1972 Olympic Games had seen athletes from 121 nations participating and the number dropped for the 1976 and 1980 editions of the Olympic Games due to political boycotts. To be sure, the IAAF's Primo Nebiolo vigorously pushed the organizing committee to ensure such a high number of participating federations.

Nebiolo had already, in 1982, commented: "It was important to have more than 100 countries represented in Helsinki, and thus make it the largest athletics event in IAAF history. As these Championships were the first, outside the Olympic Games, the entire Sports Movement would be watching to assess the success."[53] Then, shortly ahead of the championships, he sent a letter to Homén in which he pointed out that "the next 20 days are vital to ensure <u>full participation</u> of our members [emphasis added]." He required that Homén sent a report every three days so that the IAAF could chase members. The worldwide expansion of athletics became one of the key objectives during Nebiolo's reign at the helm of the IAAF and therefore it is of little surprise that he wanted to see as many federations as possible at the first world championships. However, in practical terms, it was mainly down to the organizing committee to communicate with the member federations and considering the smooth running of the event, their efforts must be highly commended. In short, the Helsinki World Championships were a highly significant sport political event – due to its lack of incidents and the primary focus remaining on the sporting spectacle.

Designing Marketing Agreements

Whereas the political influencing of the world championships was not controllable for the organizing committee, the marketing and financial aspects of the event certainly were. This was in no small part a result of the IAAF's part shift of responsibility for contracting sponsors and television broadcasters to the organizers, rather than undertaking the negotiations itself. The organizing committee

---

[52] Report, "The Official Report of the World Championships in Athletics 1983," 19.

[53] Minutes, IAAF Council Meeting in Kingston, 18–20 April 1982, Folder IAAF Council Minutes, IAAFA, 6.

was supported in this task by *West Nally*, which now worked under the framework of the *Société Monegasque du Promotion Internationale* (SMPI). In March 1982, West Nally presented nine big companies to the organizing committee, all of whom were interested in signing a sponsorship package for $1 million.[54]

However, throughout 1982, it became clear to the Finnish organizers that the processes to sign agreements were becoming drawn out. This was a concern as the organizing committee relied on the income from the marketing agreements to move forward with the planning process.[55] For example, Homén informed Nebiolo in spring 1982 that he had signed a marketing agreement with IVECO, presented to him by *West Nally*. Homén argued that it was necessary to sign the major agreements as soon as possible to ensure financial security.[56] At the same time, internal issues between *West Nally* and SMPI meant that the IAAF cut the marketing agreement in September 1982 and decided to sign contracts independently.[57] As a result, the organizing committee ended up drafting the marketing agreements that were later used also for subsequent championships.[58] This development certainly increased the responsibility of the Finnish organizers as they were now provided with the task of identifying additional sponsors. In December 1982, nine months before the start of the world championships, a new deal with *West Nally* was agreed, but by this time initial deals had already been signed. The organizers also had to deal with specific demands, such as *Coca-Cola*'s request to solely sell *Coca-Cola* products in the stadium during the competitions.[59] Another agreement with a tobacco company could not be signed due to national regulations preventing tobacco advertisements in Finland.

---

[54] Minutes, Meeting between the Organizing Committee of the World Championships and the West Nally Group, 5 March 1982, Folder "Suomen Urheiluliitto – Hbb53-MM-83 Correspondence with IAAF, A 1982–83," TAHTO.

[55] The distribution scheme of the world championships revenues foresaw that the organizing committee receive all income from ticket sales and 25% of the television and marketing sales. The IAAF would receive 75% of the television and marketing income. Report, Report to the IAAF Council by the Organizing Committee of the First World Championships in Athletics, n.d., Folder "Suomen Urheiluliitto – Hbb53-MM-83 Correspondence with IAAF, A 1982–83," TAHTO.

[56] Letter, Carl-Olaf Homén to Primo Nebiolo, 31 March 1982, Folder "Suomen Urheiluliitto – Hbb53-MM-83 Correspondence with IAAF, A 1982–83," TAHTO.

[57] Minutes, IAAF Council Meeting in Athens, 1–2 September 1982, Folder IAAF Council Minutes, IAAFA, 10.

[58] Fax, Lauri Tarasti to Luciano Barra, 4 October 1982, Folder "Suomen Urheiluliitto – Hbb53-MM-83 Correspondence with IAAF, A 1982–83," TAHTO.

[59] Fax, Luciano Barra to Lauri Tarasti, 6 October 1982, Folder "Suomen Urheiluliitto – Hbb53-MM-83 Correspondence with IAAF, A 1982-83," TAHTO.

Amongst the early, independent deals was an agreement between the IAAF/ organizing committee and Japanese electronic components manufacturer *TDK*.[60] The negotiations with *TDK* had been mainly held by the Finns and in November 1982, it was Homén who signed the original agreement and pushed the IAAF to sign it.[61] This insight is significant as since then, *TDK* has become the longest-serving international sponsor of the sport, a fact in which both the company and the IAAF take great pride.[62] In fact, *TDK*'s deal with the IAAF also marks the beginning of Asian companies' major investments into the sponsorship of international sport. *TDK* took on a pioneering role and was followed by *Panasonic* who also joined the IOC's TOP sponsor programme in 1985. What is less known, however, is that the IAAF deal with *TDK* goes back to the initiative and pressure from the Finnish organizing committee of the 1983 World Championships in Athletics. The ties between Finnish athletics and *TDK* also endured after the event. In collaboration with *Nike*, *TDK* sponsored an elite team of athletics competitors to which many Finns were recruited until the late 1980s.[63]

As with marketing agreements, the organizing committee found itself as a deal broker when it came to the television contracts for the world championships. Several correspondences between the IAAF and the Finnish organizers detail how the latter kept IAAF officials in the loop about the negotiations that eventually the IAAF itself was asked to sign (jointly with the organizers). Contracts were signed with major broadcasting companies in several countries, including *Eurovision*, *Asahi-TV* (Japan), and *NBC* (USA). Importantly, even though the organizing committee tied down large television contracts, this did not mean a faultless production of the events. For example, the Danish media complained after the world championships that results were reported very slowly to the audiences and the camera positions, all installed under the guidance of Finnish Broadcasting Company (YLE), were flawed.[64]

---

[60] Agreement, IAAF/Suomen Urheiluliitto and Daiko Advertising on behalf of TDK, 29 November 1982, Folder "Suomen Urheiluliitto – Hbb53-MM-83 Correspondence with IAAF, A 1982-83," TAHTO.

[61] Fax, Lauri Tarasti to Luciano Barra, 15 November 1982, Folder "Suomen Urheiluliitto – Hbb53-MM-83 Correspondence with IAAF, A 1982-83," TAHTO.

[62] "TDK Has Continuously Supported the World Athletics Championships," *TDK*, 14 July 2022, https://www.tdk.com/en/athletic/news/202207_01.html.

[63] Jouni Lavikainen, "'If the IOC Finds Out about This, All of You Will Be Declared Professionals': The Professionalization of Finnish Track Athletes from the 1960s to 1980s," *The International Journal of the History of Sport* 38, no. 10–11 (2021): 1050–1066.

[64] Peter Bistrup, "VM i Danmark," *Dansk Atletik* 9 (September 1983), 15.

The responsibility for marketing aspects, resulted in the organizing committee developing ambitious goals for the logo of the world championships. Already in early 1982, it had approached the IAAF to select the emblem as the permanent logo of the IAAF's world championships. In a letter to all IAAF member federation, the organizing committee hoped that the logo "could achieve a status within athletics equal to that of the Olympic rings as emblem of the Olympic Games."[65] This proposal was rejected by IAAF President Nebiolo, however, on the grounds of not wanting to see the first world championships having too big an influence on potential future competitions. Similarly, the IAAF rejected a proposal by the Finnish Athletics Federation to introduce a trophy for "the best athlete of the world championships" that could have been awarded at all future championships. The federation had a sponsor in Finnish firm Sampo to donate a silver trophy worth between $200,000 and $250,000 as a prize. The winning athlete would receive a miniature version of the trophy for his/her own possession.[66] Aware about potential conflicts with its own amateur regulations, the IAAF rejected the proposal at a Council meeting in December 1982. The meeting minutes record that Nebiolo "acknowledged that the trophy was handsome, but its presentation could potentially cause difficulties."[67] Clearly, there should not have been an incentive for potentially disrupting the restrictive amateur regulations in place.

In summary, the organizing committee of the 1983 World Championships in Athletics certainly had to take on a pioneering role in the financial aspects of the event. Importantly, their success was to be of benefit not only for the organization of the championship itself – but for the entire global athletics community. The IAAF set up a development fund to support less financially powerful federations with the surplus from the event. In future world championships, however, the hosts would not be given such an advanced role as was the case in Helsinki. In 1985, the IAAF signed a contract with marketing consultants *International Sport and Leisure* (ISL), including guarantees that the company would find sponsors for a total sum of more than $30 million to sponsor athletics events for a four-year period, rather than solely the world championships.[68]

---

[65] Letter, Carl-Olaf Homén and Lauri Tarasti to Head of Sports Division.

[66] Letter, Suomen Urheiluliitto to IAAF Council, n.d., Folder "Suomen Urheiluliitto – Hbb53-MM-83 Correspondence with IAAF, A 1982-83," TAHTO.

[67] Minutes, IAAF Council Meeting in Helsinki, 10–12 December 1982, Folder IAAF Council Minutes, IAAFA, 17.

[68] Minutes, IAAF Council Meeting in Los Angeles, 12 August 1984, Folder IAAF Council Minutes, IAAFA, 6.

Fittingly, their first sponsor became *TDK*, based on the negotiations the Finns had undertaken a few years earlier.

Women's Involvement

As outlined above, by the beginning of the 1980s, the IAAF could no longer ignore the pressure for the inclusion of the women's marathon into its competitions. Thus, it was clear early on that the Finnish organizing committee had to plan for this event. In February 1982, however, the IAAF changed the timetable for the championships and moved the women's marathon from the final weekend to the very beginning of the event. The organizing committee had to bow to this request, which meant an additional $100,000 in costs due to additional security.[69] This switch meant, however, that in the eventual winner of the marathon, the Norwegian Grete Waitz, a woman would become the first ever world champion in athletics. Considering the IAAF's historical resistance against women's engagement in athletics this must certainly be considered a landmark event – if more likely for public relations reasons than for a full commitment to women's athletics. After all, women had to continue to fight for the inclusion of more disciplines into the competition programme for several years.[70]

In contrast to the decision to move the women's marathon, guided by international developments, the Finnish organizing committee pushed independently for the involvement of women in important roles in the management of the event. This was in stark opposition to the IAAF's policy, but reflected Finland's strong push for gender equality. In 1980, the country's government implemented an Action Plan for Gender Equality that promoted gender equality in all administrative units in Finland. Against this background, the Finnish organizing committee appointed Pirjo Häggman as the "mayor" of the athletes' village for the world championships.[71] In 1981, Häggman became (together with Venezuelan Flor Isava-Fonseca) the first female IOC member. This pointed towards (slow) change within sport governing bodies. At the Olympic Games, where the Olympic village also takes on a central role in the organization of the event, only men had been appointed as mayors until

---

[69] Minutes, Meeting between the Organizing Committee of the World Championships and the West Nally Group.

[70] Krech et al., "A 'token gesture' in World Athletics governance?"

[71] Letter, Carl-Olaf Homén and Lauri Tarasti to Head of Sports Division.

1983. Thus, the Finns – as in so many other areas of the world championships – clearly took on a pioneering role in this regard.

Controversies Around Testing

With doping and sex testing, core elements of sport organization's attempts to combat potential cheaters in their sports, the Finnish organizers naturally had to coordinate such efforts at the world championships and enter unchartered territory. Support was provided through the IAAF Medical Commission's Arne Ljungvist (Sweden), who had the overall supervision over the medical procedures as well as Grégory Vorobiev (Soviet Union) and Arnold Beckett (Great Britain), who oversaw the doping and sex controls at the event.

Finding an adequate laboratory to conduct the doping analysis turned out to be the biggest challenges for the organizers. At the beginning of the 1980s, anti-doping laboratory experts under the leadership of German biochemists Manfred Donike pushed for the introduction of a new screening method to detect exogenous testosterone in athletes' bodies.[72] Moreover, Donike, who was also a member of the IAAF Medical Committee, successfully lobbied the IOC and the IAAF to accept gas chromatography–mass spectrometry (GC-MS) as the standard analytical method to identify different substances within a doping test sample.[73] The world championships in Helsinki was the first time that this technique was used in international sport.[74] It was the responsibility of the sport organization's medical bodies to ensure that those procedures were conducted adequately. Thus, accreditation procedures for anti-doping laboratories were introduced in the early 1980s.[75]

With the costs for the tests and the analyses to be carried by the organizing committee, the Finnish organizers naturally had a strong interest in the accreditation of a laboratory in Helsinki. Therefore, it sent a representative to an anti-doping workshop, held in Cologne in 1981, at which the newest anti-doping technol-

---

[72] Terry Todd, "'Anabolic Steroids: The Gremlins of Sport'," *Journal of Sport History* 14, no. 1 (1987): 100–101.

[73] Jan Todd and Daniel L. Rosenke, "'The Event That Shook the Whole World Up': Historicizing the 1983 Pan-American Games Doping Scandal," *The International Journal of the History of Sport* 33, no. 1–2 (2016): 164–185.

[74] Robert Voy and Kirk D. Deeter, *Drugs, Sports and Politics* (Champaign, Ill: Leisure

[75] Press, 1991), 5. The authors argue that this was the case in Caracas at the PanAmerican Games, but this information is incorrect. GC/MS screening was used in Helsinki, but not overseen by Manfred Donike but less GC/MS experienced scientists. It is plausible that this led to different results in Caracas than in Helsinki.

ogy was being presented and discussed. It was reported back to the organizing committee, however, that the process to becoming accredited would be costly and complicated.[76] There was also confusion as to whether the IAAF would suggest that the doping samples would be analyzed by a laboratory in Sweden. In order to keep the analysis within the country, the organizers therefore had to work closely with potential laboratories. Eventually, they settled for the private *Yhtyneet Medix Laboratoriot* in Helsinki, which was accredited by the IAAF Medical Committee in months before the championships.[77] Thus, the World Athletics Championships provided a warning example for future organizing committees on how anti-doping science would become a significant issue to be addressed. Event hosts continued to be obliged to implement sport organization's control mechanisms – without being able to influence those processes.

Despite the introduction of the official accreditation procedure and new GC/MS screening methods for testosterone, the doping controls at the 1983 World Championships did not produce any positive results. In contrast, a few weeks later, at the Pan-American Games in Caracas, Venezuela, two athletics' competitors tested positive, and a large part of the US athletics delegation – who had also competed in Helsinki – fled in fear of the more sophisticated tests.[78] This led to speculation that the tests in Helsinki were not accurate or not reported adequately.[79] Manfred Donike, though not present himself in Helsinki, later pointed to the fact that there had been unreported positive tests.[80] And indeed, archival sources highlight that two samples had a high testosterone ratio, but they were, after re-tests in Lwondon, declared negative.[81] To be clear, the Finnish organizing committee had no influence on the reporting of potential positive results as this was the responsibility of the IAAF Medical Committee representatives. However, the episode demonstrates how the organizers had to implement expensive doping control techniques to support sport organization's superficial anti-doping strategies, just for the organizers to decide whether they want to report positive controls at all.

---

[76] Krieger, *Dope Hunters*.

[77] Letter, Mauri Mattila to Carl-Olaf Homén, n.d., Folder "Suomen Urheiluliitto – Hbb53-MM-83 Correspondence with IAAF, A 1982-83," TAHTO.

[78] Minutes, IAAF Council Meeting in Helsinki, 4–5 August 1983, Folder IAAF Council Minutes, IAAFA, 2.

[79] Todd and Rosenke, "'The Event That Shook the Whole World Up'."

[80] Charles Dubin, *Commission of Inquiry into the Use of Drugs and Banned Practices Intended to Increase Athletic Performances* (Ottawa: Canadian Government Publishing Centre, 1990), 446.

[81] Voy and Deeter, *Drugs, Sports and Politics*.

Like the doping controls, the significance of the sex-testing procedures in Helsinki was only revealed in the years after the event. The Finnish organizers had to facilitate the sex chromatin sample collection and analysis procedures, but the overall supervision had the IAAF Medical Committee. Amongst the women issued a "certificate of femininity" in Helsinki was 22-year-old Spanish hurdler Mariá José Martínez-Patiño.[82] Martínez-Patiño had been raised as a girl and naturally expected to receive the certificate. Two years later, however, she forgot to bring her certificate to the 1985 Universiade in Kobe, Japan. Martínez-Patiño was re-tested and the second test proved a genetic difference in her chromosome competition that resulted in the IAAF banning her from future competitions.[83] The result had a decisive impact on Martínez-Patiño's personal life and athletic career. Irrespectively of the personal consequences for the athlete, the outcome of the test in Helsinki highlighted the inaccuracy of the sex tests at the time, adding further concerns over those who have been subject to the procedure. Controversially, the IAAF had informed the organizing committee prior to the world championships that if an athlete appeared on the list of already tested athletes, "that it is not necessary to-retest the athlete."[84] Thus, if such instructions have also been made ahead of the 1985 Universiade, Martínez-Patiño's androgenic insensitivity would have probably gone unnoticed throughout her career.

Conclusion: A Highly Underestimated Event

The 1983 World Championships in Athletics in Helsinki were a unique event, not only because it marked the beginning of the organization of independent world championships in the most popular Olympic sport. As demonstrated in this chapter, multiple exceptional circumstances resulted in the organizing committee facing unprecedented challenges. The Finns had to wrestle with processes of modernism in the sport of athletics alongside officials' crumbling conservatism. As a result, the world championships were a premiere in many ways, much beyond its official status as first international athletics world championships. Thus, like the 1948 European Championships in Athletics in Oslo (see Chapter 5 in this book),

---

[82] Minutes, "Meeting of the IOC Medical Commission's Subcommisson on Doping and the Biochemistry of Sport in Cologne, 29 September 1983," Folder IOC Medical Commission, IOC Archive.

[83] Mariá José Martínez-Patiño, "Personal Account: A Woman Tried and Tested," *The Lancet* 366, no. S38 (2005).

[84] *Ibid.*

the 1983 World Championships were a milestone in the history of athletics. The inconspicuousness of the event has contributed to the lack of academic attention towards the event. However, it appears that the modest and flawless organization – owing much down to the work of the organizing committee – must be considered the main reason for the championships' success.

The IAAF's selection of Finland as the host country during a highly politicized time proved to be a master stroke. The Finns' political neutrality and unagitated preparations of the event allowed the politically rivaling nations from the Soviet Union, the USA, West- and East Germany as well as the PRC and Taiwan to compete at the event. The world championships therefore outshone the Olympic Games in 1980 and 1984, two events that were boycotted by numerous countries for political reasons. The Finns further counted on their athletic tradition as a key argument in the bidding process and the flawless organization of the event, supported by a larger number of volunteers, proved the nations' strong interest in athletics. And if showcasing their athletics' heritage was not enough, other Finnish traditions were also introduced to the athletics community. After a meeting in Helsinki in 1982, IAAF officials thanked the organizers for their hospitality and highlighted specifically their invitation to a Finnish sauna. "Once this practice has been tried, it leaves you impatiently waiting for the next opportunity," wrote IAAF General Secretary John Holt.[85]

The world championships also had a decisive impact on the IAAF as it accelerated the processes of commerce in the sport. The revenues created from the Helsinki event provided the federation with a secure budget to operate following decades of austerity.[86] Thus, the first world championships can also be considered as the point of acceptance of capitalism in international athletics.

---

[85] Letter, IAAF Bureau Secretary B. Bedford to Lauri Tarasti, 26 July 1983, Folder "Suomen Urheiluliitto – Hbb53-MM-83 Correspondence with IAAF, B 1983," TAHTO.

[86] Letter, IAAF General Secretary John Holt to Lauri Tarasti, 17 December 1982, Folder "Suomen Urheiluliitto – Hbb53-MM-83 Correspondence with IAAF, A 1982/83," TAHTO.

CHAPTER 8

An Anti-Hero on the Running Track: The Media Picture of Sara Wedlund during the 1995 World Championships in Athletics in Gothenburg and the 1996 Atlanta Olympic Games

John Berg

Introduction

On June 11, 2021, former Swedish long-distance runner Sara Wedlund passed away at the age of 45. Wedlund, undoubtedly one of Sweden's most successful track-and-field athletes during the 1990s, had her national breakthrough at the 1995 Gothenburg World Championships in Athletics in which she set a new Swedish record at 5000 meters.[1] Before ending her elite-level career in 2003, she had won various medals in both domestic and international competitions. Her career-high moment came in 1996 when she successfully participated in the Olympic Games in Atlanta and reached the eleventh place at 5000 meters – and, for the fourth time, set a new Swedish record.

Wedlund was born on December 27, 1977. She grew up in Vällingby – a western suburb to Stockholm – and started exercising track-and-field sports at the age of thirteen right after she had quit playing football. Running quickly became her number one sport, but timely speaking, her track-and-field elite-level career became relatively short. The reason to this was mainly because of runner-related injuries that kept her away from the running track during her most performable years.

---

[1] "Så minns vi Sara Wedlund," *Svensk friidrott*, link: https://www.friidrott.se/Nyheter/allmannanyheter/2021/Juni/saminnsvisarawedlund. Accessed August 3, 2022.

In this article, focus is leaning on Wedlund as an athlete and especially on her breakthrough in the 1995 Gothenburg World Championships in Athletics, but also her following participation in 1996 Olympics in Atlanta that sort of put an end to her unparalleled breakthrough year. Wedlund's breakthrough has not yet captured the eye of Swedish sports historians, which is as a bit surprising given the fact that Wedlund was seen as somewhat different compared to other athletes at the time. As Swedish columnist Mats Wennerholm wrote regarding her death, she "came from nowhere and became a national idol."[2] Statements like this reoccur a lot when reading about Wedlund's life and career, which, despite her anonymity, paint a picture of an athlete with a significant impact in Sweden at the time. The purpose for this article will therefore be to examine and analyze how Sara Wedlund's national breakthrough was portraited in Swedish media. This will be fulfilled by a systematic reading of media sources about Wedlund, which consists of news texts, interviews and chronicles, and analyzed through theoretical concepts of hero-making in sports. Moreover, official data from competitions during Wedlund's career are used to contextualize as well as to add details to the text. Furthermore, a wider context is also important in order to understand the circumstances of which Wedlund experienced her breakthrough.

Sara Wedlund's Road to the World Championships

So let us start with Sara Wedlund and her prospective breakthrough. First of all: What constitutes a breakthrough? A couple of definitions derived from *The Britannica Dictionary* describes a breakthrough either as "a sudden increase in knowledge" or "a person's first important success."[3] Since we cannot really describe Wedlund's breakthrough in terms of "a sudden increase in the knowledge of running" – she certainly already managed *how* to run – we must stick with the second definition, which also seems to be more fitted for sports breakthroughs in a wider sense. However, the 1995 Gothenburg World Championships in Athletics was undoubtedly Wedlund's first *important* success as a runner. She was nineteen years old and still in the beginning of her career as a professional athlete, and following her successful performance at the final

---

[2] Mats Wennerholm, "Kom från ingenstans – blev en nationalidol," *Aftonbladet*, June 24, 2021.

[3] Breakthrough, Britannica, link: https://www.britannica.com/dictionary/breakthrough, 2022-05-16.

of 5,000 meters, she quickly became a household name both in Sweden and abroad. Using media sources is a good way to form an idea of a general perception of something specific, in this case a major breakthrough, but also to understand a larger context – in this case, the meaning of the 1995 Gothenburg World Championships in Athletics.

The competitions of 1995 Gothenburg World Championships in started on August 5 and Sara Wedlund arrived to the contest as a newly established, elite-level runner. Earlier in the year of 1995, she had participated in various competitions such as the Swedish Championships in cross-country running in April and the track-and-field competition *Back on Track* in June. Although she won both of these competitions and therefore had put herself in a great position to qualify for the forthcoming World Championships, she seemed to have a quite modest approach regarding her odds of actually getting there. At least this was the impression that she gave in an interview with *Göteborgs-Posten* in late May. "No, the World Championships is only something I joke about… at least so far."[4]

Whether Sara Wedlund believed it herself or not, she certainly did qualify to the World Championships. Her final test was in July, just weeks before the start of the championships, when she participated in *DN-galan* and shared the scene with track-and-field stars such as Donovan Bailey, Mike Powell and Moses Kiptanu. Wedlund performed well and set a new Swedish record at 5000 meters – a record she was going to trim only a few weeks later – and despite the star quality that surrounded the competition, Swedish journalists could not resist the nineteen-year-old rookie from Vällingby outside Stockholm. Wedlund, of course, was not used to the level of attention she was given, which, to some extent, seemed to make her even more attractive to journalists. Like many others, Swedish newspaper *Expressen* took hold off her shyness:

> Lap of honor, standing ovations, interviews… everyone is cheering, except Sara… She is a quiet girl who had just come back after four years suffering from anorexia. She is finally a whole person again. However, not whole enough for this level of attention (Öhman, 1995).[5]

DN-galan was Wedlund's first international competition. Her results at *DN-galan* eventually gave her a spot in Sweden's track-and-field team to the World

---

[4] "Vann över anorexian – och Malin," *Göteborgs-Posten*, May 31, 1995.

[5] Peter Öhman, "Du är ett mysterium, Sara," *Expressen*, July 11, 1995.

Championships, but to accept the invitation was not an easy decision both with respect to her previous health issues and her current shyness. However, another, perhaps more serious reason, was that Wedlund had a history of suffering from eating disorders. The details regarding her eating disorders are few since Wedlund almost never talked about it in public – neither during or after her career – but the problems existed and surely contributed to delay her breakthrough. Whether – or to what extent – they also contributed to shorten her career, or her life, is unknown and will not be further analyzed in this article. Anyway, Sara Wedlund's successful participation *DN-galan* proved her capacity on the international scene. In an interview with Swedish newspaper *Svenska Dagbladet* shortly after the competition, she explained her attitude towards the future and especially the upcoming World Championships.

> The World Championships is such a big competition and I am afraid that the pressure will affect me negatively. Everything has gone so fast. I need time to digest this (Olsson, 1995).[6]

Two weeks after *DN-galan*, on July 24, Wedlund finally announced her decision to be a part of Sweden's track-and-field team for the World Championships that was about to start in twelve days. The message was received with joy and happiness by media. *Göteborgs-Posten* stated that Sara had "let go of her shyness," and *Svenska Dagbladet* cheered for Sweden's new "anti-hero that had not been seen in Swedish sports since Kurre Hamrin in World Championships of football 1958."[7]

The "Greta Garbo of Sports"

Sara Wedlund entered Ullevi Stadium on August 10, which was the fifth day of the World Championships, to participate in the 5000 meters trial heat. Ullevi Stadium, inaugurated in 1958 to host the World Cup of football, had undergone severe restorations before the start of the 1995 Gothenburg World Championships in Athletics, which had resulted in a new lawn, new running tracks and a new restaurant. Moreover, the arena had expanded with a new

---

[6] Anders Olsson, "Wedlund ljuset i det svenska mörkret," *Svenska Dagbladet*, July 11, 1995.

[7] "Stjärnskottet Sara ställer upp," *Göteborgs-Posten*, July 24, 1995; Per-Olof Olsson, "…men Sara är med i VM," *Svenska Dagbladet*, July 24, 1995.

stand, allowing 10.000 additional spectators.[8] The new stand meant that Ullevi had reached a capacity of nearly 50.000 seats, which was the minimum
requirement from the International Amateur Athletics Federation (IAAF).[9]
On top of everything, a video screen measuring seventy-two square meters
to show results and presumable records had been installed on the short side.[10]
Overall speaking, Ullevi Stadium was a big arena, by far the biggest arena
that Sara Wedlund had entered so far.

This should be Sara Wedlund's third competitive attempt at the 5000 meters
distance ever. Her debut came on June 28 – less than two months earlier – at the
track-and-field *Grand Prix* in Helsinki, followed by *DN-galan* a few weeks later, and both competitions had resulted in new Swedish records at the distance.[11]
Expectations were high, and as always, Swedish newspapers took hold off her
shyness and so-called oddness. *Expressen*, who had spotted Wedlund during her
warm-up run in the nearby forest Slottsskogen, announced her appearance as
"Greta Garbo of sports," referring to the former Swedish movie star who, just
like Wedlund, had an overnight breakthrough.[12] Expressen also did an interview
with Wedlund's trainer Bosse Strandberg on the daily press conference, who did
his best to lower the expectations on her upcoming performance: "We will see
how it goes. Sara is here mostly to watch and learn."[13]

Throughout the World Championships, daily press conferences were held
where Swedish athletes were expected to participate in front of media – at least
the ones that were scheduled to compete the following day. Sara was therefore
expected to attend the daily press conference on August 9, however, she did not
show up. Instead, Bosse Strandberg stepped in to answer questions regarding
her condition and health, but also questions about her staying in Gothenburg
and feelings about her World Championships debut. According to Strandberg,
everything was normal, and the reason Wedlund did not attend the press conference was because she needed to focus on the upcoming race. Expressen asked
who had decided that Sara should not talk to media before the race, and Strandberg answered that he and Sara had made the decision in unity. Strandberg also

[8] Jonas Hedman, *VM i friidrott 1995 – Göteborg, 4 – 13 augusti* (Göteborg, Strömberg Brunns-
hags, 1995), 19.

[9] *Ibid.*

[10] *Ibid.*

[11] Stellan Kvärre, "Sara mötte vardagen på Stadion," *Dagens Nyheter*, August 16, 1995.

[12] Thomas Pettersson, "Här tränar idrottens Greta Garbo," *Expressen*, August 10, 1995.

[13] *Ibid.*

ensured that Wedlund was healthy and did not suffer at all from her previous battle against her eating disorders.[14]

Wedlund clearly did not cope with the attention. Although Strandberg stated that the reason to her absence was that she needed to prepare for the race, it was also because she felt uncomfortable standing in front of the journalists and receive questions that sometimes were way too personal. In fact, team captain Anders Gärderud, who also attended the press conference, told *Göteborgs-Posten* that Sara simply was afraid to meet journalists and the best would be to do interviews after the race.[15]

The Final and the Celebration

Wedlund's performance in the trial heat was enough to give her a spot in the final race, which was going to take place on Saturday, August 12. Unlike many athletes, Sara had arrived to the World Championships without any sponsors. Strandberg admitted that several shoe manufacturers had reached out with sponsor deals, but that they have chosen to lie low so far. So, with her own bought running shoes on her feet, she entered the running track for the final. The starting pistol went off with a bang and the athletes took off. Gabriela Szabo from Romania had an almost surprisingly strong opening and took the lead immediately. She created a long gap between herself and the rest and logged the first lap – 400 meters – on 1:05:68. However, she could not keep up with the speed and upon reaching 800 meters, the gap was slowly closed by Sonia O'Sullivan from Ireland. The current world record holder, Fernanda Ribeiro from Portugal, had established herself on a third place.

As predicted, Wedlund had no chance to keep up with the leaders who were running at almost world record speed. However, she took a stable place in the lower half of the group and kept it well throughout the race. After five laps – 2000 meters – she was at the ninth place out of thirteen runners. At about 3000 meters, Gabriella Szabo got tired and handed over the lead to Paula Radcliffe from Great Britain. Szabo, who had gone out fast, continued to decline and landed on a fourth place, while Sonia O'Sullivan managed to

---

[14] *Ibid.*

[15] "Sara smyger omkring och laddar för stordåd," *Göteborgs-Posten*, August 10, 1995.

keep herself right behind the leader. By now, Fernanda Ribeiro had taken over the lead. However, when crossing the line heading into the final lap, O'Sullivan passed Ribeiro and spent the last 400 meters only increasing the distance between them. She finished with a new championship record at 14:46:47, but ten seconds behind the world record.[16]

Wedlund kept her ninth place through the entire race and finished at 15:08:36. This meant her third Swedish record at the same number of attempts, however, she had no chance to challenge the top runners in the final. No one had expected that either. As promised, she agreed to meet the journalists to receive questions after the race:

"I was not that nervous, except from the moments just before the start. But the others looked nervous too."[17] The night after the race, *Expressen* spotted Wedlund walking around in central Gothenburg with her parents. She was surrounded by cheering fans, and between hugs and photos with passers-by, the reporter asked her about her feelings regarding the new fame: "I do not know. I guess this is the first time for me."[18]

Later that night, Wedlund went to meet up and congratulate Sonia O'Sullivan, the winner, something that *Expressen* described as "a meeting between two equal souls." The day after, she was heading back to Stockholm to continue her life as a student. Her third year of high school was about to start and she seemed fine with that, even though she returned to her hometown as a national celebrity: "It will be fun to come back to school. I do not think it will be any big difference."[19]

Wedlund's World Championships debut was now done and future challenges were laying ahead of her. Everything from now on was, sort of, up to herself. Did she want to devote herself to the run or did she have other plans?

---

[16] "Women's 5000 final, World Athletics Championships in Gothenburg 1995," *Athletics Central*, link: https://www.youtube.com/watch?v=Gy6WtDL_H_0&t=426s; "5000 meter FINAL," *Göteborgs-Posten*, August 13, 1995.

[17] Jarl Strömberg, "När jag sätter mig ner och tänker efter så kommer det att kännas fint," *Göteborgs-Posten*, August 13, 1995.

[18] Thomas Pettersson, "...Och i natt firade hon med mamma och pappa," *Expressen*, August 13, 1995.

[19] *Ibid.*

The World Championships Fever and its Consequences

> I do not want to run only. I am afraid it will be a bit boring in the long term. I would like something else to do too.[20]

Sara Wedlund had set a new Swedish record and created a fever throughout the country. Now, she wanted to continue her life as a nineteen-year-old, and she actually did not know whether she wanted to keep competing or not. The best would be to combine running with something else, preferably something that went in line with her interests in natural sciences.

The media hype around Wedlund began to fade as the World Championships came to an end. Instead, the newspapers started to summarize the Championships as a whole. The overall judgement was that the 1995 Gothenburg World Championship in Athletics, from a Swedish perspective, held a decent – but not excellent – level. High-jumper Patrik Sjöberg, whose career was in a sort of decline, ended up at sixth place.[21] Moreover, Dag Wennlund took a fifth place in javelin throw, and Claes Albihn took an eleventh place in hurdle.[22] Sara Wedlund's performance stood out so far that she not only set a new Swedish record, but she did it in her only third attempt at the distance. Her national breakthrough lighted up the World Championships, which from a Swedish perspective lacked real tops. Most important was her personality. Wedlund was one of a kind and totally unique compared to what journalists had ever seen before.

Wedlund had one race left before she headed back to school – Swedish Championships in Stockholm on August 14. She participated in the 1500 meters race and won quite easy. After the race, she was standing in front of the journalists who were wondering how it felt to go from the World Championships to the Swedish Championship in less than a week: "It feels like a relief that the World Championships is over. This is more relaxing."[23]

Wedlund admitted that it had not been easy to recharge after the World Championships. All the impressions needed to sink in and her memories were still a bit dizzy. What she remembered most clearly was the two races

---

[20] *Ibid.*

[21] In 1999, four years later, Sjöberg announced his retirement from high-jumping due to injuries.

[22] Mats Olsson, "Tronskiftet kan vara början till slutet för friidrotten," *Expressen*, August 14, 1995.

[23] Johan Esk, "Åter i vardagen – då trivs Sara," *Tidningarnas Telegrambyrå*, August 15, 1995.

and the celebration night in Gothenburg "when it was sometimes difficult to walk through."[24] Continuously, focus was leaning on Wedlund's shyness and oddness. *Tidningarnas Telegrambyrå* asked a rhetorical question on how a tiny girl with glasses could be so popular despite being so far away from the medals. The following sentence speculated that it could be because of her authenticity – Sara Wedlund was perhaps a contrast against "styled averages." Wedlund herself presented her own theory: "Maybe it is because I fight so hard in the beginning of every race. The audience like that, maybe."[25]

During the fall, Wedlund participated in several competitions such as Swedish Junior Championships and *Finnkampen*, a yearly track-and-field competition between only Sweden and Finland, and she continued to succeed. However, one big stage was still ahead of her.

Heading for the Olympic Games

The 1996 Olympic Games were held in Atlanta, US, and after her successes during the year of 1995, Sara Wedlund was self-written in the Swedish track-and-field team that was sent over the Atlantic Ocean. The Olympics were supposed to be inaugurated on July 19 and Sara Wedlund was planning to arrive two days before that. Her last competition before departure was *DN-galan* – just as the year before – which became nothing but a success, at least for her personally. She once again set a new Swedish record at 5000 meters with 15:06:90, however, she was still far away from the top and ended up at the eighth place.[26] Wedlund arrived to Atlanta as a twenty-year-old student who had just finished high school. Although the media hype from the World Championships was somewhat over, she was still one of the most exposed Swedish athletes. She was also still a bit introvert as a person and did not seem to like the attention – for instance, she had declined an inquiry to participate in the Swedish version of the TV-show *Fort Boyard*. "If I want to play, I would rather crawl around in my garden searching for spiders."[27]

---

[24] *Ibid.*

[25] *Ibid.*

[26] "Friidrottsgalan gren för gren," *Svenska Dagbladet*, July 9, 1996.

[27] Mats Wennerholm, "Tunn och skör – men urstark inuti," *Aftonbladet*, July 18, 1996.

Unlike last year, Wedlund had signed a sponsor deal with Nike, which might
had taken away some of the mystery around her person. She was now one of
the stars – and the expectations were therefore higher than before. Overall, the
Swedish representation of women athletes had increased with 50% compared
to the previous Olympic Games in Barcelona 1992.[28] Wedlund, together with
her parents, travelled to Atlanta on a plane chartered by The Swedish Olympic
Committee. Several Swedish journalists were waiting at the airport when the
plane landed, but got quite disappointed since Wedlund slipped past the que to
the passport control and disappeared without giving any longer interviews.[29]
According to *Expressen*, the further trip did not go to the Olympic Village, like
for the other athletes, but to a couple of Wedlund's relatives that lived in Atlanta. The fact that she chose to not live in the Olympic Village went in line with
the current narrative about Wedlund, and the newspaper stated that Wedlund
was "not like the rest."[30]

Off to the Olympic Final

The personal goal for Wedlund, which she mentioned in an interview with *Aftonbladet*, was to reach the Olympic final on 5000 meters.[31] To get there, she
needed to perform well in the try-out heat which took place on July 26. Wedlund went out fast and kept the lead until the final lap when the winner from
last year's World Championship, Sonia O'Sullivan, passed her and won while
Wedlund slipped down to the fifth place.[32] Despite the descent performance –
Wedlund logged 15:20:61 – it was not sure whether she would qualify to the
final, since only the best four in every three try-out heats were guaranteed a
spot. But after review, her performance and time turned out to be enough, and
Wedlund could breathe out.

On July 28, the 5000 meters final took place. Sara Wedlund stood on the starting line alongside star-runners like Junxia Wang from China, Paula Radcliffe
from Great Britain and, once again, Sonia O'Sullivan from Ireland. In total, the

[28] Mats Wennerholm, "Tjejerna har redan slagit OS-rekord," *Aftonbladet*, July 18, 1996.

[29] Thomas Pettersson, "Hon kom, hon sågs – hon smet," *Expressen*, July 18, 1996.

[30] *Ibid.*

[31] Wennerholm, *OS-rekord*, 1996.

[32] "Sara gick på knock i natt," *Göteborgs-Posten*, July 27, 1996.

final consisted of eighteen runners. The race started, and Wedlund almost immediately took the lead. However, since every runner did their best to end up in
as a good position as possible, she had trouble keeping it, which she explained
in an interview with *Expressen* after the race: "You get so many pushes and the
others step on your feet. I have not learned myself to push back yet."[33]

Cheered by the Swedish Royal Family, Wedlund did her best to keep up with
the top runners, but the race was too tough. She ended up at eleventh place with,
at least for her standards, a modest time – 15:22:98.[34] The winner was Junxia
Wang who ran at 14:59:88.[35] What was maybe most surprising was that one of
the favorites to win, Sonia O'Sullivan, did not finish the race due to illness.[36]

Back Home Again

Wedlund was clearly not happy with her results even though she had reached
her goal which was to qualify for the Olympic final. She returned to Sweden
as a twenty-year-old, well-established runner, but still quite far away from the
world elite. The intention, since she had finished school, was to invest in the
sport improve further as an athlete. Being a full-time professional runner, however, did not seem to be an option yet, and just like any twenty-year-old she
was in need for a job. Aftonbladet did their best to help her. In an article on July
30, two days after the final on 5000 meters, a sort of job ad for Sara Wedlund
was published. If readers knew something about a job that could fit a "twenty-
year-old record-holder with top grades from high school," they could just call
the attached number.[37] Even though the article was written with some sense of
humor, it seemed to have had some effect. On the following day, Aftonbladet
reported that their telephone line had "went hot." For instance, a reader had
called to offer Wedlund to work with marketing for health food products. What

---

[33] Thomas Pettersson, "Du är guld värd i alla fall, Sara," *Expressen*, July 29, 1996.

[34] *Ibid.*

[35] "Atlanta 1996, Athletics 5000M Women Results," *The official site of The Olympics*, link: https://
olympics.com/en/olympic-games/atlanta-1996/results/athletics/5000m-women

[36] "Sonia O'Sullivan," *Sporting Heroes: A photographic encyclopaedia of sports*, link: http://www.
sporting-heroes.net/athletics/ireland/sonia-o-sullivan-1821/disappointment-at-1996-olym-
pic-games_a09421/

[37] Erika Gohde, "Ring – och ge Sara ett jobb", *Aftonbladet*, July 30, 1996.

seemed to be important was that Wedlund should be able to combine the job with her running career, and for that reason, she needed a job with a flexible schedule.[38]

It is not clear whether Wedlund accepted any of the offers that came through Aftonbladet's job ad. What we do know, however, is that Wedlund was tired. It had been a heavy year with a lot of running and media coverage that had taken its toll on her. She was scheduled to participate in *Finnkampen* on August 24, but on the same day, she announced to Swedish media that she needed a break from running: "I am not ill, but I feel totally exhausted after a long and heavy season."[39]

A few days later, on August 28, Wedlund did a longer interview with *Aftonbladet*. She stated that the media attention combined with the pressure both from herself and from others had been too much to handle. Apart from becoming Sweden's most famous runner, she had also graduated from high school with top grades. With almost no days off, she had been in the center of attention for over one year. It was time to say goodbye for a while – but she also promised that she would come back in some form.[40]

Wedlund did three performances in the fall of 1996. The first one was *Lidingöloppet* – a yearly fifteen-kilometer terrain run – which took place on October 6. Here, without any significant competition, she won on 51:15, forty-three seconds ahead of Finnish runner Annmari Sandell.[41] Two weeks later, she won *Hässelbyloppet* by running ten kilometers on 31:52.[42] Wedlund's final performance in 1996 was at the European Championship in Belgium, where she ended up at second place in terrain running. 1996 was over, and no one seemed to know what was ahead of Wedlund for the upcoming year. As we know by now, Sara Wedlund's career did certainly not end here. She continued to run and compete for another seven years, however, her days as a top athlete was sort of over at the same time as she addressed her break in late 1996. The two years of being both Sweden's best female runner and a media favorite had taken its toll on her.

---

[38] Erika Gohde, "Välkommen att sälja hälsokost åt mig, Sara!," *Aftonbladet*, July 31, 1996.

[39] Göran Bolin, "Friidrott: Sliten Sara tackade nej – färdigtävlat för i år," *Dagens Nyheter*, August 24, 1996.

[40] Anna Carlsson, "Jag orkar helt enkelt inte längre," *Aftonbladet*, August 28, 1996.

[41] "Sara tillbaka – som segrare," *Tidningarnas Telegrambyrå*, October 6, 1996.

[42] "Ännu en seger för Sara Wedlund," *Helsingborgs Dagblad*, October 20, 1996.

An Anti-Hero on the Running Track

Let us now return to Wedlund's breakthrough in the 1995 Gothenburg World Championships in Athletics, where one big reason to her popularity likely was that Sweden actually lacked successes. As *Göteborgs-Posten* wrote in its exhaustible chronicle after the championships, the Swedish effort was mediocre – with Wedlund as one rare exception.[43] Among medal hopes that did not deliver, the chronicle listed Patrik Sjöberg – who suffered from injuries – and hurdler Sven Nylander. According to the chronicle, he "never found the rhythm" and it was also stated that he showed signs of age.[44] Wedlund, who still was in her early career, was a positive surprise compared to the rest.[45]

One way to describe Wedlund's impact on the Swedish track-and-field sports can be in terms of hero-making. According to Swedish historian John Hellström, sports heroes are often created by media, and to become one, there are three aspects that needs to be fulfilled. The first one is that the athlete needs to succeed in a sport that is highly valued. The second one, besides being successful, is that the athlete should have a personality that goes in line with the surrounding society. The third one consists of the audience. A national sports hero needs a national audience that can identify itself with the athlete.[46] Among sports heroes that ticks all the three boxes, Hellström points out the fighters Harry Persson and Ingemar Johansson, tennis player Björn Borg, skier Ingemar Stenmark and heptathlon athlete Carolina Klüft.

It can be argued that also Sara Wedlund ticked almost every one of the boxes set up by Hellström. First, she competed in an athletic discipline with a long tradition in Sweden, and she did it with great success. Moreover, her personality – at least the personality that the audience could take part of through media – was both different and attractive. If we put Wedlund in a context of other Swedish track-and-field athletes in the 1990s, she stood out with a humble and shy personality, which likely contributed to her popularity. As a contrast, high-jumper Patrik Sjöberg, whose career was in somewhat decline, was known for a profligate living and a more offensive attitude towards journalists.

---

[43] Göteborgs-Posten, *VM i friidrott 1995* (Göteborg: Göteborgs-Posten, 1995), 59.

[44] *Ibid*, 63.

[45] *Ibid*, 60.

[46] John Hellström, *Den svenska sporthjälten: Kontinuitet och förändring i medieberättelsen om den svenska sporthjälten från 1920-talet till idag* (Malmö: Bokförlaget idrottsforum.org, 2014).

Wedlund was something else. She was *both* an upcoming star that no one really knew anything about, and she combined that with a personality that no one had seen in this context before. If Sjöberg represented a non-Swedish, rock star attitude, Wedlund was leaning towards a traditional, low key Swedishness that had previously been carried out by athletes such as Ingemar Stenmark or Harry Persson. Perhaps Sweden needed athletes like Sara Wedlund – an individual, successful athlete without a big ego, but with a high level of mysticism. Who was she? Where did she come from? The curiosity did not know any limits.

Understanding Wedlund can also be done with inspiration from Diana Luiza Dumitriu, who had studied media's role in the making of sport heroes. She suggests that sport heroes should be seen as both celebrities and national heroes. Both of these appeals to emotions and unites people as much as they divide, which is closely connected to identification mechanisms.[47] Making a sports celebrity, or a sports hero, is as much a question of the athlete's own performances as the media context in which the athlete operates. Dumitriu's exemplifies with Romanian tennis player Simona Halep, who had her breakthrough in the 2014 Roland Garros tournament – also known as the French Open – which was a mega sport event in parity with other similar. Halep, who was completely unknown for the masses before the start of the tournament, went straight to the final where she got beaten by Marija Sharapova after a tight game. Her extra ordinary performance in a tournament that most often revolves around established, experienced athletes, was one reason to her hero status. Another, at least as important, was her attitude towards being a celebrity. Dumitriu states that Halep "challenged the celebrity laws" and became sort of an "anti-star."[48] Unlike more established star tennis players, she showed no signs of vanity or impertinence. Instead, she was focusing on her performance on the center court.[49]

Dumitriu's analysis of Simona Halep's breakthrough can also be transferred to Wedlund's experience from the 1995 Gothenburg World Championships in Athletics. Wedlund could be seen as an "anti-star" or an "anti-hero," since she did not behave as sports heroes normally did. However, the buzz that her behavior generated was – combined with her performances on the running track – enough to actually portrait her as a national hero. Wedlund, according to media, also seemed focused on her task and did not let anything bother her prior to the

---

[47] Diana Luiza Dumitriu, "Media Construction of Sports Celebritites as National Heroes," *Romanian Journal of Communication and Public Relations* 20, no. 2 (2018): 21 – 33.

[48] *Ibid.*

[49] *Ibid.*

races. Dumitriu also points at another reason relevant in the case of Wedlund – just like in the 1995 Gothenburg World Championships in Athletics, the 2014 Roland Garron tournament lacked successes from a Romanian perspective, which also contributed to Halep's breakthrough.[50]

Drawing upon Hellström and Dumitriu, Wedlund was made a national hero by the media to some extent through the way she acted, but perhaps above all through the way she *did not* act. At the same time, through her behavior and attitude, she was constructed as an anti-hero. Compared to track-and-field stars that entered the scene a few years later, for instance Carolina Klüft, Wedlund was not half as extrovert towards fans and media. Another part of Wedlund's status as an anti-hero was her previous eating disorders, even though media rarely elaborated further around them. However, when the disorders were mentioned – and that she had overcome them – they often functioned as elements in the successful "against all odds"-story of her running career.

To further understand how Wedlund could be made a "national anti-hero," it is important to view both the 1995 Gothenburg World Championships in Athletics and the 1996 Olympics in a wider context. How did the circumstances contribute to the media picture of Sara Wedlund's?

A Reflective Summary – Media pictures of Sara Wedlund during the 1995 Gothenburg World Championships in Athletics and the 1996 Atlanta Olympic Games

Sara Wedlund was by far the biggest Swedish success during the 1995 Gothenburg World Championships in Athletics, even though she was not even close to reach any top places. Her anti-hero status might have had a compensative function, meaning that her appearance and attitude was more important than her actual competitive results. To some extent, this was also the case during the 1996 Olympics, where Wedlund once again could not challenge the top runners and ended up in the lower places. What is interesting is that Swedish media almost never addressed Wedlund's potential as a runner solely – in case they did, it was embedded in descriptions that also involved her looks, especially her glasses, or her positive attitude. From a media perspective, expectations on her actual performances were probably limited, even though her Swedish records of course added something to

---

[50] *Ibid.*

the narrative. On the other hand, as mentioned, newspapers had likely troubles finding other presumptive medal hopes in the Swedish track-and-field team during the time, meaning that Sara Wedlund were given more attention than she would have had if her breakthrough had come a few years earlier – or later.

What about the two big international competitions Wedlund performed in? On August 5, 2020, *Dagens Nyheter* posted an article in which they pointed out that twenty-five years had passed since the 1995 Gothenburg World Championships in Athletics. The article stated that the World Championships had paved the way for a golden era of Swedish track-and-field sports.[51] Some of the future Swedish stars was on site to watch the competitions, but also to work as officials. That included the fifteen-year-old triple-jumper Christian Olsson, who witnessed Jonathan Edwards set a world record at 18.29 – a record that still stands. Six years later, Olsson had his own breakthrough during the World Cup in Edmonton 2001, in which he ended up at second place right behind the same Edwards. Olsson and Edwards then became the two biggest stars of triple-jumping during the early 2000s. With this in mind, Sara Wedlund was somehow squeezed in between two successful eras of Swedish track-and-field sports, since her breakthrough came during Patrik Sjöberg's decline, but before the breakthrough of stars such as Christian Olsson and high-jumper Kajsa Bergqvist.

To put the 1995 Gothenburg World Championships in Athletics in a wider context, it is up until today still the biggest sporting event in Swedish history. Despite being the starting shot of the golden years of Swedish track-and-field sports, it also became somewhat an economic disaster for the Swedish Athletes Federation. The financial loss ended at 20 million Swedish crowns, while the federation had calculated with a profit of 25 million. One reason to the major loss – and miscalculation – was due to a contract with the entrepreneur for the World Championships village which made the village 50 million more expensive.[52] However, looking at the 1995 Gothenburg World Championships in Athletics from a socio-economic perspective, it was a success. Beer tents and pop up-restaurants filled the streets of Gothenburg and the parties went on for nine days straight.[53] A major revenue also came from the ticket sales – the daily tickets to Ullevi cost between 565 and 1100 Swedish crowns – and together

---

[51] Jens Littorin, "Miljonfiaskot i Göteborg blev svensk friidrotts lycka," *Dagens Nyheter*, August 5, 2020.

[52] *Ibid*; Peter Thunborg, "Fiaskot som la grunden för det svenska friidrottsundret," *Expressen*, January 23, 2020.

[53] Göteborgs-Posten *VM i friidrott*, 90.

with all visitors that had travelled to Gothenburg to participate in the festivities connected to the World Championships, the final income to the Swedish state landed on 250 million Swedish crowns. 11,3 million of the income was donated to the federation in goodwill, which mitigated its financial situation a bit.[54] With that in mind, Sweden probably did not have to rely on competitive successes as much as if the World Championships were hosted somewhere else. For nine days, Gothenburg was the center of the world's absolute best athletes such as triple-jumper Jonathan Edwards, hurdle-racer Kim Batten, runner Fernanda Ribeiro and sprinter Michael Johnson – and, not to forget, sprinter Carl Lewis, who unfortunately had to leave Gothenburg due to injuries before the competitions had begun. Gothenburg also showed its best side in terms of weather – the 1995 Gothenburg World Championships in Athletics was indeed a sunny story and an important sporting event for Sweden and Swedish track-and-field sports.

Sara Wedlund's participation in the 1996 Olympics was somewhat different compared to the World Championships. The mystification regarding her personality had faded a bit since everyone already knew who she was. In Atlanta, she was treated more like a rock star as reporters were waiting in the arrival hall at the airport – likely disappointed over the fact that she left the building through a backdoor. Media still tried to get a glimpse of her, however, in a different way compared to the situation during her breakthrough year. Wedlund, in their eyes, was still different and interesting, but she had also arrived as an established runner with higher expectations on both being successful on the running track and being accessible for media. The expectations on being accessible was seen as fulfilled to some extent. Various newspapers reported that Wedlund seemed to have gotten rid of her shyness and showed a more relaxed attitude towards journalists. *Svenska Dagbladet*, for instance, stated that Wedlund "happily accommodates the photographers requests" and was "open and with a completely different confidence than last year when she felt hunted and wanted to hide from media."[55] *Expressen*, who likely reported from the same spot, wrote that Wedlund was "far from a shy girl who made a lightning career in the World Championships last year" and that she had become "a professional" in handling media.[56] Being more confident and relaxed was seen as positive by media, since that enabled another successful story

---

[54] *Ibid*, 88; Thunborg, *Friidrottsundret*, 2020.

[55] Anders Lindblad, "Sara har lämnat sin skyddade tillvaro – nu är hon en i gänget," *Svenska Dagbladet*, July 25, 1996.

[56] Thomas Pettersson, "Sara flyttar hemifrån. 'Det är här i OS-byn som stämningen finns'," *Expressen*, July 25, 1996.

to be written – a story of a shy girl that suddenly had turned into a mature, confident woman. On the other hand, it also meant that Wedlund to a higher extent was
seen as an athlete among others.

So, what is clear is that the media picture of Sara Wedlund changed a bit
between the 1995 Gothenburg World Championships in Athletics and the 1996
Olympics, depending on both Sara as an individual person and the fact that the
competitions was seen differently from a Swedish perspective. In Gothenburg,
the competitions were framed in a context of party and enjoyment. Swedes
could follow the competitions either on site or via radio and television. In Atlanta, competitions were broadcasted nighttime for Swedish people, making it
more difficult to keep up with Wedlund and the other Swedish athletes. Most
likely, this also contributed to a difference in how Wedlund was portraited by
Swedish media.

Lights Out

What also contributes to the legacy of Sara Wedlund is of course the fact that
she totally left the track-and-field world at the same time she quit running on
elite-level. It is not uncommon that former athletes remain within sports and
continue their careers as trainers or media experts, but Wedlund did nothing
like that. In fact, she disappeared from the celebrity sphere completely, and
only did a few interviews during her remaining life. One was with *Aftonbladet*
in 2003, the same year as she officially quit, in which she admitted that her
eating disorders still bothered her. Wedlund was now twenty-seven years old
and almost eight years had passed since her enormous breakthrough in the 1995
Gothenburg World Championships in Athletics. She had not completely closed
the door to a comeback but did not seem confident regarding her odds. The two
years – 1995 and 1996 – on top-level had continued to left its marks: "I competed for two years and then it ended. It still feels like I have a lot to give, but it
is a real mental challenge to want to but not be able to."[57]

In the interview, Wedlund also opened up about the injury that were com-
municated as the main reason for her ended career – spasms in the groin that
resulted in a crooked running step. According to Wedlund, no one knew what
the injury was caused by, but it clearly frustrated her.

---

[57] Daniel Nyhlén, "Jag är inte frisk från anorexin," *Aftonbladet*, July 15, 2003.

> I started with track-and-field sports at the age of 13. Before that, I played foot-
> ball. I have always been doing sports, and now it is over. I get to go for walks
> and cycle instead, so boring (Ibid).[58]

At the end of the interview, the reporter asked a general question about Wedlund's life goals, and her answer was that she wanted to keep them for herself.

The interview with *Aftonbladet* in 2003 was the last one that Wedlund did.
In the coming years, several of her Swedish records were broken, however, her
indoor-record at 5000 meters – set in early 1996 – still stands up until today.
The only times she appeared in media, roughly speaking, was when her records
were broken, or when newspapers decided to publish flashbacks from the 1995
Gothenburg World Championships in Athletics. Other young athletes such as
high-jumper Kajsa Bergqvist and Carolina Klüft took her place in the spotlight,
and Wedlund became somehow forgotten.

On June 11, 2021, almost eighteen years after she did her last interview,
Swedish media announced the death of Sara Wedlund. Apart from countless
articles that reported about her death, there were also those who tried to dig
deeper in her life after the career. The TV-broadcaster *Discovery Plus* did an
interview with her former trainer, Bosse Strandberg, who said that Wedlund after finishing her career spent several years trying different things. For instance,
she tried to study at dental school, but according to Strandberg, she suffered
from mental illness that kept her from doing everything she wanted to do.[59] To
a great extent, however, Wedlund's life after her career ended is still shrouded
in mystery.

---

[58] *Ibid.*

[59] Vendela Ögren, "Tränaren om Sara Wedlunds liv efter idrottskarriären," *Expressen*, June 21,
2021.

CHAPTER 9

The Emotionalization of Sports for Children and Young People in Swedish Athletics

Jens Ljunggren

During the first half of the nineteenth century, physical education for children and young people was conducted in Swedish schools; subsequently, in the sports clubs that gained momentum in the late nineteenth century, young people played an important role. Public funds were allocated to sports on a regular basis from 1913, and during the post-war period, especially from the 1960s onward, sports for children and young people grew explosively to become the most important association-led activity for young people in Sweden. However, from this point on, a noticeable change in the view on sports for children and young people took place. Prominent sports researchers began to question whether it was appropriate to let children and youth conduct competitive sports, and this discussion is still going on today.[1]

Focusing on athletics, this study examines how, as well as why, new approaches to sports for children and young people have taken shape in Sweden from the time around 1970 until today. Athletics is an ideal topic for analysis. Early on, the Swedish Athletics Association (SAA) organized competitions to attract young people, and during the post-war period it invested heavily in youth sports.[2] Not only did the SAA take the lead in advancing new training methods in general; from the 1980s onward, it also adopted much of the new

---

[1] Johnny Wijk, *Idrott, krig och nationell gemenskap: Om riksmarscher, fältsports och Gunder Hägg-feber* (Östlings bokförlag Symposion, Eslöv, 2005), 233–237; Riksidrottsförbundet, 2019-idrotten-i-siffror---rf.pdf (https://www.rf.se/Statistikochforskning/Statistik/idrottsrorelsenisiffror), 63; Jan Toftegaard Støckel, Åse Strandbu, Oskar Solenes, Per Jørgensen & Kristin Fransson, "Sports for children and youth in the Scandinavian countries," *Sports in Society* 13, no 4 (2010), 626–627.

[2] Leif Yttergren, *Träna är livet: Träning, utbildning och vetenskap i svensk friidrott, 1880–1995* (Idrottsforum.org, Malmö, 2012); Göran Patriksson & Claes Annerstedt, "Barn- och ungdomsidrott – en bred översikt," in *Idrott: Hundra år i Göteborg*, eds. Cege Berglund & Gudrun Nyberg (Carlssons, Stockholm, 2019), 34–35, 41–43, 46–47.

sports pedagogy for children and young people. The purpose of this chapter is to analyze, from an emotional-historical perspective, how and why adults' attitudes regarding sports for children and young people changed during the period and how this affected the activity. The chapter's main argument is that, because new emotional norms prevailed in society, dominant attitudes and practices in children's and young people sports were challenged and new pedagogical ideas adapted. To understand this process, and to complement the two already established analytical notions in Swedish sports research (*association* and *competition education*), this study introduces the analytical concept of *personality education*, which points out how the upbringing of the young athletes was aimed at developing them as individuals.

Perspectives on late Twentieth-Century Swedish Sports for Children and Young People

As a consequence of the 1960s left-wing movement in Sweden, fierce sports criticism came to the fore. Although the left-wing criticism soon faded, the discussion on how children and young people were affected by competitive sports continued. The fact that sports for children and young people expanded in society, and reached further down the ages, led to increased concerns among many adults from the 1970s onward. It was a common standpoint in professional and public debate that the performance aspect of sports for children and young people had been overemphasized and that children had become far too achievement oriented.[3]

Examining exclusion and questioning competitive sports for young people, sports researcher Lars-Magnus Engström became a dominant voice in the debate during the 1970s and 80s. Since then, several researchers have pointed out that competitive sports have intensified, arguing that this has had a negative effect on sports for children and young people. In the 1990s, sociologist Tomas Peterson launched the two analytical notions of association education and competition education. Association education accentuated how sports club members collaborated democratically for the common good. Meanwhile, Peterson placed the part of the club activity that was directed at improving results and achieving competition success under the notion of competition

---

[3] Jonny Hjelm, *Idrott, tävling och allvar: En kritisk granskning av svensk idrottsforskning* (Idrottsforum.org, Malmö, 2015), 35–48, 57.

education. When introducing this model, he contended that a shift had taken place in Swedish football clubs from association to competition education.[4]

This study reverses the perspective by instead asking why the competition element in sports for children and young people was problematized at the time. The few historians who have already approached this question have not contented themselves with the notion that the development of the activity can explain the change in attitude. According to historian Johnny Hjelm, an important driving force behind the criticism of competition in sports for children was the development of sports science at the time. By criticizing the element of competition, researchers established themselves in sports science and, one might add, also made themselves heard and influential in physical education and sports by pointing out problems that they – due to their competence as researchers – claimed to be able to solve. It is worth noting, however, that the notion of young people's negative experience of competition was also questioned in research.[5]

The fierce criticism of competition in sports for children and young people at the time can also be analyzed with the help of historical and sociological childhood research perspectives. Historian Susanna Hedenborg argues that, in order to explain changing stances toward children's and youth sports, we must analyze how attitudes toward children and young people developed in society in general. For instance, when child labor was written off as a suitable method of upbringing during the interwar period, sports were instead perceived to be a positive educational alternative for young people. Likewise, the criticism of children's sports from the 1970s onward was not as much rooted in the fact that the activities changed as in the fact that new notions of childhood were taking shape in society, according to Hedenborg.[6] Following this line of reasoning we could argue, for instance, that sports researchers were a subgroup of an increasingly influential cluster of childhood experts in society, whose profession it was to emphasize children's exposure to risks.[7]

[4] Tomas Peterson, "En allt allvarligare lek: Om idrottsrörelsens partiella kommersialisering," in *Ett idrottssekel: Riksidrottsförbundet 1903–2003,* eds. Jan Lindroth & Johan R. Norberg (Informationsförl, Stockholm, 2002), 397–399, 407–409. See also Karin Redelius, *Ledarna och barnidrotten: Idrottsledarnas syn på idrott, barn och fostran* (HLS Förlag Stockholm, 2002), 201.

[5] Hjelm, *Idrott, tävling och allvar.* 19–23, Göran Patriksson questioned the negative depiction of children's experiences of sports in *Idrottens barn: Idrottsvanor, stress, "utslagning"* (Stockholm: Friskvårdscentrum 1987).

[6] Susanna Hedenborg, "Barnet och det idrottande barnet," in *Är idrott nyttigt? En antologi om idrott och samhällsnytta,* ed. Johan Hvenmark (SISU idrottsböcker, Stockholm 2012), 90–109.

[7] Sandin, Bengt & Gunilla Halldén, "Välfärdsstatens omvandling och en ny barndom," in *Barnets*

In this study, I have chosen to analyze sports for children and young people from the context of the history of emotions. Historians of emotions analyze how emotional norms have prevailed in society as well as what people have actually felt. Emotions are innate. How people relate to their emotions has, however, been largely affected by external circumstances. Social settings contain emotional norms for what people should feel and express. How emotions are named, responded to and made sense of affect how people feel and manage their emotions privately as well as publicly. The history of emotions deals with how such processes work, and how and why they change over time.[8]

Historical research shows that how children and young people have been attributed emotions and emotional needs, and how these needs have been met, have varied over time, and taken different forms under different circumstances. From the middle of the nineteenth century, increased attention was paid to children's emotions in children's literature and manuals on upbringing. Instead of conveying unambiguous top-down moral messages, from this point on these texts have rather invited readers to gain insight into, and to better understand, how and why children acted and felt like they did. Along with the children, the adults were now also encouraged to learn more about their emotions and how to deal with them. Through being emotionalized, children were also empowered; particularly during the left-wing wave of the 1960s, children's books emphasized the importance of strengthening children's position in society by letting them live out their feelings and be authentic.[9]

Long before both the left-wing wave of the 1960s and the sports pedagogical debates of the 1970s, in Sweden it had been argued that competitive sports, unlike the old-fashioned Ling gymnastics, had a strong emotional appeal that could be used to lure young people away from negative and harmful temptations in society. For instance, in 1942 a manual pointed out that to involve the youth in proper and constructive education, it was necessary to satisfy their intense "need for joy," and that sports were an excellent means to do this.[10] Certainly, children and young peo-

---

bästa: En antologi om barndomens innebörder och välfärdens organisering, eds. Bengt Sandin, & Gunilla Halldén (Eslöv: B. Östlings bokförl. Symposion, 2003); Astri Andresen, Barnen och välfärdspolitiken: Nordiska barndomar 1900–2000 (Stockholm: Dialogos, 2011).

8. For an overview, Jan Plamper, The history of emotions: An introduction, (Oxford University Press, 2015)

9. Pascal Eitler, Stephanie Olsen & Uffa Jensen, "Introduction," in Learning how to feel: Children's literature and emotional socialization, 1870–1970, ed. Ute Frevert (Oxford University Press, 2014), 14–17.

10. Yngve Östberg, Ungdom och idrott: Råd och anvisningar för ledare av ungdomsavdelningar (Riksidrottsförbundets Ungdomskommitté, 1942), 5–7.

ple in sports have been ascribed different emotions and emotional needs far back in time. However, today we know little about the extent to which, in what way, and under what circumstances sports have fostered young people emotionally. In this study I will show that, during the last third of the twentieth century, new ways of approaching emotions took shape in society and that this is an important reason why the element of competition in sports for children and young people was questioned.

New Emotional Norms in a Post-Industrial Society

At the end of the 1950s and into the beginning of the 1960s, prominent Swedish intellectuals complained about what they perceived to be an emotional deficit in society. To get away from the emotionally dehydrated society they believed they were living in, these intellectuals searched for strong and overwhelming emotional storms, a longing that at least some of them satisfied by becoming politically active. Yet another consequence of this emotional yearning was that the notions of *alienation* and *authenticity* were deeply and excessively deliberated in the public debate. The concept of alienation pointed out that modern life had divided human nature into different spheres of existence, such as work, leisure, and domestic life. To counteract this negative development, people ought to become authentic by harmoniously developing themselves into well-balanced entities of emotion, morality, and reason. Important carriers of these ideas were, for instance, the alternative movements of the 1970s, which in order to realize the vision of the whole and free human being advocated moving to the country, experimenting with new forms of housing and cohabitation, and protecting forests, nature, and the environment from utilitarianism and excessive rationalization.[11]

As the material standard of society increased and became a relatively less important political issue, the notion of *quality of life* was instead given emotional and psychological meaning far more than it had previously had. Researchers have explained that this was a consequence of the fact that the industrial soci-

---

[11] Martin Wiklund *I det modernas landskap: Historisk orientering och kritiska berättelser om det moderna Sverige mellan 1960 och 1990* (Östlings bokförlag Symposion Eslöv 2006); Kristoffer Ekberg, *Mellan flykt och förändring: Utopiskt platsskapande i 1970-talets alternativa miljö* (Historiska institutionen, Lunds universitet, Lund, 2016); Jens Ljunggren, "Inledning: Känslor, tid och förändring," in *Känslornas revolution: kärlek, ilska och lycka på 1970-talet*, ed. Helena Bergman; Christina Florin & Jens Ljunggren (Appell förlag, Stockholm, 2017), 20–22; Jens Ljunggren, "The boosting and molding of anger: Swedish Social Democratic emotional policy from the 1880s to the 1980s," *Labour History Review* 83, no. 3 2018, 266–268.

ety was being replaced by a post-industrial economy, which due to its growing service sector, academicization, and expanding information technology placed new demands on how human relations and attitudes should be shaped. This was a multifaceted social process that, based on various motives and goals, moved away from the radical initiative's ambitions to build a new society and whose common denominator was instead to empower individuals by giving them an opportunity to grow and develop on their own.[12]

Some scholars have even argued that at the heart of this lay fundamental structural changes that thoroughly reshaped the human subject as such and allowed for various forms of modernity to exist in parallel. When traditional patterns of family and work life, career paths, gender roles, sexualities, and so on were broken down, individuals had to shape their life biographies with far less certainty than before. On the one hand, the new capitalist order required individuals to continuously adapt to new conditions. On the other hand, the individuals themselves did their best to maintain their flexibility so as not to get stuck in the limiting patterns of the past. Already in 1996, sociologist Zygmunt Bauman distinguished an "avoidance of being fixed" in society.[13]

The 1970s teachings on human self-realization paved the way for what many have called the psychologizing of society and led to a growing market for various forms of therapies and human self-optimization cultures. From the late 1960s, initiatives were taken in several areas of society to examine, comprehend, and improve people's emotional experiences. Experts engaged themselves in understanding how, for instance in work and family life or in connection with parenting and love relationships, to advance people's quality of life by guaranteeing them positive experiences in the form of pleasure as well as meaning and a sense of community. This was rooted in basic attitudes that spread internationally and sometimes also led to esoteric teachings and new forms of spirituality.[14]

---

[12] Linnea Tillema, *Övningar i frihet: Pedagogiseringen av känslolivet och mellanmänskliga relationer i 1970-talets Sverige* (Göteborg & Stockholm: Makadam förlag, 2021), 22; Philipp Sarasin, *1977: Eine kurze Geschichte der Gegenwart* (Berlin: Suhrkamp Verlag, 2021), 211–219.

[13] Zygmunt Bauman, *Tourists and Vagabonds: Heroes and Victims of Postmodernity* (Reihe Politikwissenschaft/Political Science Series No. 30, 1996), 12. For an overview of this debate see Heiner Keupp & Joachim Hohl, "Einleitung," in *Subjektdiskurse im gesellschaftlichen Wandel: Zur Theorie des Subjekts in der Spätmoderne*, eds. Heiner Keupp & Joachim Hohl (Transcript Verlag 2006), 8–9, 16.

[14] Pascal Eitler & Jens Eberfeld, "Von der Gesekkshaftsgeschichte zur Zeitgeschichte – und zurück," in *Zeitgeschichte des Selbst: Terapeutusierung – Politisierung – Emototionalisierung*, eds. Pascal Eitler & Jens Elberfeld (Transcript Bielefeld 2015, p. 29); Philipp Sarasin, *1977: Eine kurze Geschichte der Gegenwart* (Berlin: Suhrkamp Verlag, 2021), 211–219.

However, caring for people's emotions and quality of life also had the aim of releasing productive societal resources; therefore, human capital as such increasingly became a resource to be shaped and improved. The idea behind these efforts was that an organization that managed to satisfy its employees' desire for self-realization and well-being, and at the same time succeeded in enriching them with meaningful work and well-functioning social relationships, would gain in efficiency and development power. Therefore, it was believed to be of crucial importance to educate people to be empathetic and considerate as well as flexible and open to change. In this way, not only should the individual's self-realization and independency be harmonized with the collective's coexistence; foreseen here was also a virtually endless educational process, which meant that everyone was expected to constantly develop his or her personality. Attitudes such as these have survived and flourished in late 1900s and early 2000s workplace psychology, management, and self-improvement teachings.[15] As we will see in this chapter, these ideas also greatly affected sports for children and young people.

Personality Education in Leadership Manuals

This study's main research objects are coaching and leadership manuals for children and young people, published by the (SAA) during the period 1975–2020. The sports study and education association (SISU) were founded in 1985, and in 1992 established the publishing house SISU Sports Books to produce educational materials for the SSC. Most of the examined manuals were published by SISU and many of them were printed in several editions, which indicates that they were used for educational purposes and had commercial potential. From the 1980s onward, an increasing number of manuals were published, but apparently the genre was about to change shape. From the 1950s to the early 1970s leadership manuals consisted almost exclusively of practical exercise instructions or organizational matters.[16] Thereafter, they

---

[15] Kristoffer Ekberg, "Om lyckokänslor i arbetslivet i skiftet mellan 1970- och 80-tal," in *Känslornas revolution*; Linnea Tillema, *Övningar i frihet*, 97–104, 239–246.

[16] Gösta Holmér, *Hopp: Modern teknik och träning för vuxna och ungdom* (Stockholm: Lindqvist, 1959); Gösta Holmér, *Löpning: Modern teknik och träning för vuxna och ungdom* (Stockholm: Lindqvist, 1959); Gösta Holmér, *Kast: Modern teknik och träning för vuxna och ungdom* (Stockholm: Lindqvist, 1959); Hazze Jönsson, *Friidrottsskolan: Råd och anvisningar i friidrott för ungdom samt administration och organisation av friidrottsskolor* (Bjästa: Cewe-förl., 1975), Lennart Jönsson, *Friidrottsskolan: Råd och anvisningar i friidrott för ungdom* (Bjästa: Cewe-förl., 1975).

developed toward discussing leadership in general and including reasoning on children's and young people's psychological, intellectual, social, and moral development. This kind of normative material helps in analyzing changing attitudes in sports as well as in society. However, it is far more difficult to substantiate the extent to which it influenced the activity, not least as research has shown that the SSC's policy documents have far from always been implemented in practice.[17] Sports associations consist of different motivations and interests and we should therefore not assume that this normative material represented the entire SAA.

Based on the changing emotional norms in society outlined above, I contend that in order to analyze these leadership manuals we need to add to the concepts of competition and association education (here, also civic education) yet another analytical notion. Personality education, as I call this added concept, contains the moods and new emotional norms that prevailed in the post-industrial society. While association or civic education emphasizes societal benefits in terms of, for example, public health and democracy - and competition education promotes improvement in results - personality education instead stresses people's individual development and self-realization.

Alternately, these three forms of education have stood in opposition to, and overlapped, each other. Nothing excludes the possibility that the public bodies' mandatory civic education, or the competition education within the SSC, have in practice also been ways for people to shape and develop themselves personally. Equally, we should not assume that any of these forms of education could have worked without a measure of social competence or pleasure in work. It may be consistent to understand personality education as a new kind of civic education for a new society in which self-realizing individuals were expected to provide increased returns in working life by being creative and socially capable. Personality and competition education differ in that the former focuses primarily on human capital and on developing the personality as a whole, whereas the latter is directed at the development of results, measurable performances, and execution techniques, and is based on specialization. The model below is an abstract analytical tool, based on three ideal types, for scrutinizing the discussion on sports for children and young people; thus, it is not an exact depiction of reality:

---

[17] *Idrotten vill - en utvärdering av barn- och ungdomsidrotten* (F&U-rapport 2007: 1).

Civic Education	1. Public health
	2. Fostering of youth
	3. Respectability
	4. Democratic competence
	5. Good habits
Competition Education	1. Focus on results
	2. Specialization
	3. Top-down relationship between the leader and the active person
	4. Fixed rules
	5. Physical strength and ability
	6. Rationality and technological development
Personality Education	1. Focus on the development of the personality
	2. Holistic thinking
	3. Self-realization
	4. Emotional satisfaction
	5. Emotional and social skills
	6. Flexibility and creativity

Motivation, a Scarce Resource

As a consequence of the new emotional norms becoming established in society, the 1970s onward prompted a new kind of risk awareness to be voiced in the debate on sports for children and young people. Even more forcefully, not only the physical but also the psychological well-being of sporting children and young people was emphasized. In one of the typical dissertations of the time, the concern for young people's emotional lives was expressed as follows: "Physical education teachers have a narrow view of man as a work machine, which is only discussed in physiological terms. The mental part is completely forgotten, but a lot happens on the psychological level."[18] It was thus considered crucial to be able to understand how and why negative feelings arose in connection with competitive sports and, not least, to be able to

---

[18] Bert Aggestedt, & Ulla Tebelius, *Barns upplevelser av idrott* (Göteborg: Acta Universitatis Gothoburgensis, 1977), See also Göran Patriksson, *Idrottens barn: Idrottsvanor, stress, "utslagning,"* 1987, p. 6.

empathetically comprehend what low-performing children and young people were experiencing.[19] Within the framework of the physically based understanding of risk, it had been taken, more or less, for granted that children and young people were naturally inclined to compete in sports. By instead emphasizing the need to motivate young people, the emotion-based understanding of risk became a new challenge for Swedish children's and youth sports. In athletics, as we will see, this challenge was dealt with by emotionalizing sporting activity for young people.

In Swedish athletics leadership manuals, great effort was devoted to how to motivate children and young people to engage in sports. When instructor Lennart Jönsson discussed how to recruit young people to athletics in 1975, he concluded that the sports activity needed to be well organized and run by well-informed leaders.[20] In the manuals that followed during the 1980s and onward, the issue was dealt with in much more detail. From then on, instead of "recruitment" the manuals talked about "motivation," and in a fashion that resembled contemporary work psychology. Instead of assuming that young people were automatically inclined to engage in competitive sports, these manuals insisted that active efforts were needed to elicit the right emotions and willingness to play sports among youths.[21]

When one looks back at the development of sports for children and young people during the post-war era, an exceptional success story emerges. In 1943, boys devoted 19% and girls 4% of their spare time to sports. In 1998 the same figures were 30% and 19%, and now sports were the most popular organized leisure activity for children and young people. In 2007, more than 65% of children aged ten to eighteen participated in sports activities in clubs or associations each week.[22]

Still, there were reasons other than membership numbers to seriously consider young people's motivation for sports. Continuously during the period, issues of exclusion, stress, early specialization, competition, and dropout from sports

---

[19] Johnny Hjelm, "Skolidrottens tävlingsfostran 1930–1980," in *Fostran i skola och utbildning: historiska perspektiv,* ed. Anna Larsson (Uppsala: Föreningen för svensk undervisningshistoria, 2010), 165–166; Hjelm, *Idrott, tävling och allvar,* 47–48.

[20] Lennart Jönsson, *Friidrottsskolan,* 7–8, 28–32.

[21] Ylva Bergström; Ulrik Mattisson & Toralf Nilsson, *Friidrottens ungdomstränarutbildning: Ett studiecirkelmaterial: Bas allmän* (Stockholm: Svenska friidrottsförb., 1993), 13–15.

[22] Göran Patriksson, *Idrottens barn,* p. 57; Johnny Wijk, *Idrott, krig och nationell gemenskap,* 236; *Levnadsförhållanden rapport 116* (Statistiska centralbyrån 2009, 14).

were deliberated.[23] In 1995, the Swedish Sports Confederation adopted the policy document *Idrotten vill* (What Sport Wants), conveying common guidelines for, among other things, how to treat children and conduct sports for young people appropriately. From 2004 to 2007, the governmental program the *Handslag med idrotten* (Handshake with sports) was underway to make more sports available to more young people, and soon thereafter in 2007 was followed by yet another governmental program with similar intent, *Idrottslyftet* (the Promotion of Sports). In 2009, the UN Convention on the Rights of the Child was introduced in the regulation of the state's support for sports as well as in the SSC's statutes. From 2009 to 2011 the SSC had the Promotion of Sports program evaluated, and in 2015 the parliamentary Committee on Cultural Affairs decided to review the state's sports politics regarding children and young people.[24]

In other words, children's and youth sports were intensively monitored by government institutions as well as by a plethora of public debaters and researchers in sports science. Behind this lay particularly high ambitions regarding how to integrate children and young people into sports. In 2014, a survey showed that in terms of physical activity among young people Sweden was at the top among the European Community countries.[25] Still, Swedish authorities were not satisfied. They wanted even more young people to play sports. This, however, presupposed that the sports for youths were conducted in a way that could attract children outside of those most interested in competitive sports.

In the 1960s, to ensure an influx of young talent, the Swedish Athletics Association increased the number of competitions for young people.[26] Subsequently, recruitment ambitions were expanded further, and in leadership manuals published from the 1980s, it was pointed out that competition and motivation did not always go hand in hand. Although there could be no doubt that the competitive element remained the lifeblood of athletics, it was now also emphasized that to motivate as many young people as possible, the hitherto dominant focus

---

[23] Göran Patriksson, *Idrottens barn*, 1, 7, 61–65.

[24] Johan R. Norberg, *Statens stöd till idrotten: Uppföljning 2011* (Centrum för idrottsforskning, Stockholm, 2012), 50–51; Håkan Larsson, "Konsten att stänga dörren: Strategier för att få unga att vilja fortsätta," in *Spela vidare: En antologi om vad som får unga att fortsätta idrotta*, eds. Christine Dartsch Nilsson & Johan Pihlblad (Centrum för idrottsforskning 2013: 2), 123, 129.

[25] Charlotte van Tuyckom, "Youth Sports Participation: A comparison between European member states," in *Routledge Handbook of Youth Sports*, eds. Ken Green & Andy Smith (London: Routledge 2016), 61–71.

[26] Göran Patriksson, *Idrottens barn*, p. 9.

on performance needed to be toned down. For example, leadership manuals emphasized that children felt anxious about being excluded from the team or not being able to live up to performance standards, and that their personal concerns and needs must therefore be taken into account. In this respect, the reasoning was that overly goal-oriented training and an overemphasis on performance and results easily lead to performance anxiety, which causes young people to lose interest in sports. In addition, it was emphasized that it was necessary to let children and young people play games in a less pressured environment - that the main reason why they took part in sports was not a desire to win. Thus, the competition situation had to be adapted to the training situation instead of the other way around.[27]

Occasionally, the competition element in children's and youth sports was also discussed in more abstract terms. A 1993 textbook analyzed the issue by breaking it down into a few polar relationships. This was done by, for instance, contrasting expressive and instrumental approaches to sports. When children participated in physical activities of joy and found pleasure in having a well-functioning body, they acted in a physically expressive way. When leaders instead emphasized the competitive element and exclusively rewarded achievements, they promoted an instrumental approach to sports activities. In a similar fashion, the textbook considered the relationship between measurable values on the one hand and the children's inner experiences on the other. It was argued that in such a quantifiable activity as sports, it can easily happen that children's and young people's inner experiences are overlooked. Ultimately, however, the existential significance of sports lay in the fact that it could convey meaningful emotional experiences to its practitioners, and when this was no longer possible, its meaning was at stake, For example - "The experience of sports – the existential value of sports – is at least as important for the elite athlete as for those who practice exercise sports. The desire to achieve – the perfect – is an ability that we establish at a young age." So far, young people's positive experiences of sports were defined in terms of achievement, perfection, and success. However, the reasoning was incongruous. By drawing attention to young people's possi-

---

[27] Ulf Larsson, ed., *Psykologi och pedagogik* (Stockholm: Svenska fri-idrottsförb. 1985), 26–27; Ylva Bergström, Ulrik Mattisson, & Toralf Nilsson, *Friidrottens ungdomstränarutbildning: Ett studiecirkelmaterial. Introduktion* (Stockholm Svenska friidrottsförb. 1992), 11, 15; Helen Svan, *Friidrott för barn: 7–10 år* (Farsta: SISU idrottsböcker, 2000), 15, 23; Elin Sundlöf, & Peter Wikström, *Friidrott för barn* (Farsta: SISU idrottsböcker, 2011), 6, 12, 34; Håkan Widlund, *Friidrott för ungdom: 14–17 år* (Farsta: SISU idrottsböcker, 2003), p. 20.

ble negative experiences of sports and what this could lead to in terms of lack of motivation, the importance of always succeeding was relativized. Young people "must be allowed to fail, to play games [rather than sports], to always dare to try and challenge [their] limits." Accordingly, young people's motivation in sports should be promoted not only through opportunities for success but also through joy, togetherness, variation in training, and participation in the planning and evaluation of activities.[28]

Due to the ever-increasing recruitment demands and the firm belief in sport's positive effects on youths and society, adults' concerns about young people leaving sports intensified. Therefore, it was now considered more important than ever to understand the sporting children and young people from within by caring about their thoughts, worries, longings, and joys. We find the most detailed analysis of why children and young people left sports in the leadership manual *Friidrott* för *ungdom: 14–17* år (Athletics for Young People Aged 14-17), from 2003. This manual tried to come to terms with why children and young people preferred activities other than sports "within the framework of the traditionally organized sports movement." Its analysis indicated that young people long for experiences and sources of commitment other than those that association sports within SSC can offer. Instead of fixed and predetermined rules, young people want to decide for themselves when and how to play sports. Likewise, they expect to be immediately rewarded, which is the exact opposite of association-based sports' long planning horizons. In addition, it was argued that as a result of human identities being disconnected from the social class, young people strove to form their individual identities. In all this, it was concluded that the old-fashioned association sports with their "methodical patterns" had fallen short.[29]

The Sports Leader, an Emotional Worker

Just like the work motivation in contemporary work psychology, young people's motivation for sports was treated as something that needed to be actively enthused through external stimuli. As a consequence, a new form of leadership was called for. The leadership manual that dug deepest into understanding why

---

[28] *Friidrottens ungdomstränarutbildning* (1993), 12–14.

[29] *Friidrott för ungdom: 14–17 år* (2003), 2.

children and young people left competitive sports, *Friidrott* för *ungdom: 14–17* år (Athletics for Young People Aged 14–17) in 2003, was also the one that most thoroughly discussed the new leadership role. It emphasized that a significant reorganization of leadership practice was needed, which, however, presupposed that older sports leaders' alleged opposition to the necessary development must be broken down. This ambition was presented as a demand as well as a hope for the future: Now we need to educate young people, who,when they are older, will take over the leadership role and thus renew it.[30]

During the analysis period, the sports leader was increasingly portrayed as an *emotional worker*. The concept of emotional work comes from sociologist Arlie Russell Hochschild's pioneering study of flight attendants' working conditions in the US in the 1970s. She defined emotional work what people do when they moderate, adapt, and shape their emotions according to obligatory patterns in order to influence other people's feelings as well.[31] However, more was expected of leaders in children's and youth sports in Swedish athletics than merely adapting to external norms through their posture and facial expressions. They were encouraged to care for the children's and young people's mental, social, and physical well-being and to build deep relationships with them. Sports leaders thus needed to act as surrogate parents by taking an overall responsibility for children's and young people's education and personal development: "Leadership can be likened to parenthood or to wisdom," as one leadership manual pointed out.[32] It was even suggested that sports leaders were better reference persons for youths than their actual parents, who often pressed them too hard and had unrealistically high demands on their sporting development.[33]

To motivate the youths, the leader needed to be able to read their mood. The leadership manual *Psykologi och pedagogik* (Psychology and Pedagogy) stated in 1985 that the leader must be able to interpret the "motivational situation" and design the training practice so that all participants, taking into account their

---

[30] *Friidrott* för *ungdom: 14–17* år (2003), 8, 32.

[31] Arlie Russell Hochschild, *The managed heart: Commercialization of human feeling* (Berkeley: Univ. of California Press, 1983), Chapter 1.

[32] Leif Dahlberg; Rolf Asplund, & Maude Hjelte, *Idrottsskola för flickor och pojkar 7–10 år* (Stockholm: Svenska fri-idrottsförb. 1985, 7–9). See also Håkan Widlund, *Grundträning i friidrott 10–14 år* (Farsta: SISU Idrottsböcker, 2011).

[33] c (1985), 17; *Grundträning i friidrott 10–14 år* (Stockholm: SISU Idrottsböcker, 2011), 7.

level of performance as well as their gender, perceived it as meaningful.[34] Just as vehemently, the leadership manual *Friidrottens ungdomstränarutbildning* (Athletics' Youth Coaching Education) (1992) emphasized that the leader's task was primarily to "educate, enthuse and motivate" and that the crucial element of sports leadership was to "create the right attitude to training and competition." Only thereafter did the manual list what knowledge of physiology and technical skills the sports leader needed.[35] In a study manual from 1993, course participants were asked to discuss what they could do to strengthen young participants' level of motivation.[36] And as pointed out in yet another manual, it was the leader's responsibility "to create an atmosphere around the competition that makes it fun and exciting for everyone in the group to participate."[37]

However, the athletic leader's emotional work needed to go much deeper than that. He or she also had to be empathetic and able to understand how the children and young people felt in their lives in general. Already in the leadership manuals of the 1980s and 90s, this ambition came to the fore. In one of them, leaders were asked to be aware of what they exposed the children to and to ask themselves what feelings this might arouse in the young athletes.[38] In addition to planning and carrying out the training program, the leader must "have time and energy left over" to engage "on a personal level with the young people."[39] During the often-difficult years of youth, the leader must be able to understand the young people and their problems, but at the same time also be fully aware of and communicate their own values to them.[40] The emotionalization of the sports for children and young people leadership continued with undiminished strength into the twenty-first century. Now, it was emphasized that during the period in life when young people were driven by strong and

[34] *Psykologi och pedagogik* (1985), 28–32, 49–50.

[35] Ylva Bergström, Ulrik Mattisson & Toralf Nilsson, *Friidrottens ungdomstränarutbildning: Ett studiecirkelmaterial. Introduktion* (Svenska friidrottsförb., Stockholm, 1992), 5.

[36] *Friidrottens ungdomstränarutbildning* (1993), 3, 6.

[37] Elin Sundlöf & Peter Wikström, *Friidrott för barn* (Stockholm: SISU idrottsböcker, 2011), 6, 12, 34.

[38] Nils-Egil Rosenberg, *Träningsprogram för uppbyggnadsstadiet. D. 1* (Stockholm: Svenska fri-idrottsförb., 1987), p. 13.

[39] *Friidrottens ungdomstränarutbildning* (1992), 6–7; cf. *Idrottsskola för flickor och pojkar 7–10 år* (1985), 7–9.

[40] *Friidrottens ungdomstränarutbildning* (1992), 9–10; *Idrottsskola för flickor och pojkar 7–10 år* (1985), 7.

conflicting emotions and were simultaneously confronted with increased external demands from the surrounding society, the sports leader must be able to meet and talk to them.[41] These high expectations of what positive personal development and the interaction between the leader and the young athletes would result in were maintained through general reasoning about children's and young people's mental and social development.[42]

Although the leadership manuals called for understanding of and openness to children's different emotional states, they were also normative in that they conveyed a clear-cut principle of enjoyment. On the one hand, it was argued that even though negative and strong emotions could be hard for the adults to handle, it was necessary to let children "show their feelings." On the other hand, it was emphasized that the leader must always guarantee the children positive shared experiences.[43] Whether the children were happy, sad, confident, insecure, stubborn, or lazy, it must be the task of the leader to let them experience the maximum "joy, fellowship, excitement and development."[44] One of the leadership manuals summarized what it was all about as follows: "Having fun is one of the main reasons why children choose sports. But sometimes in sports, children experience something completely different. They may feel unfairly treated, there might be a difficult moment, it can be one-sided and boring. This is where your ability is put to the test. It is now that you have the chance to offer what is fun."[45]

An obvious problem with the principle of enjoyment, of course, is how best to deal with the disappointment of defeat. Some of the manuals touched on how to deal with losses and explained that the leader must learn to de-dramatize young people's feelings of failure. In this matter, the leadership manuals were influenced not only by work psychology but also by current sports psychology. Still, on this issue they were also contradictory. For example, in the event of a loss, the sports leader was instructed to care for everyone equally and to

---

[41] *Friidrottens ungdomstränarutbildning* (1992), 9–10; *Idrottsskola för flickor och pojkar 7–10 år* (1985), 7.

[42] *Friidrott för barn* (2011), 21–24.

[43] *Friidrott för barn* (2011), 13, 22–24, 26, 29. See also Nils-Egil Rosenberg, *Träningsprogram för uppbyggnadsstadiet* (Stockholm: Svenska fri-idrottsförb., 1987), p. 13; Daniel Bergin, *Friidrottens tävlingar för barn: Regler och riktlinjer för tävlingsverksamhet för barn* (Stockholm: Svensk friidrott, 2019), 2019, 3.

[44] *Friidrott för barn* (2011), 6.

[45] Helen Svan, *Friidrott för barn: 7–10 år* (Farsta: SISU idrottsböcker 2000), 29.

emphasize that there is no shame in losing.[46] In a leadership manual for young people aged fourteen to seventeen, failure was instead almost treated as taboo, while simultaneously the responsibility for dealing with it was placed on the young athletes themselves. The young athletes were encouraged to control their emotions and to learn to erase memories of failures with the help of mental training.[47]

From the 1970s onward, children's and youth sports thus faced new challenges. While the element of competition was repeatedly questioned in both professional and public debate, it was still a priority for SAA to organize as many children and young people as possible and to ensure that they were properly taken care of. To meet these challenges, measures were taken to emotionalize sports for children and young people in a positive way, which led to three important consequences. First, the sporting child was defined as an emotional subject. Second, the sports leader was defined as an emotional worker. Third, the activity was designed based on the principle of enjoyment, which did not leave much space for difficult, challenging emotions and experiences in connection with the practice of sports. Still, in all this there was a contradiction. Through positive emotional work, children and young people would be motivated to take part in competitive sports; however, as a result of the positive emotionalization, the elements of competition and performance in children's and youth sports were problematized and downplayed.

Athletics' Personality Education

There was, however, more to the sports leader's emotional work than simply recharging children's and youth sports with positive emotions as a reaction to heightened emotional risks. It was also about forming and developing the character of children in a certain way. Determinedly, and completely in step with the spirit of the times, several personality education goals were expressed in the sports leadership manuals. Occasionally, these goals were expressed in terms of various psychological developmental ladders. *Psykologi och pedagogik* (Psychology and Pedagogy), from 1985, was inspired by psychologist Abraham H. Maslow's hierarchy of needs. Maslow had present-

---

[46] *Psykologi och pedagogik*, 1985, 15: *Friidrott för barn 7–10 år* (2000), 33.

[47] *Friidrott för ungdom: 14–17 år* (2003), 9, 21, 23–24, 28–29.

ed his ideas as early as 1943 in the article "A Theory of Human Motivation." At the bottom of the hierarchy of needs we find physical demands, and then in ascending order the human needs for security, belonging, and love. Thereafter follows respect (self-confidence, self-respect, and recognition) and finally, at the top of the pyramid, self-realization.[48] Additionally, the brochure *Friidrott för barn: 7–10 år* (Athletics for Children Aged 7-10) of 2000 presented a development ladder for young athletes' personal and social education. Here the ladder consisted of four steps: "joy," "fellowship," "stimulus," and "self-worth."[49]

We have already seen that the sports leadership manuals conveyed the view that the pedagogical task of sports for children and young people – as well as the relationship between sports leaders and young athletes – must entail self-realization in close human relationships characterized through inner satisfaction and emotional and social competence. Creativity and intuition, as well as the opportunity for young people to develop freely to become independent, innovative, trusting, and responsible individuals were also added to these original principles. As noted above, it was believed that showing young people trust, compassion, and respect and providing them a safe environment would allow them to "develop and grow" on their own. To promote their creativity and problem-solving ability, it was also important to make them feel affirmed and convey to them that they had the ability to develop.[50]

Repeatedly in the leadership manuals, a holistic educational ideal for the sporting children and young people was highlighted. For instance, one of the manuals explained that the human being consists of different parts – physical, cognitive, and emotional – and that sports educators must therefore strive to maintain a holistic view of the children and their development.[51] Or, as articulated elsewhere: "We want to emphasize once again that children's development should be seen from a holistic perspective. By adapting the activities to each child's conditions and creating a positive environment, the children's development is stimulated."[52] In another manual, it was stressed that the young

---

[48] *Psykolog och Pedagogik* (1985), 26–27

[49] *Friidrott för barn: 7–10 år* (2000), p. 27.

[50] *Idrottsskola för flickor och pojkar: 7–10 år* (1985), p. 7; *Friidrottens ungdomstränarutbildning* (1992), 9–10; *Friidrott för ungdom: 14–17 år* (2003), 7, 11–12, 17; *Friidrott för barn* (2011), 21–24.

[51] *Friidrottens ungdomstränarutbildning* (1992), 3–4, 9–10.

[52] *Friidrott för barn: 7–10 år* (2000), p. 10. See also *Idrottsskola för flickor och pojkar 7–10 år* (1985), 7–9.

athletes naturally needed to improve their technique and practice specific skills, but that they must also be given space for their emotions, intuition, and creativity. If the sports leader noticed that the participants were overprioritizing the left hemisphere of their brain by focusing on "logic, analysis, technology and strategic thinking," it was necessary to compensate for this by letting them play games, music, sing, paint and draw pictures, or just be creative - for instance, encouraging them to create their own exercises. A number of measures such as technical exercises, analysis, planning, and statistics, were also listed as optional techniques for development.[53]

It is worth noting here that the emphasis on the holistic understanding of young athletes did not directly lead to specialization, and that none of the developmental ladders referred to above, conveyed anything about competition education in the form of careful preparation, goals, competition, or combat. Nor did they have anything to say about being disciplined or learning to uphold routines. As a consequence of the personality education ambitions in the reviewed leadership manuals, they instead articulated a divergence between the children and young people on the one hand, and the elements of competition and performance on the other. It is telling, for example, that while a 1993 leadership manual stated that it was both natural and meaningful for children to develop their capability to perform in sports, it also questioned whether it might not be more important for them to "develop their skills" than to achieve "competitive success."[54]

Most clearly, the opposition between personality and competitive education was accentuated in the leadership manuals of the twenty-first century. The authors behind *Friidrott för barn: 7–10 år* (Athletics for Children Aged 7-10) (2000) explained that with "psychological and social development, we want to point to children's intellectual, social and emotional development." They also emphasized that it "becomes important to pay attention to the children for who they are and not for what they can achieve."[55] In the introduction to a manual from 2011, it was stressed that play (in contrast to organized competitive sports) was important for children's personal social and intellectual development.[56] Even more sharply, in a leadership manual for children aged ten to

---

[53] *Friidrott för ungdom: 14–17 år* (2003), 19–20.

[54] *Friidrottens ungdomstränarutbildning* (1993), 4–5.

[55] *Friidrott för barn; 7–10 år* (2000), 15.

[56] *Friidrott för* barn (2011), 18.

fourteen years from 2011 it was argued that if "the active person feels that he/ she is appreciated and respected by the leader regardless of his or her athletic success during training and competition, it becomes clear that human value is the most important thing of all."[57] Not letting too much of the participant's well-being and the perception of their human dignity be governed by how well they performed was also a reason why the leader must take care of the young athlete's inner life and pay attention to their personhood as individuals.[58]

Most eloquent on the subject was, again, *Friidrott för ungdom: 14–17 år* (Athletics for Young People 14-17). In long sections of this text, no strict competition education - in terms of ranking and continuous performance improvements - was expressed at all. Instead, it focused on developing each individual's personality. Under the heading "Our guiding stars," an account was given of how to create "personal and social stimuli" for the children. Sports, it was argued here, must be based on the notion of equal human dignity and an activity for "personal development." In practice, this meant that sports for children and youth should enable progress and development according to each participant's actual abilities. In addition, the youths must also be allowed to be and dream without having to live up to external demands. The manual defined "external attention" in terms of training, competition, the development of skills, and results. "Internal attention" instead involved 'nurturing thoughts and fantasies and drawing attention to the young person's interests outside sports. Perhaps this is what sports must ultimately strive for, one of the brochure's contributors deliberated: "Our educational goals will then be directed toward human issues such as personal development, social and emotional competence."[59]

In all examples above, we can see that there has been a shift in focus from performance to the young athlete's personal development. But sports leaders, too, were required to develop their personalities. Basically, a good leader must embrace being a leader, and a good reason for choosing this position was to "be able to develop as a person." While this was considered an intrinsic value in sports leadership, the leader's personality education was also depicted as a duty. The leader, it was argued, must be able to create the right conditions for his or her "own personal development."[60] Children's and youth sports as such

---

[57] *Grundträning i friidrott: 10–14 år* (Stockholm: SISU Idrottsböcker, 2011), 18.

[58] *Friidrott för ungdom: 14–17 år* (2003), 20.

[59] *Friidrott för ungdom: 14–17 år* (2003), 4, 20, 29.

[60] *Friidrott för ungdom: 14–17 år* (2003), 10, 14. See also, *Friidrott för barn 7–10 år* (2000), 28.

thus took the form of a unit for personality education for all, and in this respect no distinction was made between children and adults.

A New Concept of Sports

Throughout the analysis period, of course, the element of competition education continued to be the main motivating factor for the leadership manuals. However, as shown above, significant elements of personality education were also gradually added to the sports pedagogy for children and young people in Swedish athletics. Consequently, as we have also seen, a contradictory relationship arose between competition and personality education. Repeatedly, leadership manuals underlined that children's mental well-being, self-esteem, and personal development must be decoupled from performance thinking and a one-sided focus on competition. If we consider the ongoing emotional-historical development that was behind the ideal of personality education, especially from the 1970s onward, it becomes clear that this was a way of adapting sports for children and young people to changing societal demands. Problematizing the element of competition for youths was partly about protecting them. However, it was also a matter of encouraging them to grow and develop to eventually become as highly-functioning, efficient, and productive citizens in the post-industrial society as possible.

To a great extent, the leadership manuals examined in this study overlapped the SSC's policy documents. For example, *Idrotten vill* (What Sport Wants) emphasized that everyone had the right to participate regardless of their physical or mental condition. It explicated the case that children's all-round development should be the primary goal, and that young people should be allowed to participate and compete against themselves instead of others. The combination of competition and personality education that the leadership manuals conveyed was even more in line with the SSC program *Strategi 2025* (Strategy 2025), which called for "new approaches to training and competition." These approaches involved less specialization and more individualization. The strategy accentuated that the association sports organized by the SSC must renew themselves by not merely highlighting competition and only focusing on the result. In short, "sports where we focus on ourselves instead of just comparing ourselves with others. All clubs – regardless of sport – should be inspired by it."

At the moment, we know much less about how the young people themselves perceived the matter; however, some studies have shown that personality development has been an important motive for many young people in Swedish association sports. According to a recent opinion poll, children and young people in association sports are more involved in non-profit organizations than others. Furthermore, the most important motive for those engaged in non-profit activities is personal development.[61] According to a qualitative study, young people find meaning in sports mainly because they feel they can develop and learn new things. Although children and young people value competition, they often do so based on personal development. The competition element engages them and becomes a way for them to grow and measure their abilities. Still, winning and succeeding in competitions are far from always the most important motive for them. Many are more attracted by what the competition offers now than by long-term elite investments, while others adapt to competition practice in the sports associations because it is the only option.[62]

I argue here that in the leadership manuals, the SSC's policy documents - and the young people's attitude to sports - a new conceptualisation of sports took shape, incorporating the element of competition into a personality education framework. The notion of personality education was supported by an ideal for individual development. Based on their actual abilities, and in line with the holistic understanding of the human being, children and young people were encouraged to play sports to realize themselves in an environment that would be characterized by emotional competence and satisfaction. Taken together, this promoted a form of individualism that could not easily be adapted to the traditional competition education in Swedish association sports. It is therefore worth noting that much of what contemporary sports leaders actually stood for – such as the importance of stimulating children's winning instincts, that it was a positive upbringing experience for children to deal with losses, that young people's motivation was based on success, or that competition was a prerequisite for learning – had no prominent place in the leadership manuals studied here.[63] Indeed, it seems that there was a conflict between different levels within the organization regarding how to define sports for children and young people.

---

[61] *En engagerad idrottsgeneration?* (Ungdomsbarometern & Centrum för idrottsforskning 2020), 28–29.

[62] Britta Thedin Jakobsson, "'Därför vill vi fortsätta:' Om glädje, tävling och idrottsidentitet," 70–71, 77–78, in *Spela vidare.*

[63] Redelius, *Ledarna och barnidrotten,* 190–191; Larsson, "Konsten att stänga dörren," 123–152.

However, the emerging conceptualisation of sports was not entirely new. Throughout the nineteenth century and well into the twentieth, Swedish gymnastics had been based on a holistic understanding in combination with an idea of constant individual self-improvement.[64] At the end of the twentieth century, these ideals reappeared. An important difference, however, was that while the twentieth-century model had been stable and predetermined, the late twentieth-century personality education ideal instead presupposed a virtually endless developmental process of the individual. The ideal of personality education thus combined a holistic thinking that we recognize from early Swedish gymnastics along with a dynamic element that we recognize from competitive sports. As a predominantly individual sport, athletics appears to be a particularly interesting case when it comes to personality education.

Summary

The great bulk of research on the development sports for sports for children and young people from the 1970s onward has focused on how and why competitive sports intensified. In this study, I have instead analyzed how and why competitive sports for children and young people were questioned during the period. From the perspective of emotional history, this study examines both why the competition element was perceived as problematic and what consequences this had for children's and youth sports in Swedish athletics. In the post-industrial society, the importance of emotions increased and new norms for what people had the right to feel (and what they should not need to feel) were defined. But at the same time, emotions were also used as productive resources more than ever before.

Regarding risk awareness in sports for children and young people, the emphasis was no longer exclusively on the physical dangers but increasingly also on the emotional strains the young people were arguably exposed to in connection with competitive sports. At the same time, however, emotions also became a way to overcome young people's reluctance to participate in competitive sports. In leadership manuals for young people, emotions were treated as something that was open, mobile, and possible to influence and change, and there-

---

[64] See for instance, Jens Ljunggren, "Linggymnastics: The masculine road through modernity: Ling gymnastics and Male Socialisation in Ninteenth-Century Sweden," *European Sports History Review: European Masculinities: Sport, Europe, Gender,* vol 2 (2000).

fore something that could be used to make competitive sports attractive. Consequently, the sporting child was increasingly defined as an emotional subject and the leader as an emotional worker. However, along with high expectations of how to get young people to play sports and how to attract more than only those who were most interested in competitive sports, the emotionalization of sports for children and young people led to the element of competition being problematized and moderated.

To further deepen the understanding of why the competition element was questioned, in this study I have introduced the concept of personality education, which, I claim, helps us understand how the education of young athletes in Swedish athletics was adapted to changing societal norms concerning how to behave and what to strive for in life. In the post-industrial society where such things as flexibility, creativity, emotional fulfillment, and emotional and social competence were highly valued, old-style competition education became somewhat outdated. Relatively speaking, the focus shifted from body techniques and performance to emotions, relationships, and the development of the individual as a whole.

What emerged, I argue, was a new concept of sports that integrated the element of competition into a context of personality education. Overall, it was about protecting young people and recruiting them to sports. However, understanding the criticism of competition and achievement in children's and youth sports solely as a means of liberating or shielding the children and young people would be too one-sided. Given the historical context it was, not least, a matter of making them suitable for and able to contribute as efficiently as possible to the new post-industrial society. It has been thoroughly demonstrated here that this was the case in normative leadership manuals. However, we know less about the extent to which new ideas were implemented in the clubs.

CHAPTER 10

Technological Innovation and Performance Enhancement in Norwegian Running

Anne Tjønndal and Frida Austmo Wågan

During the last two decades Norwegian elite runners have managed to set several new European records in middle- and long-distance running. As of 2023, more Norwegian runners than ever before are able to compete at an elite international level. This recent success has also contributed to increased recruitment of new athletes, media coverage as well as general fan interest in the sport of running in Norway. For instance, participation rates from the national Norwegian Athletics Championships demonstrate that in a twenty-year time period (2003–2022), participation in the running events increased by 52.4%. Some have called the uplift in running performances, increased participation at grassroots levels, and fan-interest the "Ingebrigtsen-effect", since the technologically advanced and scientifically prescribed training regimes of Jacob Ingebrigtsen – himself an Olympic gold medalist and European champion at 1500 meters– has been successful in inspiring other Norwegians to use biomedical and self-tracking technology for training.[1]

Norwegian training philosophies in athletics and other sports have changed substantially during the last three decades. In particular, the development of training philosophies have been shaped by an increased *scientification*. By scientification we refer to the use of specialized, scientific training methods favored by Ingebrigtsen and the increasing importance of knowledge derived from sport science in the training and development of elite athletes.[2] This includes the sys-

---

[1]   Egil Ø. Nærland, "Ingebrigtsen-effekten: Ventelister hos hjemklubben i Sandnes," *Aftenposten,* August 18, 2018, https://www.aftenposten.no/sport/i/0n9yzE/ingebrigtsen-effekten-ventelister-hos-hjemklubben-i-sandnes.

[2]   See for example: Marius Bakken, "The Norwegian model of lactate threshold training and lactate controlled approach to training," *Mariusbakken.com,* July 28, 2022, http://www.mariusbakken.com/the-norwegian-model.html; Håkon Hapnes Strand, "Terskeltrening gjør deg til løpsmaskin," *Forskning.no,* October 29, 2012, https://forskning.no/menneskekroppen-partner-sport/terskeltrening-gjor-deg-til-lopsmaskin/674625; Daniel Svensson, "*Scientizing performance in endurance*

tematic usage of lactate threshold training, and the reliance on lactate measures when controlling for training intensity and training load in elite runners. Since the early 2000s, lactate threshold training has increased in popularity, and is now recognized as an important asset of "the new Norwegian model," and has become the dominant approach to training in a vast majority of running clubs and groups in Norway.[3] International athletes from other countries, like Sweden and USA, has also copied the model with great success in more recent years.[4]

The scientification of training in 'the new Norwegian model', combined with technological innovations related to equipment, biomedical and self-tracking technology, are not unique to Norway, but have been promoted as crucial factors in athletics globally since the middle of the twentieth century.[5] A contemporary example of one influential technological innovation is the invention of carbon fiber soles in running shoes, resulting in the development of more energy-returning and performance enhancing shoe technology.[6] Advances in performance enhancing technology, such as the aforementioned carbon fiber running shoes, are often debated in the media and within the scientific community.[7] However, with the high speed of technological development in a globalized world, scientific research often lags behind public debate, and there are few scholarly investigations of the impact of recent technological innovations on performance enhancement in elite running, especially in a Scandinavian context.

sports: The emergence of 'rational training' in cross-country skiing, 1930–1980, " (PhD diss., KTH Royal Institute of Technology, 2016).

[3] Trine Mjåland, "Terskeltrening er trendy og effektivt. Slik anbefaler idrettsforsker at du gjør det," Aftenposten, January 26, 2021, https://www.aftenposten.no/sport/sprek/i/47mqdq/terskel-trening-er-trendy-og-effektivt-slik-anbefaler-idrettsforsker-a.

[4] Runar Gilberg, "Kalle Berglund så til Norge og begynte med doble terskeløkter," Kondis.no, September 4, 2019, https://www.kondis.no/kalle-berglund-saa-til-norge-og-begynte-med-doble-terskeloekter.6244051-393386.html.

[5] Nigel Balmer, Pascoe Pleasence, and Alan Nevill, "Evolution and revolution: Gauging the impact of technological and technical innovation on Olympic performance," Journal of Sports Sciences 30, no. 11 (2012): 1075–1083, https://doi.org/10.1080/02640414.2011.587018; Giuseppe Lippi, Giuseppe Banfi, Emmanuel J. Favaloro, Joern Rittweger, and Nicola Mafulli, "Updates on improvement of human athletic performance: Focus on world records in athletics," British Medical Bulletin 87, no. 1 (2008): 7–15, https://doi.org/10.1093/bmb/ldn029.

[6] Geoffrey T. Burns, and Nicholas Tam, "Is it the shoes? A simple proposal for regulating footwear in road running," British Journal of Sports Medicine 54, no. 8 (2020): 435–443, https://bjsm.bmj.com/content/54/8/439.

[7] Amby Burfoot, "Those Superfast Nike Shoes Are Creating a Problem," New York Times, October 18, 2019, https://www.nytimes.com/2019/10/18/sports/marathon-running-nike-vaporfly-shoes.html.

In this chapter we examine how recent technological innovations in bio-medical, wearable self-tracking training technology and the scientification of running in general has impacted performance enhancement in middle- and long-distance running in Norway. Specifically, we aim to investigate how coaches approach technology for performance enhancement in elite running. The following research question is examined: *how do Norwegian elite running coaches approach novel technologies and what are their experiences of risks and benefits for the athletes?* Empirically, we base our chapter on qualitative interviews with coaches in Norwegian running, focusing on their experiences of technology, scientification of training and performance development.

The next part of the chapter gives a brief summary of previous research on scientification, technological innovation, and performance enhancement in running. This is followed by a description of our theoretical framework: Giddens' globalization hypothesis, before an outline of the methodological process.[8] The second half of the chapter is comprised of our findings and discussion, before some concluding remarks are presented.

Scientification, technological innovation and performance enhancement in running

The use of scientific approaches and biomedical technologies in sports have significantly escalated in recent decades.[9] This includes an intensification of the use of scientifically derived knowledge from sport psychology, sport physiology and biomechanics applied to systematic analysis of biometrical data (e.g heart rate, lactate levels, speed).[10] In running, such a scientific approach to training is seen as necessary for the development of elite athletes.[11] The lack of scientification is, in

---

[8]   Anthony Giddens, *The Consequences of Modernity,* (Stanford: Stanford University Press, 1990).

[9]   Andy Miah, "Rethinking enhancement in sport," *Annals of the New York Academy of Sciences* 1093, no. 1 (2006): 301–320, https://doi.org/10.1196/annals.1382.020; Barry Drust, and M. Green, "Science and football: evaluating the influence of science on performance," *Journal of Sports Sciences* 31, no. 13 (2013): 1377 – 1382, https://doi.org/10.1080/02640414.2013.828544.

[10] Svensson, *"Scientizing performance in endurance sports."*

[11] Benjamin B. Houston, "Creating the consumer-runner: The impact of medicine, commercialization, and public awareness on the popularization of long-distance running in the United States during the twentieth century," (PhD diss., Western Illinois University, 2015).

some cases, blamed for shortcomings in athletic performance.[12] Two examples of
the latter are the studies by Li and Mao who, in studies of Chinese athletics, explain
the lack of performance enhancement and world-level performances by emphasizing the missing link between new scientific knowledge and exercise planning and
monitoring on the part of coaches in Chinese athletics training philosophies.[13]

Previous research has found that technological innovation significantly impacts performances in many Olympic sports, including javelin,[14] swimming,[15]
pole vault,[16] and cycling.[17] In many sports, the use of various technologies is
essential to practice the sport itself. However, running is a sport with minimal need for technology in terms of equipment.[18] Despite this, technological
advances in running shoes, systematic use of biomedical tools such as lactate
measures accompanied with scientifically derived knowledge about exercise
physiology, have each played an essential part of performance advancement in
recent years.[19] For instance, all world records in distances ranging from 5000m
to marathons have been broken since the 2016 shoe innovation where Nike
added a combination of a carbon fiber plate and high-energy return foam in
production of their running shoes.[20] The biggest improvements are seen in the
longest distances, and the finish times of top international marathon runners

[12] Hong Li, "Research on the Status Quo and Countermeasures of Scientific Training of Track and
Field Sports," *Insight-Sports Science* 2, no. 2 (2020): 58–61; Peng Mao, "Scientific, confident
and painstaking training innovation–the inevitable way to the development of track and field in
China," *Journal of Physical Education* 16, no. 8 (2009): 14–17.

[13] *Ibid.*

[14] Lippi et al., "Updates on improvement of human athletic performance."

[15] Todd A. McFall, Amanda L. Griffith, and Kurt W. Rotthoff, "The Impact of Technology and
Rule Changes on Elite Swimming Performances," in *The Economics of Aquatic Sports Sports
Economics, Management and Policy,* ed. Jill S. Harris (Springer Cham, 2020): 77–92, https://
doi.org/10.1007/978-3-030-52340-4_9.

[16] Balmer et al., "Evolution and revolution."

[17] Steve J. Haake, "The impact of technology on sporting performance in Olympic sports," *Journal
of Sports Sciences* 27, no. 13 (2009): 1421–1431, https://doi.org/10.1080/02640410903062019.

[18] Joel T. Fuller, Clint R. Bellenger, Dominic Thewlis, Margarita D. Tsiros, and Jonathan D. Buck-
ley, "The effect of footwear on running performance and running economy in distance runners," *Sports Medicine* 45, no. 3 (2015): 411–422, https://doi.org/10.1007/s40279-014-0283-6.

[19] Burns and Tam, "Is it the shoes?"; Borja Muniz-Pardos, Shaun Sutehall, Konstantinos Angelou-
dis, Fergus M. Guppy, Andrew Bosch, and Yannis Pitsiladis, "Recent Improvements in Marathon
Run Times Are Likely Technological, Not Physiological," *Sports Medicine* 51, (2021): 371–378,
https://doi.org/10.1007/s40279-020-01420-7.

[20] Stéphane Bermon, Frédéric Garrandes, Andras Szabo, Imre Berkovics, and Paolo Emilio Ada-
mi, "Effect of advanced shoe technology on the evolution of road race times in male and female elite runners," *Frontiers in Sports and Active Living* 3 (2021), https://doi.org/10.3389/
fspor.2021.653173.

have improved by 2% for men and 2.6% for women after the 2016 innovation in shoe technology.[21]

Research on biomedical and wearable self-tracking technology in running has mainly focused on athletes' use of this technology in relation to performance enhancement and injury prevention.[22] This literature indicates that male runners are more likely to use wearable self-tracking technology compared to female runners.[23] Furthermore, runners motivated by goals of performance enhancement and competition success, as well as young athletes, report more frequent use of self-tracking technology compared to recreational runners, and older athletes.[24] Clermont and colleagues found a difference in intentions for using self-tracking technology and preferred running technology when comparing competitive and recreational runners in Canada. In this study, competitive runners were operationalized as runners that ran more than four times per week and that had athletic competition as motivation for running (self-identified). These runners preferred GPS-tracking watches and were interested in tracking personalized data to optimize running efficiency. Recreational runners were operationalized as runners who ran less than three times per week and had health-related motivations for their running. They found that recreational runners used apps and wristband activity trackers to increase motivation for exercise. Common for both recreational and competitive runners was the belief that basic metrics found in self-tracking technology was important for injury prevention.[25]

[21] Jonathan Senefeld, "Technological advances in elite marathon performance," *Journal of applied physiology* 130, no. 6 (2021): 1635-2024, https://doi.org/10.1152/japplphysiol.00002.2021.

[22] Mark Janssen, Ruben Walravens, Erik Thibaut, Jeroen Scheerder, Aarnout Brombacher, and Steven Vos, "Understanding Different Types of Recreational Runners and How They Use Running-Related Technology," *International Journal of Environmental Research and Public Health* 17, no. 7 (2020) 2276, https://doi.org/10.3390/ijerph17072276; Christian A. Clermont, Linda Duett-Leger, Blayne A. Hettinga, and Reed Ferber, "Runners' perspectives on 'smart' wearable technology and its use for preventing injury," *International Journal of Human-Computer Interaction* 36, no. 1 (2020): 31–40, https://doi.org/10.1080/10447318.2019.1597575.

[23] Martin Wiesner, Richard Zowalla, Julian Suleder, Maximilian Westers, and Monika Pobiruchin, "Technology adoption, motivational aspects, and privacy concerns of wearables in the German running community: field study," *JMIR mHealth and uHealth* 6, no. 12 (2018), https://doi.org/10.2196/mhealth.9623; Marijke Taks, Roland Renson, and Bart Vanreusel, "Social stratification in sport: A matter of money or taste," *European Journal for Sport Management* 2, no. 1 (1995): 4–14.

[24] Clermont et al., "Runners' perspectives"; Janssen et al., "Understanding Different Types of Recreational Runners and How They Use Running-Related Technology"; Mark Janssen, Jeroen Scheerder, Erik Thibaut, Aarnout Brombacher, and Steven Vos, "Who uses running apps and sports watches? Determinants and consumer profiles of event runners' usage of running-related smartphone applications and sports watches," *PLOS ONE* 12, no. 7 (2017), https://doi.org/10.1371/journal.pone.0181167.

[25] Clermont et al., "Runners' perspectives."

Research on running coaches' experiences of performance enhancing technology are still scarce,[26] with a few notable exceptions. For instance, Fleming and colleagues found that 92% of elite coaches and runners sampled (N= 62) believed that wearable self-tracking technology was essential to improving performance, especially in terms of preventing injuries and improving technique.[27] Another study on North-American college athletics by Rauff and colleagues,[28] examined coaches' perspectives on gathering and using scientific data in athletics, and found that a majority of coaches (54%) felt that collecting data could support them when designing training regimes for their athletes, while 61% felt that they would benefit from monitoring progress in their athletes through data from self-tracking technology.

Most literature in the field focuses mainly on the positive effects of technological innovation on running performances.[29] Yet, some critical concerns have been raised by scholars.[30] These perspectives highlight the possible harmful and unintended consequences of applying self-tracking technology to athlete performance, such as reducing movement and performance to ra-

---

[26] Roger S. Jaswal, Pro Stergiou, and Larry Katz, "How Canadian High-Performance Coaches Adopt and Implement Technology: Exploring the Antecedents of Intra-and Interorganizational Trust, Technological Proficiency, and Subjective Norms and Social Influence on Technology Adoption," *International Sport Coaching Journal* 9, no. 1 (2021): 234–243, https://doi.org/10.1123/iscj.2020-0088.

[27] Paul Fleming, Colin Young, Sharon Dixon, and Matt Carré, "Athlete and coach perceptions of technology needs for evaluating running performance." *Sports Engineering* 13, no. 1 (2010): 1–18, https://doi.org/10.1007/s12283-010-0049-9.

[28] Erica L. Rauff, Augustine Herman, Douglas Berninger, Sean Machak, and Sarah P. Shultz, "Using sport science data in collegiate athletics: Coaches' perspectives," *International Journal of Sports Science & Coaching* 17, no. 3 (2022): 500–509, https://doi.org/10.1177/17479541211065146.

[29] Luke Jones, Tim Konoval, and John Toner, "Sport and Surveillance Technologies," in *Sport, Social Media, and Digital Technology: Sociological Approaches,* ed. Jimmy Sanderson (Bingley: Emerald Publishing Limited, 2022), 165–183, https://doi.org/10.1108/S1476-285420220000015020.

[30] Joseph Mills, Jim Denison, and Brian Gearity, "Breaking coaching's rules: Transforming the body, sport, and performance," *Journal of Sport and Social Issues* 44, no. 3 (2020): 244–260, https://doi.org/10.1177/0193723520903228; Luke Jones, and Jim Denison, "A sociocultural perspective surrounding the application of global positioning system technology: Suggestions for the strength and conditioning coach," *Strength & Conditioning Journal* 40, no. 6 (2018): 3–8, https://doi.org/10.1519/SSC.0000000000000367; Jim Denison, Luke Jones, and Joseph Mills, "Becoming a good enough coach," *Sports Coaching Review* 8, no. 1 (2019): 1–6, https://doi.org/10.1080/21640629.2018.1435361; Jo Little, "Running, health and the disciplining of women's bodies: The influence of technology and nature," *Health & place* 46, (2017): 322–327, https://doi.org/10.1016/j.healthplace.2016.11.011; Shaun Williams, and Andrew Manley, "Elite coaching and the technocratic engineer: Thanking the boys at Microsoft!," *Sport, Education and Society* 21, no. 6 (2016): 828–850, https://doi.org/10.1080/13573322.2014.958816.

tional systems where the body functions as a machine.[31] Furthermore, the normalization of the use of self-tracking technology in sport settings are problematized, and seen in relation to trends of "technology optimism" in many societies,[32] and a constant search for "the most effective" solution in every given setting.[33]

Theoretical framework: Giddens' globalization hypothesis

The increasing normalization and legitimization of technology-use across all societal areas has been highlighted by many sociologists as a key feature (or result) of globalization processes.[34] In many sports, at all levels, the use of both scientific approaches and new biomedical technologies have escalated the last decades,[35] as sport generally has become increasingly globalized.[36] Technological innovations in media and communication, as well as in sport science are viewed as central drivers for the transnational development of sport: with intensified mediatization, commercialization and professionalization of sports as prevailing consequences.[37] Based on this notion, Giulianotti and Robertson argue that sport functions as an increasingly significant subject for studies on globalization in more general terms, because of its dual role as a long-term motor – and metric – of transnational change.[38] Sociological analysis of the globalization process incorporates a range of different conditions, such as the development of new media communication technologies, world economy integration, political transformations, transnational corporation growth, and cul-

---

[31] Williams and Manley, "Elite coaching and the technocratic engineer;" Jim Denison, Joseph Mills, and Luke Jones, "Effective coaching as a modernist formation: A Foucaudian critique," in *Routledge handbook of sports coaching*, eds. Paul Potrac, Wade Gilbert, and Jim Denison (London: Routledge, 2013), 388–399.

[32] Douglas Kellner, "Theorizing Globalization." *Sociological Theory* 20, no. 3 (2002): 285–305, https://doi.org/10.1111/0735-2751.00165.

[33] Denison et al., "Becoming a good enough coach."

[34] Kellner, "Theorizing Globalization." Anthony Giddens, *Runaway World: How Globalisation Is Reshaping Our lives*, (Routledge, 2002).

[35] Miah, "Rethinking enhancement in sport."

[36] Richard Giulianotti, and Roland Robertson, "Sport and globalization: transnational dimensions," *Global networks* 7, no. 2(2007): 107–112, https://doi.org/10.1111/j.1471-0374.2007.00159.x.

[37] Barry Smart, "Not playing around: global capitalism, modern sport and consumer culture," *Global networks* 7, no. 2 (2007): 113–134, https://doi.org/10.1111/j.1471-0374.2007.00160.x.

[38] Giulianotti and Robertson, "Sport and globalization."

tural change, while new technology, scientification, and economic growth are viewed as the most central driving forces behind these processes.[39]

Giddens highlights three main dimensions of globalization processes: 1) expansion of trading, 2) increasing transnational economic activity, and 3) better and faster communication networks across the globe.[40] Furthermore, he defines globalization as the dynamic character that colours modern societies, and "the intensification of worldwide social relations which link distant localities in such way that local happenings are shaped by events occurring many miles away and vice versa".[41] Such disembedding mechanisms require the creation of *symbolic tokens*, especially money and money transactions, defined as mechanisms to control time and space.[42] They also lead to the establishment of *expert systems*. According to Giddens, expert systems are "systems of technical accomplishment or professional expertise that organize large areas of the material and social environments that we live in today."[43] These systems disembed further, because they provide abstract guarantees of expectations across time and space: impersonal tests and public forms further "stretch" social systems. They also imply a different kind of trust. The concept of trust is a central element in Giddens' thinking about modernity. He defines trust as 'confidence in the reliability of a person or system, regarding a given set of outcomes or events, where that confidence expresses a faith in the probity or love of another, or in the correctness of abstract principles "technical knowledge."[44]

In the case of athletic performance enhancement, novel technologies combined with scientific knowledge of highly-specialized scholarly fields – such as medicine or exercise physiology – may constitute a type of expert system in a Giddensian understanding of the term.[45] These expert systems denote new forms of trust as they require coaches and athletes to have confidence in the veracity of the technical knowledge behind performance enhancing technologies and the scientific principles of a training regime. An example could be the need for trust that the data produced by wearable self-tracking technology is accurate, useful and reliable.

---

[39] Anthony Giddens, *The Consequences of Modernity*; Ulrich Beck, *Individualization: Institutionalized individualism and its social and political consequences,* (SAGE Publications Ltd, 2002).

[40] Giddens, *The Consequences of Modernity.*

[41] *Ibid.,* 64.

[42] Anthony Giddens, *Modernity and self-identity. Self and society in the Late Modern Age* (Cambridge, UK: Polity Press, 1991), 22.

[43] *Ibid.,* 27.

[44] Giddens, *The Consequences of Modernity,* 34.

[45] Giddens, *Modernity and self-identity. Self and society in the Late Modern Age*; Giddens, *The Consequences of Modernity.*

According to Giddens, another example of globalization processes is the tendency towards increased reflexivity in modern societies, both at an institutional, and an individual level.[46] This reflexivity helps us produce knowledge about our practices and institutions through science, public administration, volunteer organizations and media technology, which further enables us to reorganize and manage these practices and institutions in more efficient and effective ways. Taken together with other mechanisms behind globalization processes like capitalist values, increased reflexivity has, according to Giddens, led to a growing individualism in western societies, with a trend towards specialization and professionalization of different roles.[47]

Methods

In order to examine how coaches approach technology for performance enhancement in running and their experiences of risks and benefits for the athletes, qualitative interviews were conducted with coaches and leaders integral to Norwegian elite running.

Sample and interview procedure

The sample consisted of semi-structured interviews with seven coaches and leaders. Among our seven interviewees, four are elite coaches and three hold leadership positions in Norwegian running (such as the Norwegian Athletics Federation and organizations responsible for major national running events). The interviewees were recruited strategically and contacted through the professional e-mail addresses provided as their contact information on organizational websites.

The interviews focused on topics related to performance enhancement and technology, current training regimes and scientification, as well as risks and benefits associated with the implementation of new technological advancements in running equipment and training. A description of the interviewees is presented below, in Table 1. All participants were assigned pseudonyms to ensure anonymity. These are based on their position in Norwegian running. Coaches have been given C-names, leaders are given L-names, and event managers E-names.

---

[46] Giddens, *The Consequences of Modernity.*

[47] *Ibid.*

Table 1: interview sample

Pseudonyms	Age	Gender	Current position in Norwegian running	Running experience
Carlos	30s	Male	Coach	Active runner, still competing
Calvin	40s	Male	Coach	Earlier athlete competing in running among other sports
Cooper	60s	Male	Coach	Earlier athlete competing in running among other sports
Clinton	60s	Male	Coach	Earlier runner, competing at a high level
Ernest	70s	Male	Event manager	Earlier athlete competing in running among other sports
Lydia	40s	Female	Organization/ leader	Earlier runner, competing at a high level
Lloyd	60s	Male	Organization / leader	Earlier athlete competing in running among other sports

Analysis

The interview material was analyzed using a thematic approach.[48] In the first part of the analysis, interview transcripts were read through to achieve famil-

[48] Virginia Braun, and Victoria Clarke,"Using thematic analysis in psychology," *Qualitative research in psychology* 3, no. 2 (2006): 77–101, https://doi.org/10.1191/1478088706qp063oa.

iarity with the data. Codes were placed on content that provided meaningful indications of coaches' and leaders' perspectives on the development seen in Norwegian running. After the initial coding seven recurring categories were developed: (1) commercialization and sponsors, (2) innovations in running technology, (3) scientifically prescribed training regimes, (4) role models, (5) gender differences, (6) performance, and (7) Norwegian running history.

In this chapter we focus on the parts of the interview material that relate to the categories scientifically prescribed training and innovations in running technology, as these stood out as the most dominant themes from the data gathered.

Findings and discussion

In this section we present findings from the analysis of the interviews. We split the findings into two sub-sections: 1) the impact of technological innovation on running performances, and 2) development of scientifically prescribed training regimes.

The impact of technological innovation on running performances

The interviews demonstrate that the Norwegian running coaches' experiences align with notions found in previous theoretical work on training technology and performance enhancement in elite sport,[49] in that they view novel sports technology as fundamental for the improvement of athlete performance in running:

> I suppose that all of the technological innovations contributes to better quality in the daily training. We witnessed a improvement in performances before the carbon-shoes was fully introduced in 2020, although they have been an important factor for performance enhancement in running (Lloyd).

> Technology is the key to improving performance and training in running (Ernest).

> There is motivation in just trying new technology and wearable gear, and that this motivation may influence performances in a positive manner (Calvin).

---

[49] Balmer et al., "Evolution and revolution;" Lippi et al., "Updates on improvement of human athletic performance;" McFall et al., "The Impact of Technology."

The quote from Lloyd illustrates how the impact of technological innovation on running performance is related to quality improvement in training regimes and scientification. Ernest's quote can be interpreted as an expression of 'technology optimism', which Kellner described as a feature of many globalized societies.[50] Through a Giddensian perspective, it can also be read as an example of how expert systems (in this case the scientification of elite athlete training) denote new forms of trust. Both Lloyd and Ernest's quotes imply that further technological innovation is the key to more progress in performances.[51]

Calvin adds to these perspectives by connecting the introduction of self-tracking technology to athlete motivation. In this way, Calvin illustrates how the athlete benefits of self-tracking technologies in elite running may go beyond the performance data such technological tools produce. According to previous research, by Janssen and colleagues as well as Clermont and colleagues,[52] runners who are motivated by goals related to performance enhancement and competition success, are more likely to use self-tracking technology compared to other athlete groups. Based on Calvin's quote and the findings of Clermont and colleagues self-tracking technology might impact performance in different ways for different athlete groups.[53] This was highlighted by several coaches and leaders in our interviews. For instance, Lloyd and Lydia said:

> Sometimes new technology, such as lactate measures, heart rate measures and GPS watches are introduced too early to younger athletes. It might not really impact their performance. The performance models that we (the Norwegian Athletics Federation) use that are developed for adult athletes. Younger athletes' bodies work different, since they don't really produce any lactate, not in the same way as adults do. So when a thirteen or fourteen year old athlete uses such technology it's a joke, because it's more important that the athlete learns to "know" their body and own intensity zones (Lloyd).

> The technology may have different functions for different groups of runners, whereas top athletes are using technological measures in order to maximize their performances, while regular exercisers use it primarily for motivational reasons (Lydia).

---

[50] Kellner, "Theorizing Globalization."

[51] Lippi et al., "Updates on improvement of human athletic performance."

[52] Janssen et al., "Understanding Different Types of Recreational Runner;" Janssen et al., "Who uses running apps and sports watches?;" Clermont et al., "Runners' perspectives."

[53] Clermont et al., "Runners' perspectives."

Here, Lloyd recognizes the value of using self-tracking technology such as GPS watches, lactate measures and heart rate monitoring for adult athletes. Several of the coaches and leaders we interviewed explained that the widespread commercial use of these technologies was seen as important for performance enhancement, although with different functions for athletes at various levels of performance. In this case, our findings resonate with interviews featuring coaches from different college sports in North America, also indicating that coaches find these technologies to be beneficial for performance enhancement.[54] However, others have highlighted that applying such self-tracking technology may come with harmful and unintended consequences for some athletes because they reduce athletic movement and performance to rational and quantifiable systems.[55] Lloyd's skepticism toward using such technology on younger athletes illustrates how these technologies might not always contribute to performance enhancement in running, and that there is a need to tailor technology to specific groups of athletes. Similar concerns are also highlighted in STS literature outside of elite sports coaching. For instance, Benjamin describes in detail how the 'New Jim Code' outcomes of racist technology severely impact peoples' lives.[56]

Regarding the impact of technology on performance enhancement, the technological innovation the coaches discussed most frequently and in-depth during our interviews, was the new running shoe technology. The introduction of shoes with a carbon-fiber plate and foam with a greater energy return was highlighted as the most significant innovation in relation to enhanced performances by all interviewees. Clinton described how carbon-fiber shoes were beneficial for elite runners:

> Carbon-fiber shoes impact running performances in two ways. First, you run faster and reduce the race-times in competitions. There is a big difference in race-times for the marathon distance after the development of the shoes. The other aspect of it is the effect they have on training. If athletes use them frequently during training, it reduces the risk of injuries, and they may tolerate more hard sessions (Clinton).

Of course, the carbon-fiber running shoes do not represent a technological innovation exclusive to Norway and Norwegian running. Carbon-fiber running shoes have revolutionized elite running globally and represent an example of

---

[54] Rauff et al., "Using sport science data in collegiate athletics."

[55] Denison et al., "Effective coaching."

[56] Ruha Benjamin, *Race after technology* (Polity Press, 2019).

Gidden's three main dimensions of globalization processes applied to elite sport.[57] Through increases in trading and transnational economic activity, as well as better and faster communication networks, carbon-fiber shoes have quickly become the shoe technology of choice for elite runners globally. In 2018, the world records for 100km, marathon, half-marathon and 15km were all set by runners using Nike carbon-fiber shoes (*Vaporfly 4%*). Since then, Burns and Tam have claimed that the *Nike Vaporfly* 4% and the *Nike Alphafly* shoes represent the greatest technological innovation in running shoes to date.[58] Carbon-fiber running shoes became increasingly popular after Kenyan runner Eliud Kipchoge became the first human to run a marathon under two hours using the *Nike Alphafly* shoes in October 2019. Although not an official record, many regard Kipchoge's performance as a result of the Alphafly shoe technology, which has been suggested to improve running speed by 3.4% in elite runners.[59] In addition to the improvements in running speed, the coaches interviewed had experienced that the carbon-fiber shoes could also contribute to injury prevention:

> It seems like the athletes can withstand more training with the carbon-fiber shoes. We have used these shoes to prevent repetitive strain injuries, both in training and competitions, and if that means that the athletes run faster in competitions when using such shoes it's just a bonus (Cooper).

While public and scientific debates have mainly focused on improvements in running speed with the new carbon-fiber shoes,[60] the coaches and leaders we interviewed mainly highlighted direct effects of the shoes, such as the reduction of injury risk and reduction of recovery time after training, as the quote from Cooper illustrates. If athletes train more and at higher intensity with fewer injuries they will likely improve their performance. Hence, the contribution of the new shoe technology is twofold, as Clinton also describes. Firstly, because the shoe allows elite runners to run fast, and secondly because it contributes to further scientification of training through the development of new and improved sports equipment.

---

[57] Giddens, *The Consequences of Modernity.*

[58] Burns and Tam, "Is it the shoes?"

[59] Burns and Tam, "Is it the shoes?;" Wouter Hoogkamer, Shalaya Kipp, Jesse H. Frank, Emily M. Farina, Geng Luo, and Rodger Kram, "A Comparison of the Energetic Cost of Running in Marathon Racing Shoes," *Sports Med* 48, (2018): 1009–1019, https://doi.org/10.1007/s40279-017-0811-2.

[60] Burns and Tam, "Is it the shoes?;" Fuller et al., "The effect of footwear."

The informants in our study distinguish between motivational and instrumental effects of technology for elite and recreational runners, where technological innovations are perceived to have a motivational effect on recreational runners in contrast to an instrumental effect on elite runners' performances. Some of the coaches reported that female athletes were less motivated by new technologies and perceived this as a contributing factor to the lack of performance development among female Norwegian runners. For instance, both Lloyd, Calvin and Lydia observed female athletes to be less interested in measurements and new innovations in self-tracking technology, whilst both progression in measurements and testing of new technologies was viewed as a central factor for long-term motivation in male athletes. Such gender differences in motivational effects of new technology are also found in other studies on recreational athletes, which show that men, to a greater degree than women, use sports technologies like GPS-measures and watches.[61] Other scientific literature highlights that novel sports technology may lower gender differences in elite sport performance,[62] demonstrating a greater performance enhancement in female athletes compared to male athletes following the introduction of new sporting technologies.[63] Although this is not the case in our sample, nor in the number of records broken, or average percentage of improvement in race times for Norwegian men and women between 2001 and 2021, it has been the case in middle- and long-distance running in a global context.[64] Still, our analyses support the overall notion that the introduction of new carbon-fiber technology in running shoes in 2016 have led to new records and time-improvements in longer running distances, particularly in male athletes.

Development of scientifically prescribed training regimes

Within our sample, scientifically prescribed training methods and self-tracking technologies were identified as commonly used by the best performing athletes. The interviewees regarded this as crucial for the current advancements in international performances occurring among Norwegian runners. Similarly,

---

[61] Wiesner et al., "Technology adoption."

[62] Kutte Jönsson, "Sport beyond gender and the emergence of cyborg athletes," *Sport in society* 13, no. 2 (2010): 249–259, https://doi.org/10.1080/17430430903522962.

[63] Lippi et al., "Updates on improvement of human athletic performance."

[64] Bermon et al., "Effect of advanced shoe technology"; Senefeld, "Technological advances in elite marathon performance."

Houston argued that scientifically derived training regimes was the most important factor for the performance enhancement during the American "running boom" in the 1970s.[65] Especially, advancements in sports medicine and technologies capable of systematically monitoring physiological factors known to affect performance (e.g., heart rate, lactate levels and pacing) are perceived as crucial to ensure quality in training over long periods of time. Carlos explained the importance of scientifically prescribed training regimes for performance enhancement in Norwegian running:

> The systematic approach to training and the improved quality in training regimes is the main cause of performance enhancement in running. Knowledge and use of systematic data gathering of factors that influence performance is more important than the use of technology to control intensity in training (Carlos).

This perspective, as illustrated by Carlos' quote, contributes to current research literature, which has focused primarily on how scientific approaches and the use of self-tracking technology could prevent injuries, improve technique, and monitor progression.[66] Our data contrasts previous findings by Rauff and colleagues on studies of college sports coaches' (N= 13) perspectives on such technology. While they found that 54–61% of coaches perceived technology as beneficial to monitor athletes' performance, all of the coaches and leaders in our sample saw scientific approaches and self-tracking technology as crucial factors in the performance enhancement seen in Norwegian running lately.[67] It should be noted that neither Rauff et al.'s study nor our study provide a big enough sample of coaches in the interview process to generalize these findings across other coaching contexts.

The fact that scientific knowledge about training and performance have become increasingly accessible globally over the last decades, through media and the internet, was brought up by several of the informants. They highlighted this in two ways. First, in relation to the emergence of the "new Norwegian training model" and greater cohesion among coaches about what training regimes that are the most effective for elite running performance. Second, in relation to the recent overall enhancement in performance levels nationally due to the fact that

---

[65] Houston, "Creating the consumer-runner."

[66] Fleming et al., "Athlete and coach perceptions;" Rauff et al., "Using sport science data in collegiate athletics."

[67] Rauff et al., "Using sport science data in collegiate athletics."

a majority of athletes are conducting their training based on scientifically prescribed regimes that have been popularized through the international success of
Team Ingebrigtsen:

> The training philosophy developed by Team Ingebrigtsen with high levels of
> threshold training is popular. And, most importantly: it seems to be effective for
> runners at all levels. It has become the new Norwegian training model (Cooper).

Having immediate access to relevant information that is disembedded from the
context the knowledge derived from, is a key aspect of Giddens globalization
hypothesis.[68] The spread and adoption of Team Ingebrigtsen training philosophy, following the success of Olympic gold medalist Jakob Ingebrigtsen, exemplifies 'disembedding' through the separation of time and space in athletic development in modern elite running. The characteristics of Team Ingebrigtsen's
training regime may also be interpreted as an expression of expert systems in
the coaching of elite runners. This is illustrated through Cooper's quote when
he describes the importance of threshold training in this approach to coaching
elite runners – a method associated with scientification of training.[69] Scientification of training also became apparent when the coaches described their own
use of technology and scientific measures in coaching practice:

> We monitor heart rates for all strides during interval sessions, and some-
> times we also measure lactate-levels. Then I plot this data into a spreadsheet
> and compare it to measures from previous sessions in order to modify the
> speed and intensity in a progressive manner. For many athletes it gives them
> motivation because they see that "okay, I run a lot faster now compared to
> training sessions two months ago". I use the data to show them their prog-
> ress (Calvin).

Although perceptions of scientifically prescribed approaches to training were mainly positive among the interviewees, some were critical about the current use of the
technologies involved in such training regimes. For instance, Calvin worried that
these technologies sometimes over-complicate training principles in sport:

> Some over-complicate things. The principles behind effective training are quite
> easy. You need to introduce the body to a certain physiological stress before it
> adapts to the stress and then becomes better. Yet, this could be done very com-
> plicated by introducing technology, which I see more and more often. It is im-

---

[68] Giddens, *The Consequences of Modernity;* Giddens, *Modernity and self-identity.*

[69] Svensson, *"Scientizing performance in endurance sports."*

portant to use the technology the right way, by sorting out data that is relevant from the data that is not relevant. Often, it is a process of learning to understand what is useful and what is not (Calvin).

Calvin's quote also implies that coaches and athletes who use self-tracking technology as a part of their training regimes need the necessary competence to use such technologies in the "right way." Other coaches also mentioned an over-reliance on technological measures, especially for young athletes with little experience and competence, and that young athletes risk alienation from their own bodily sensations as a consequence of this. Such worries are in coherence with findings from critical studies on sports technology, that have highlighted how large-scale use of sports technology may substantiate a mechanic and dualistic perspective on the athletic body, rather than an intuitive relationship with bodily sensations.[70]

Despite the notion that relevant information about running and exercise in general have become more readily available, the theme "competence" was discussed by several of the informants. This was brought up indirectly by the coaches by mentioning the need for a certain knowledge and 'know how' in order to understand the underlying mechanisms that the "new model of training" is built on, and to use monitoring technologies the "right way." These aspects also align with research on coaches' use of new technologies, which have demonstrated the need for additional coach education when implementing new sports technologies.[71] This also supports claims that athletes and coaches are becoming increasingly professionalized, and that only small groups of privileged individuals have the competence needed to use the technology and scientific knowledge about training in a productive way.[72] This further reflects the increasingly tendency towards specialization and reliance on "expert knowledge" that often characterizes globalized societies.[73] Using the same approach to training. while not having necessary knowledge of sports technology and scientifically prescribed training regimes. may "(Re) complicate" the sporting practice, resulting in an unintended negative effect on performance.[74]

---

[70] Mills et al., "Breaking coaching's rules"; Little, "Running, health and the disciplining of women's bodies."

[71] Jaswal et al., "How Canadian High-Performance Coaches."

[72] Anne Tjønndal, *Idrettsteknologi*, (Fagbokforlaget, 2023).

[73] Giddens, *Modernity and self-identity*; Giddens, *The Consequences of Modernity.*

[74] Pam R. Sailors, "More than a pair of shoes: Running and technology," *Journal of the Philosophy of Sport* 36, no. 2 (2009): 207–216, https://doi.org/10.1080/00948705.2009.9714757.

Despite increasing standardization and scientification of different areas aspects of society being a part of the globalization process, standardized and universal training regimes based on scientific research can be perceived as problematic if this becomes the "only" or "right" way to do running, because it might not be the most suitable training regime for all athletes.[75] Here, some of the informants discussed gender differences and the urgency for more scientific knowledge regarding manipulation of female athletes' training and performance enhancement. For instance, Cooper mentioned:

> While I have some ideas that female athletes, at least in a certain age (referring to the period when athletes are between 15–25 years old), should train in different ways than male athletes regarding strength and intensity on running sessions, I have no documentation on this although I wish that there was more research covering the theme (Cooper).

This is in line with existing reviews on the elaboration of exercise and sport science in general,[76] but also in relation to technology in running and exercise knowledge, where most studies on the effects of new technology on physiological measures are exhibited with male athletes only.[77]

Conclusion

This chapter investigates how Norwegian elite running coaches approach novel technologies and what their experiences are in terms of risks and benefits for athletes. A main finding from the interviews is that the coaches have an

---

[75] Giddens, *The Consequences of Modernity*; Sophia Nimphius, "Exercise and sport science failing by design in understanding female athletes," *International Journal of Sports Physiology and Performance* 14, *no.* 9(2019): 1157–1158, https://doi.org/10.1123/ijspp.2019-0703.

[76] Nimphius, "Exercise and sport science failing;" Emma S. Cowley, Alyssa A. Olenick, Kelly L. McNulty, and Emma Z. Ross, "Invisible sportswomen: the sex data gap in sport and exercise science research," *Women in Sport and Physical Activity Journal* 29, no. 2 (2021): 146–151, https://doi.org/10.1123/wspaj.2021-0028.

[77] Fuller et al., "The effect of footwear"; Dustin P. Joubert, and Garret P. Jones, "A Comparison of Running Economy Across Seven Carbon-Plated Racing Shoes," *Kinesiology and Health Science, Faculty Publications.* 33 (2021), https://scholarworks.sfasu.edu/kinesiology/33; Dustin P. Joubert, Caleb Garcia, and Blake W. Johnson, "A case study comparison of two carbon-plated running shoes on running economy and running mechanics," *International Journal of Exercice Science* 89, no. 2 (2021), https://digitalcommons.wku.edu/ijesab/vol2/iss13/89/; Wouter Hoogkamer, Rodger Kram, and Christopher J. Arellano, "How Biomechanical Improvements in Running Economy Could Break the 2-hour Marathon Barrier," *Sports Medicine* 47, (2017): 1739–1750, https://doi.org/10.1007/s40279-017-0708-0.

overall positive attitude toward the increased used of performance enhancing technologies and scientification of training in elite running. Technologies used by the coaches in this sample include wearable self-tracking technologies, carbon-fibered running shoes and scientifically prescribed lactate measures during training. The latter represents the clearest example of scientification of training in our data.

The coach's positive position regarding performance enhancing technologies could be interpreted as an expression of the "technological optimism" that dominates many globalized societies.[78] There are two reasons for this. First, by their tendency to mainly focus on the positive aspects of the biomedical and wearable self-tracking technologies,[79] and second by implying that further technological innovation is the key to further progress in performances.[80] From a Giddensian perspective, the strong belief that novel technologies are the key to improving performances and training in running, illustrates how expert systems, such as the scientification of athletic training, denotes new forms of trust. Trust is a central element in Giddens' thinking about modernity, and in this case implies the need for coaches and athletes to have confidence in the correctness of the "abstract principles" or "technical knowledge" behind the data produced by performance enhancing technologies, and the reliability of scientifically prescribed training regimes.[81]

The interviews with Norwegian middle- and long-distance running coaches also exemplify some risks and benefits implementing new technologies may have for elite athletes. In terms of benefits, the coaches emphasize three things. Firstly, the importance of the new carbon-fiber running shoes. Their experiences are that these shoes allow athletes to run faster due to innovations in the materials of the shoe, as well as contribute to performance enhancement by allowing athletes to train harder for longer times without risking injury. Secondly, that self-tracking technologies that produce biometric data may contribute to better motivation among some athletes, and thirdly, that it allows the runners to gain new insight about their own bodily performance.

The coaches mention two risks associated with the increased use of technology for training in running. First of all, that these technologies are mainly designed and adapted to male adult athletes, and that this diminishes their use-

[78] Kellner, "Theorizing Globalization."

[79] Jones et al., "Sport and Surveillance Technologies."

[80] Lippi et al., "Updates on improvement of human athletic performance."

[81] Giddens, *The Consequences of Modernity.*

fulness for other athlete groups, such as youth athletes and female athletes. For instance, Lloyd goes as far as to call the use of self-tracking technology for teenage athletes 'a joke'. Another risk for the athletes is the over-complication of running training. As coach Calvin says in his interview "the principles behind effective training are quite easy (…). Yet, this could be done very complicated by introducing technology'. Over-complicating training regimes becomes a risk as the scientification of training regimes implies a need to use technology 'the right way' (Calvin's words). In order to use technology the right way, coaches and athletes need the knowledge and expertise to interpret the data produced by these technologies in a meaningful way. The risk associated with this is misleading interpretations and falsely objectification of athletic performance.

Norway is one of the countries with the tightest bond between scientific sports institutes and elite sports organizations.[82] This may partially explain why Norway has witnessed a tremendous increase in the level of performances, even with the global increase in running performances in mind. The peculiarity of the case of course means that the findings from our study are not necessarily transferable to other countries and empirical contexts. Yet, there are some similarities between Norwegian running and developmental trends seen in elite running worldwide. The dominant view of scientific knowledge about exercise physiology and performance as crucial to perform at a high level, underlines our finding that Norwegian running have gone through a substantial "scientification." This is in line with research on other sports like triathlon,[83] as well as an overall tendency in the global society.[84] Similarly, the technology-optimism expressed by coaches and leaders in our interview data align with findings from other countries and other sports.

Other countries may also have witness similar enhancement in running performances without relying heavily on scientification and technology, as the case is with Norway and the Team Ingebrigtsen training regimes. In these cases, performance improvement could be explained by other factors, such as general improvement in the sport over time and the democratization of sport participation, for example. That is, our point is not that scientification and technology is the

---

[82] Lena Øyen, "To hus tett i tett: om forskningssamarbeid og prestasjonsutvikling," *Norges Idretshøgskole,* November 25, 2021, https://www.nih.no/om-nih/aktuelt/nyheter/nih-podden/2021/om-forskningssamarbeid-og-prestasjonsutvikling/.

[83] Gregoire P. Millet, David J. Bentley, and Veronica E. Vleck, "The relationships between science and sport: application in triathlon," *International journal of sports physiology and performance* 2, no 3 (2007): 315–322, https://doi.org/10.1123/ijspp.2.3.315.

[84] Giddens, *The Consequences of Modernity.*

only explanation for performance enhancement in running in Norway or other places. Rather, our aim is to investigate how coaches approach new technologies and the meaning they give to the usefulness, benefits and risks associated with them. For instance, access to science and knowledge about running and performance enhancement has informed Norwegian coaches in their approaches to training and competitions, leading to new European records. Similar studies of elite sports context with leading international performances may continue to expand our knowledge of the impact and scientification of training regimes and technological innovation on participation, development, and performance enhancement in elite athletics.

www.ingramcontent.com/pod-product-compliance
Lightning Source LLC
Chambersburg PA
CBHW040422110426
42814CB00008B/331